DEPARTMENT OF HEALTH

ON THE STATE OF
THE PUBLIC HEALTH

THE ANNUAL REPORT OF
THE CHIEF MEDICAL OFFICER OF
THE DEPARTMENT OF HEALTH
FOR THE YEAR 1996

LONDON: The Stationery Office

ISBN 0 11 322097 9

CONTENTS

INTRODUCTION

Rt Hon Frank Dobson MP
Secretary of State for Health

Sir,

I have pleasure in submitting my Report on the State of the Public Health for 1996, together with some comments on the more important developments and events in the first half of 1997. This Report is the 139th of the series which began in 1858.

I am pleased to report that health has continued to improve overall during the year. Infant mortality reached its lowest recorded rate and perinatal mortality also fell in 1996. Progress continued to be made towards more integrated working to maintain the public health, and for more efficient communications between all those involved. The importance of an underlying strategy to enhance public health, not just to treat illness, was recognised in the 1992 White Paper *The Health of the Nation: a strategy for health in England*[1], and has been further emphasised by the appointment of a Minister for Public Health, who set out a new public health strategy[2] on 7 July "to tackle the underlying causes of ill-health and to break the cycle of social and economic deprivation and social exclusion".

As I have discussed in previous years, this Report is not simply a document of record, but must also try to interpret and to explain changes in those factors that are known to influence and to determine health, and should identify areas where improvements could be made. In recent Reports, I have highlighted some issues for special mention, with the intention that they would be followed up: topics identified in earlier years have been acted on and progress is discussed in this Report. As well as a broader discussion of the potential for health, four other key issues are identified for particular attention during the coming year: health of disabled people, consent, domestic violence and air pollution. It is hoped that over the next year these topics will stimulate interest, and I shall report back on them in next year's Report. The multidisciplinary nature of health care has also been addressed by the Chief Nursing Officer and her colleagues on the theme of joint working for health.

I wish to acknowledge the help and support given to me by numerous colleagues in the Department of Health and the Office for National Statistics, as well as other Government Departments and Agencies, in the preparation of this Report, and the assistance of The Stationery Office, Norwich, which arranged the printing and publication.

I am, Sir,
Your obedient servant

Sir Kenneth Calman

September 1997

LONG TERM STRATEGIC AIMS

Previous Reports[3,4,5,6] set out a series of long-term strategic aims which also underpin the content of this Report:

— To promote efforts to ensure health for all;

— To achieve the targets in a strategy for public health;

— To involve patients and the public in choices and decision-making;

— To establish an effective intelligence and information system for public health and clinical practice;

— To ensure a health service based on an assessment of health needs, quality of care and effectiveness of outcome; *and*

— To provide a highly professional team of staff with strong education, research and ethical standards.

These six points continue to provide the strategic direction and intent of the Report.

HEALTH IN ENGLAND

Key indicators of the overall health of the population indicate that the substantial health gains of recent years have been maintained during 1996. Provisional crude death rates fell in England in 1996 among males and females alike. The average expectation of life at birth was estimated in 1995 to be 74.3 years in males and 79.5 years in females; projections for 1996 suggest slightly higher figures than in 1995. The infant mortality rate for 1996 reached its lowest ever level of 6.0 per 1,000 live births. Perinatal mortality (stillbirths plus deaths under one week-of-age) also fell in 1996, to 8.6 per 1,000 live births.

Although such broad measures of health status are at or near their best-ever levels, it is important to consider the scope for further improvement, the existence of striking inequalities between particular population groups within this country, and to take account of international comparisons where appropriate.

For example, international data indicate substantially greater average expectation of life at birth in countries such as Japan (76.6 years in males, 83.3 years in females), France (82.8 years in females) and Sweden (76.3 years in males), and considerably lower rates of infant mortality in Japan (4.2 deaths per 1,000 live births), and in Finland and Sweden (4.0 deaths per 1,000 live births)[7] (see Appendix Table A.11). These figures indicate the scope for further improvements in public health.

Inequalities exist across a wide range of health indicators. Some are longstanding and are widespread across the world, but this does not mean that they are inevitable and cannot be addressed and reduced. Initial results based on the 1991 Census presenting mortality by social class (based on occupation) have now been published for England and Wales[8]: between the 1981 and 1991 Censuses, although mortality rates fell in each social class, the fall was least in social class V and the mortality gradient therefore widened over this period. Around the time of the 1981 Census the all-causes mortality rate in social class V was almost 2.5 times that in social class I; the more recent figures indicate an almost three-fold difference. Equivalent data relating to child injury death rates again show a fall in each social class, but the reductions in social classes IV and V were substantially less than in social classes I and II, leading to an increase in the gradient of child injury death rates between social classes I and V which now represents a five-fold difference[9].

Other important inequalities also exist and persist in relation to gender, ethnicity and area of residence. For example, mortality rates in this country are around twice as high among infants of mothers born in Pakistan and the Caribbean Commonwealth as those found in infants of mothers born in the United Kingdom (UK)[10]. Major differences in life expectancy also exist across England: for example, life expectancy at birth in males in Manchester has been estimated to be over six years shorter than in Surrey; for females the difference of four years is slightly smaller but still substantial[11]. Based on self-reported assessment of 'chronic illness' in the 1991 Census, the number of years of life in good health that a man can on average expect to live has been estimated to be over ten years better in Surrey than in Manchester (based upon area of residence at the time of death or Census)[11].

Research into the nature and possible causes of the new variant of Creutzfeldt-Jakob disease (nvCJD), identified by the UK's National CJD Surveillance Unit in 1996[12,13], remains a priority. The Spongiform Encephalopathy Advisory Committee (SEAC) considered the research findings which have emerged on the possibility of a link with exposure to bovine spongiform encephalopathy (BSE) at a meeting in May 1997. The Committee's statement, published on 1 July[14], concluded that the evidence that has accumulated since March 1996 is consistent with the hypothesis that nvCJD is caused by exposure to the BSE agent, and that no evidence refuting the hypothesis has yet come to light. However, the SEAC regarded the evidence to date as insufficient to constitute formal proof of a causal link, and further data are required before a definitive conclusion can be reached.

Up to the end of 1996, 13 patients were identified as having died from nvCJD in the UK, and there were a further two cases in patients who were still alive (confirmed by brain biopsy), making a total of 15 definite and probable cases of nvCJD up to the end of December 1996. A further 6 cases have been identified since then, making a total of 21 definite and probable cases of nvCJD up to the end of June 1997. These figures are updated by the Department on a monthly basis[15], and sent to clinicians quarterly in *CMO's Update*[16], but are subject to revision as new cases are identified and confirmed by the CJD Surveillance Unit. At present, there are insufficient data to make soundly based predictions of the likely future course of the disease.

THE STRATEGY FOR HEALTH

The Health of the Nation White Paper[1] outlined five key areas to promote the public health in respect of coronary heart disease (CHD) and stroke, cancers, mental health, HIV/AIDS and sexual health, and accidents. Progress has been made towards most of the targets set, some of which have already been met, but in others - particularly obesity, teenage cigarette smoking and alcohol consumption among women - further measures need to be taken to counter clearly adverse trends.

On 7 July, Ms Tessa Jowell MP, the Minister for Public Health, set out a new public health strategy "to tackle the underlying causes of ill-health and to break the cycle of social and economic deprivation and social exclusion"[2]. Work on health inequalities will be emphasised, and the role of public health will be enhanced. The impact on health of factors such as poverty, unemployment, poor housing, social isolation, pollution and ethnic minority status and gender will be emphasised, and communication between Government Departments and Agencies, local authorities and social services, other sources of support (including the voluntary sector) and individuals will be further enhanced.

Sir Donald Acheson, formerly Chief Medical Officer of the Department of Health, will undertake an independent review, set within the broad context of the Government's overall financial strategy, to identify priority areas for future policy development based on available evidence, following a review by the Department of Health (DH) and the Office for National Statistics (ONS) on inequalities in health and expectation of life in England.

Meanwhile, the Department will produce a Green Paper on the new health strategy in Autumn 1997; this will be followed by consultation with a view to production of a White Paper by Summer 1998. The White Paper will include a focus on health inequalities informed by Sir Donald's work, as well as an emphasis on local as well as national targets. It will look at particular population groups (such as older people), and at particular settings such as healthy schools and healthy workplaces.

JOINT WORKING FOR HEALTH

Health is about people, not just patients; and about patients, not diseases. Effective delivery of health care services is a multidisciplinary exercise, not just a medical one; effective interventions to improve the public health require, and receive, the co-operation of many Government Departments and Agencies and the support of many people from various disciplines. The principle that health care itself must become more pluralistic and less disease oriented was recognised in May 1996 by a World Health Assembly resolution that countries should work to strengthen the role of nursing and midwifery, a resolution supported by the UK.

Health care does not just start and end at the hospital or surgery door. Greater awareness of the need to encourage and enhance team-working, community development programmes and support for people to encourage healthier lifestyles has led to greater awareness of all the contributions from individuals within health care teams. Developments in nursing, midwifery and health visiting now offer a template to widen the scope of professional health promotion and preventive services, and the contribution of nurses, midwives and health visitors towards public health is well established in hospitals, general practice, and the community (including schools and the workplace).

Pre-registration education and training prepares nurses and midwives for a role in health promotion; health visiting has had a public health role since its origins at the end of the last century, and district nurses and midwives have long provided community-based health care, often serving the most vulnerable members of the community. Current developments in nursing build upon these strong traditions.

The number of nurses working in primary care has shown an overall increase of 25% between 1984 and 1994, and in some groups - such as general medical services, practice nurses, community psychiatric nurses and community learning difficulties nurses - numbers have more than doubled over this period. Such growth has enabled the extension of a range of services in general practice, including the development of screening, health promotion and chronic disease management programmes. Nurses have also developed their roles through the establishment of nurse-led minor injuries clinics, the introduction of nurse prescribing and provision of other more specialist services - including immunisation, child health surveillance, home care schemes to enable people to be cared for in their own homes and nurse-led specialist services such as clinics for leg ulcer care, dermatology and parenting skills. Midwives continue to provide a central role in the provision of maternity services, in line with *Changing childbirth*[17].

The broad nature of the work of health visitors enables familiarity of and close co-operation with the work of local authorities and voluntary organisations, to enhance alliances to further the improvement of public health and to help their patients. This work ranges from community health needs assessment, to inform how and where local resources should be targeted, to working with individual clients and particular vulnerable groups, but also takes account of specific health issues that affect whole communities. Their insights into the impact of social aspects, such as poor housing and other environmental effects on the health and well-being of individuals, will contribute to the understanding of health inequalities, and ways to minimise them.

In addition to the specialist public health role of health visitors, all nurses and midwives contribute to the advancement of public health. *Making it happen*[18], the 1995 report of the Standing Nursing and Midwifery Advisory Committee, provided some useful pointers to how the National Health Service (NHS) could further develop this role.

School nurses provide a unique contribution to child health and development and their public health role will contribute to the health of future generations. The report *In a different light*[19], published in December 1996, explored the role of school nurses and noted that they are the only health professionals exclusively concerned with the health needs of school-age children and the wider school community; the planning of future services for school-age children will require collaborative working between health authorities and educational establishments, and should be based on the health needs of the children and available resources, in co-operation with primary health care teams.

Although historically associated with cancer care, the nature and approach of specialist palliative care is increasingly recognised as an integral part of care for many chronic illnesses. Following extensive consultation, *A policy framework for commissioning cancer services*[20], published in October 1996, placed emphasis on recent advances in pain and symptom management in support of patients and families alike, and stressed the importance of continuous support and advice from multiprofessional teams, including those from the voluntary sector, who have played a vital and valued role in the provision of cancer and palliative care services. A shift in the focus of palliative care towards primary care services should help practice nurses to support patients and to facilitate rapid and appropriate referrals to specialist teams.

The health of disabled people is discussed elsewhere in this Report (see pages 20 and 104). Disability can arise through various causes, and its effect on individuals and their families, in the context of their lives and relationships, may range from minor to devastating. The priority is to help those individuals and their families to balance their chosen lifestyle with the challenges that may arise. Many, but not all, disabled people want to be at the centre of decision-making about services designed to meet their needs, and various organisations have helped to enhance the development of nursing roles to support the management of particular disease processes. Any services to maximise individuals' options for independence and choice require all health care professionals to adopt a rehabilitative approach; this not only requires the provision of information to the individuals concerned in a manner which is useful to them, but also close collaboration between health and social services and other sources of care, including voluntary agencies and informal carers, and between the many professionals who may contribute to that care.

Incontinence remains a taboo subject: despite a national public awareness campaign, 32% of men and 39% of women who reported bladder problems had not sought advice from a health care professional. The management of incontinence is most effective when approached on a multidisciplinary basis, and the 1997 theme of a national 'Pelvic Floorathon' to encourage women of all ages to take up pelvic floor exercises to prevent incontinence in later life will strengthen the advice given by physiotherapists and continence advisers.

The importance of effective multidisciplinary teamwork cannot be overstated yet it can be difficult to achieve. The range of professionals within the NHS alone is diverse and each group has a particular role to play, the balance of which may change with different patient groups and in different service settings. The emphasis now being given to the planning and delivery of integrated services offers the opportunity to get teamwork right within the NHS and in collaboration with other sources of care. Teams need to contain the right balance of skills and knowledge and develop the flexibility to share their expertise; the foundations for such an approach need to be laid down during initial professional education and training, and reinforced in continuing professional development. Multidisciplinary education and shared learning across the health professions is increasing and should help to ensure more effective working within health care teams, and with other agencies and across sectors. It is a daunting challenge, but such collaboration is integral to the effective promotion of the public health.

PROGRESS ON ACTION POINTS IN PREVIOUS REPORTS

Each year, topics which have been highlighted in previous Reports are reviewed and any action noted.

Progress on topics identified in 1993

Health of adolescents: Given the key importance of education in young people's lives, DH has worked closely with the Department for Education and Employment (DfEE) on various activities aimed to improve the health and well-being of young people; these include the Young People's Health Network and the European Network of Health Promoting Schools. The Young People's

Health Network, launched on 24 June 1996, has created considerable interest. The Health Education Authority (HEA), which manages the Network, has some 5,000 organisations registered on its database. Projects to evaluate health promotion activities and to involve young people in health promotion work have been commissioned through the Network. The English research project within the European Network of Health Promoting Schools is in its final phase and a report will be published later in 1997. As part of this initiative, the HEA is assessing the potential benefits of the development of a national association of health promoting schools. During 1995-96, the Health Select Committee of the House of Commons carried out an inquiry into children's health[21]. Among its conclusions were that the rewards of good health care in childhood, especially health promotion and preventive interventions, are unique because the benefits may last a lifetime and may be passed on to future generations.

Asthma: DH continues to accord high priority to services for people with asthma. October 1996 saw the launch of the 'Control your asthma' card, produced by jointly with the National Asthma Campaign to help people with asthma to manage their condition.

Genetic factors and disease: The pace of advances in genetics continues to escalate. Since 1993, the House of Commons Select Committee on Science and Technology have published two reports[22,23] on human genetics, emphasising the need to address ethical aspects of developments and to improve public understanding of genetic science. The Human Genetics Advisory Commission, set up in 1997, will advise on these and on wider ethical issues arising from developments in genetics. The Advisory Committee on Genetic Testing, set up in 1996, is developing a Code of Practice on 'over-the-counter' genetic tests and will continue to advise on developments in genetic testing.

Changing patterns of infectious disease: Some of the recent changes in the epidemiology of infectious diseases are referred to in the sections on emerging and re-emerging infections (see page 207) and travel-related disease (see page 208). Although international preparedness for novel and emerging infectious diseases (including drug-resistant disease) continues to dominate international discussions, the evolving epidemics of established conditions such as malaria, tuberculosis, cholera and HIV/AIDS continue to be the major infectious disease challenges world wide.

Progress on topics identified in 1994

Health in the workplace: The special chapter in the Report for 1994[24] outlined some of the important effects of work on health, the effects of health on work, and the value of health promotion in the workplace. Risks from chemicals, radiation and other physical agents, and from biological factors, were outlined, and risk assessment and management highlighted, and progress was followed up last year[25]. Continued progress by the Department and the Health and Safety Executive (HSE) is described on page 83. The Minister for Public Health has announced that healthy workplaces are to be a key strand of the public health strategy, which will be set out in a Green Paper[2].

Equity and equality: The 1994 Report[26] raised the important issue of equity and equality, and set out a framework for considering such topics. The analysis was supported in 1995 by a report[27] to the Chief Medical Officer on variations in health in England related to the five key areas in the Health of the Nation strategy[1] and the NHS. Equity, of course, has been at the heart of the NHS from its beginning, and is incorporated into its priorities and planning guidance[28,29], and the Research and Development Directorate has set aside specific funding to support research into variations in health status. Aspects related to the potential for health are discussed on page 14.

Food poisoning: For the second year in a row, food poisoning notifications have remained fairly stable after increases in 1992-94. The number of laboratory-confirmed reports for England and Wales showed varying trends for different foodborne pathogens, especially for *Salmonella* infections - which overall stayed roughly the same, but with notable changes among reports of different serotypes and phage types (see page 213). Whilst the total number of confirmed *Escherichia coli* O157 cases in England and Wales fell in 1996, a serious *E. coli* O157 outbreak in Lanarkshire, Scotland, at the end of the year resulted in almost 500 cases, with over one-third admitted to hospital and 20 deaths. The expert group which investigated this outbreak made a number of recommendations in its final report which have been accepted by the Government[30]. Food safety, including food poisoning, remains a key concern, and work is being taken forward as a priority to establish a Food Standards Agency which will incorporate some areas of work currently undertaken by DH and the Ministry of Agriculture, Fisheries and Food (MAFF).

Drug and solvent misuse: The DH tasks related to drug and solvent misuse arising from the three-year strategy for England, *Tackling drugs together*[31], include various initiatives. Local drug action teams have been set up across England together with local community networks and drug reference groups; since late 1995, there has been an HEA national anti-drug publicity campaign particularly targeted at young people, and including the launch of a parents' guide to drugs and solvents[32]. The Task Force to Review Services for Drug Misusers report[33], published in May 1996, was well received and its findings have assisted in the preparation of purchasing guidance for services for drug misusers. The 24-hour freephone National Drugs Helpline was opened in April 1995, and received over 500,000 calls in its second year. Shared care arrangements for drug misusers between providers of primary and secondary health care have been reviewed by all health authorities, and medical and nursing professional bodies are helping to improve staff training and education. Deaths due to solvent misuse rose steeply from 1984 to a peak of 151 in 1990, and subsequently fell in successive years to 58 deaths in 1994, but rose to 68 in 1995[34]; a further publicity campaign on the hazards of solvent misuse is due later this year. Concern over alcohol misuse by young people was heightened following the appearance on the market from Summer 1995 of a range of new alcoholic drinks colloquially known as 'alcopops'. In May 1997, the Home Secretary convened the Ministerial Group on Alcopops to examine what measures were needed to prevent or inhibit the inappropriate marketing, promotion and sale of alcoholic drinks to individuals under 18 years-of-age. The Ministerial Group issued a press release and statement on 17 July which set out the action the Government expects the alcohol industry to take in order to tackle this problem over the next year[35]. The Ministerial Group will keep progress under review, and has not ruled out further action if steps taken by the industry prove ineffective.

Progress on topics identified during 1995

Risk communication and the language of risk: Last year's Report[36] discussed how the language of risk may be used and understood, and the need to pay close attention to these factors when communicating about health risks. Poor communication can have serious consequences, exaggerating fears unnecessarily or desensitising the public to real risks. The 1995 Report discussed the need to make small probabilities understandable, and set out for debate a scale of probabilities to underpin the consistent use of terms such as 'severe' or 'moderate' risk; a later suggestion is to scale risks by use of familiar, everyday comparisons - for example, 'one person in a small town' as a rough equivalent to '1 in 10,000'[37].

However, the topic of risk communication runs much wider than the expression of probabilities and has been the subject of a DH programme, with the co-operation of other interested parties. A one-day conference in October 1996 brought together a wide range of participants from Government, industry, academia and interest groups. A number of useful key themes emerged, which are being taken forward in the Department and through a further conference to be held in November 1997.

Within the Department, an extensive work programme has concentrated primarily on risks to public health, though it is also relevant to communication with individual patients. The programme involves four interlocking elements:

General guidance on risk communication: Guidelines on risk communication for use throughout the Department are being developed. A study of risk communication on public health issues has summarised relevant research and its implications for practice, and has been circulated widely within the Department, and to other Government Departments via the Inter-Departmental Group on Public Health (IDGPH) and the Inter-Departmental Liaison Group on Risk Assessment (IDLGRA). It focuses interest in risk communication, has spread awareness of the relevant research and offers general guidance on management of the communication process. More prescriptive guidelines, based on existing material and work outlined below, are being developed.

Developmental workshops: These events develop the ability of key staff to identify and manage risk communication issues. Guided by internal and external facilitators, participants work on fictional but realistic cases, structured to bring out points of particular interest - both to promote personal learning and to indicate possible improvements to Departmental practice. Following a pilot workshop, a series of events now under way will ensure the participation of nearly 50 staff across the Department and its Agencies, and Regional Offices; further events will involve participation by other Government Departments.

Case study seminars: These are based on discussions of real cases, and involve members of staff who managed the episode concerned. At each event, the case in question and the draft guidelines on risk communication are evaluated against each other; lessons are drawn from each case, and the guidelines themselves are progressively refined.

Support for key risk communication decisions: Methods developed for strategic planning provide ways to structure and analyse current issues, often used in decision-support workshops. The methods help to identify the policy options available, the key stakeholders and how they may respond, and what the most important sources of uncertainty are. They provide a clearer view of how the case is liable to develop, and the effectiveness or otherwise of different communication strategies.

This programme complements more detailed work on risk communication and management in specific areas. In the field of microbiological risk, for example, a working group of the Advisory Committee on Dangerous Pathogens (ACDP) has carried out a study leading to recommendations for risk assessment. An interim report[38] was followed up by a major seminar organised by the Department.

Inter-Departmental fora such as the IDGPH and the IDLGRA have a major role in spreading attention to risk communication across Government, and help to co-ordinate progress. Two current programmes, both funded by the HSE, are of particular relevance: work on 'benchmarking' of risk communication, which will draw conclusions from case studies from various Departments, including DH, and complements the internal studies referred to above; and an investigation of the role of the mass media in either amplifying or attenuating public responses to risks.

All these elements provide ways to improve the practice of risk communication. Throughout, the Department's work is guided by three general principles:

- *While public reactions to statements about risk can seem surprising, they are not totally unpredictable:* a good deal is known about why different types of risk cause more or less alarm and, when working to inform the public, awareness of this can help the Department to identify particular challenges in advance;

- *Effective communication is necessarily a two-way process:* it is essential to identify and communicate with the key stakeholders involved in each case and to pay attention to their values and beliefs. The point is not only to express the Department's view, and those of its expert advisors, most effectively, but also to learn from those with different and legitimate perspectives - so openness in the policy process must therefore be encouraged; *and*

- *Good risk communication requires a coherent strategy, rather than ad-hoc reaction to events:* overall aims must be clearly formulated and kept under review, particularly as they relate to other key stakeholders; an assessment must be made of possible outcomes; and the results of particular risk communication episodes - successful or otherwise - must be monitored and acted upon.

Mental health: Following last year's special chapter on mental health[39], further progress has been made in this key area, with a focus on users' needs and views, the NHS workforce and the quality of services. In January 1997, *The patient's charter: mental health services*[40] was launched, and plans to spend over £1.4 million nationally are being developed to increase knowledge and understanding about mental health and to combat the stigma of ill-health. Over 500 responses to the Green Paper *Developing partnerships in mental health*[41] published in February 1997, have been received, and highlight the importance of inter-Agency working and integrated planning in mental health services. Following last year's consultation on a revised version of the Mental Health Act 1983[42] Code of Practice, approximately 200 responses are now being analysed. In March 1997, the House of Commons Health Select Committee published their report on child and adolescent mental health services[43], and work on the development of the Health of the Nation Outcome Scales for Children and Adolescents (HoNOSCA) was completed. In May 1997, *The primary mental health care toolkit*[44,45] was published, giving guidance on basic primary mental health assessment, diagnosis and management. In recognition of the special challenges in London, an independent Advisory Panel, due to report in Autumn 1997, has been established to advise on planning mental health services. Further attention has also been given to the NHS workforce: a full consultation process about professional development will provide the basis for a strategy to equip staff with the skills to deliver modern, comprehensive mental health services. The new education and training consortia, with their focus on integrated planning across the medical and non-medical workforce, are already playing an important role.

Antibiotic-resistant micro-organisms: The increasing proportion of bacteria developing resistance to antibiotics to which they were previously sensitive is now causing international concern. Although immediate control measures are important, in the longer term refinement of the usage of antibiotics must be the key feature of a strategy to address this challenge. In many countries, antibiotics are freely available over the counter, and their usage extends far beyond medical, dental and veterinary practice because of their effect as growth promoters in agriculture; achieving change in all these areas is a daunting task. Nevertheless, experience in Denmark, which has seen a dramatic reduction in the prevalence of antibiotic-resistant micro-organisms, indicates that much can be done. During the past year, many parts of the Department have been involved in discussions about how best to effect such a change in the UK, and further progress should be reported next year. New guidelines on methicillin-resistant *Staphylococcus aureus* (MRSA) control in hospitals, and guidance on the management of tuberculosis which is drug resistant or associated with HIV infection, should be published during 1997, and a report from the Advisory Committee on the Microbiological Safety of Food (ACMSF) on the role of food in the acquisition of antibiotic-resistant infection is being prepared.

Information technology: Information technology (IT) and the use of computers has revolutionised the way in which patient care is delivered and health improved[46]. Rapid developments indicate that, over the next few years, the pace of change will become even faster, providing greater potential benefits to patients and the public, with likely improvements in public health, health care, education, research and management effectiveness. However, there are also potential disadvantages in the process and, in particular, a need to maintain the confidentiality of individual patient information. Aspects of progress in information and in discussion of ethical issues are addressed elsewhere in this report (see pages 247 and 245, respectively).

HIV infection and AIDS: Last year's Report[47] outlined the success of actions taken to control the spread of this novel disease after its identification in the early 1980s. Health promotion campaigns are still crucial to the control of HIV/AIDS, but the recent introduction of combination therapy is a very promising development. Zidovudine, the first drug used to treat HIV infection, loses its therapeutic benefit as the virus becomes drug-resistant. Combination therapy - the use of two or more antiretroviral drugs - is based on the hypothesis that HIV is unlikely to develop resistance to more than one drug at the same time, especially if they affect different stages of the viral life-cycle. Combination therapy is not a cure for HIV infection and, although clinical trial results are promising, the long-term effects are unknown. However, evidence including data from randomised trials indicates that these treatments provide clinical benefit and may delay the onset of AIDS[48,49], and has prompted clinicians to produce guidelines for the antiretroviral treatment of HIV and AIDS[50]. Although there is no room for complacency, emerging epidemiological evidence of a recent decline in AIDS cases since the introduction of combination therapies is encouraging - but public health measures aimed at prevention of infection remain central to the containment of this condition.

NEW TOPICS IDENTIFIED DURING 1996

Each year a small number of issues will be identified as topics of particular importance, to be followed up in subsequent Reports. It should be recognised that the actions needed to ensure progress on these topics may be the responsibility of a wide range of organisations and individuals.

The potential for health

Just a glance at the Reports on the state of the public health over the past 139 years shows clearly how public health in England has changed for the better. Life expectancy, infant mortality and maternal mortality have all shown striking improvements. The quality and range of health care provided, the support from other sources, the volume of research - all have been greatly enhanced. But a review of this year's Report still shows some disturbing features.

Mortality among males aged 15-44 years is still as high as it was in 1986 - a sad loss of young lives. Excess winter mortality still occurs in England, particularly among elderly people. Deaths related to drug misuse and accidental poisoning increased almost six-fold among men aged 40-44 years since 1986, and cigarette smoking by children, particularly by girls, continues to increase. Lung cancer has now overtaken breast cancer as the predominant cause of cancer deaths among women in some parts of the country, and is strongly associated with cigarette smoking. Many chronic diseases remain serious challenges for individuals, their families and society alike. Death rates from heart disease and stroke, while falling, remain too high; obesity is increasing; regular participation in exercise remains disappointing; and some evidence indicates increased alcohol consumption - most disturbingly among teenagers. All of these data require explanation and action to improve health. The contention is that, with existing knowledge, health can be improved - and that the potential is there if only it can be realised. Nevertheless, it should be made clear that the determinants are mainly social and economic, and that solutions need to be found at personal, local and national levels.

The concept of 'potential' for health is used deliberately, and should be more widely recognised: potential is associated with the concept of energy - the capacity to work and play; it implies an ability to transform, to change one form of energy into another; it suggests empowerment of individuals - a crucial factor in improving public health; it acknowledges a gap between what is now and what could be.

What are the determinants of health and the factors which influence health care, and how might individual and public health be improved?

The objective is to improve the health of the people of England by setting out a clear strategy, based on available evidence and with the involvement of individuals, organisations and Government alike. Health cannot be narrowly defined; it is not just the absence of sickness, nor just about living longer, but about a better quality of life. Good health is perhaps the ultimate 'feel-good' factor, and should be encouraged. Any strategy for public health must take into account these factors and be broadly based and holistic. Improving health is as much about employment, occupation, housing, transport, the environment, education and living standards - including poverty - as it is about treatment within the health service[51]. This is a wide canvas, and can always be refined; the process is one of continual revision and renewal, and must therefore be grounded in values which are long-lasting and durable.

The values and principles which underpin this approach are those which have been set out in each Report for the past five years (see page 2)[3,4,5,6]. They are re-stated here, and developed further.

Health for all: This principle involves the whole population, not as empty rhetoric, but implying the need to ensure that the whole population - no matter where they live, who they are, their age, gender, lifestyle, or what they believe in - should not be disadvantaged. As a key principle of social justice, everyone should have the opportunity to realise their potential for health, and they need to be involved in the process.

The value of people: Resources, enthusiasm, energy and skills must be focused on individuals: services to improve health do not exist to please doctors, nurses, managers, or politicians, but for the public, and involve a wide range of contributors, including voluntary agencies. The involvement of patients and the public in this process is essential. Self care, and care by relatives and friends, should not be overlooked or unacknowledged. It forms the greatest proportion of overall health care.

Intelligence and surveillance: Changes in health and the outcome of health care should be identified early and acted upon, which requires an effective system of monitoring and surveillance and must incorporate continual evaluation of the results of interventions.

Evidence-based decision-making: A scientific approach and recognition of the importance of the knowledge base are essential to make rational decisions about health and health care - although the limits of scientific knowledge, and the need to deal in some circumstances with uncertainty, should be recognised.

Education and research: A knowledge base continually revised and updated by research represents the bedrock of information for professionals, patients and the public alike.

Ethics and moral issues: At the heart of the effective and equitable delivery of health care services, these provide the framework within which decisions should be made. Informed principles of equity, human rights, social justice and concern for the individual should be held by all those involved in making decisions about health and health care.

How do these six key principles form a value base to further a strategy to improve the health of the people of England? They point to a need to consider: holistic aspects that cover physical, social, psychological and spiritual aspects of life, putting the patient and community first; ecological aspects, in that they put the health of human beings within the context of the world as a whole, and relate human activity to animal and plant life and the wider environment; inter-sectoral working, in that they acknowledge that a wide range of agencies and individuals need actively to pursue the potential for health; and equity, in that existing variations and inequalities in health must be tackled.

Any strategy to improve public health requires an understanding of what factors influence health and ill-health, and of how outcomes of health care can be influenced. What, then, are the determinants of health?

Genetic factors: These are of considerable importance to our understanding of health and diseases and, as more genes are recognised to have an impact on health, so the implications will become increasingly important - although ethical aspects of population screening must be fully addressed.

The environment: Attention must be paid to factors in the external world which might have an impact on health - such as quality of air, water, soil, and exposure to radiation or infectious disease - as discussed in Agenda 21, the strategy developed by the United Nations (UN) to link environment and sustainable development at the UN Conference on Environment and Development (the 'Rio Summit') in June 1992.

Lifestyle: Many aspects of how we live and behave affect our health and should be better recognised; dietary habits, cigarette smoking, drug misuse, excessive alcohol consumption and sexual behaviour are all relevant.

Social and economic factors: These affect health in many ways, sometimes as key determinants. The influence of different cultural backgrounds, employment status, income, housing and social class are all relevant; the effects of education and the opportunities this may provide to further public and individuals' health are also important.

Health services: The provision of a health care service contributes to health by effective treatment and, where cure is not possible, by reducing disability or improving the quality of life.

In the development of any specific disease, some or all of these factors will be relevant. For many diseases, the contribution of health care - although crucial to the individual - may have a relatively minor role in the furtherance of public health. This concept of considering health can be extended to look at those factors which influence the outcome of health care. As with the determinants of health, five major factors are all relevant.

Health status of the individual: The health and fitness of an individual at the time of diagnosis is relevant to the treatment which may be given, and its outcome.

The diagnosis: The natural history of a disease, and its stage at diagnosis, strongly influence prognosis and may predicate the outcome. Accurate diagnosis is essential.

Treatment and rehabilitation: For some illnesses, available treatment is very effective, and may be the major determinant of outcome; for others, treatment may only have a limited effect on outcome.

The skill-mix of those providing care: The skills of all health care professionals are clearly relevant and training does not end after qualification; the skills and contributions of other carers must not be overlooked.

Facilities and resources to provide health care: These are not just financial but also relate to skills, expertise and equipment.

A model for health and health care

The determinants of health and those factors which influence health outcomes may be incorporated into a model which can be used to assist decision-making and to identify priorities. Models are always over-simplifications - but they do help to interpret data, predict outcome and help to communicate the way forward. By use of this model, a strategy to improve health can be more easily defined, and regularly updated and evaluated (see Figure I.1).

Figure I.1: *A model of health*

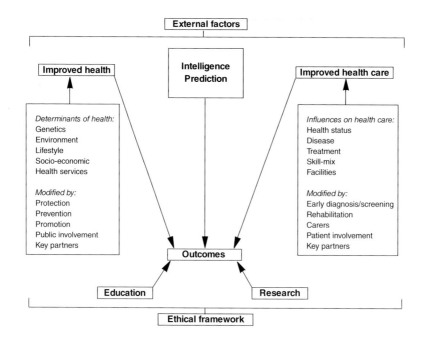

The basic model integrates the determinants of health and outcomes of health care, linking these with methods to assess the outcome of any intervention. Such measures might range from improved health, reduction in mortality or disability, recovery from illness or a change in quality of life; added to this is the impact of research and education; and ethical issues provide a broad framework within which the model should operate, reflecting the importance of moral values; external factors beyond health and health care are also relevant.

The determinants of health can be modified to include health protection and health promotion, disease prevention, and public involvement. Those factors which influence health care are modified by early diagnosis and screening, by the importance of rehabilitation, by the role of carers and by patient and public involvement. In each case it is important to consider key partners (including relatives, social services and local authorities, and the voluntary sector) who may be crucial in assisting the process of recovery. The model is further refined by consideration of information, intelligence systems and surveillance, and methods to predict health.

Use of this model needs a topic to be identified - which could be a disease, a hazard or a lifestyle issue - then consideration of whether or not there is a particular patient or population group to be investigated. In a systematic way each of the components should be reviewed, recording the information available and its possible impact upon outcome; where evidence is not available, or where gaps in knowledge occur, it will help to identify areas for further research. Finally, the whole model is considered and priorities identified which are both practical and lead to improvement in health or the outcome of health care. Some examples may help to illustrate this more effectively, but are presented for discussion only and there is scope for informed debate about the conclusions; that is the purpose of the exercise.

Dementia: The subject needs careful definition as many forms of disease may lead to similar symptoms, some of which may be effectively treated; many not. The population is generally elderly, but younger people may be affected. There is a need for more epidemiological data, and more research. In the 'health box', genetic factors may be relevant, but most others are not; among modifiers, health promotion may have little place, but public involvement and understanding are crucial; under 'health care', major issues include progression of disease, lack of effectiveness of treatment, the importance of trained staff and the role of carers. Priorities that can be identified include a need for staff training, carer support, and more epidemiological data and research.

Lung cancer: The main causal factor is cigarette smoking, which is influenced by familial, social, educational and economic factors. Health promotion, and smoking cessation are relevant. The disease is very difficult to treat and represents a classic example of prevention opportunities, with identifiable priorities including a co-ordinated approach to smoking control (including advertising and economic regulation), more research on treatment, and further encouragement of smoking cessation.

Childhood accidents: The environment, parental lifestyles and social factors are all relevant. Health promotion and public involvement are central. Acute treatment is generally effective, and there needs to be an emphasis on rehabilitation where required. Priorities that can be identified include social and economic factors, secure play areas, local involvement and community development projects.

Use of this model of health, which can be applied to individuals or populations, is relatively simple to operate, but there is no substitute for detailed investigation. However the model can help to identify key challenges and priorities for different groups, such as patients, professionals, managers and politicians.

Experience across the world has shown that to improve health, a strategic long-term approach is required. In general, a limited number of topics are chosen to reflect major health problems. Targets are set, and a wide variety of groups and organisations from all sectors are involved in the process of change. There should be a regular process of monitoring and evaluation.

The root causes of ill-health such as poverty, social factors, employment status, poor housing, transport and environmental pollution, and level of education need a national focus. Community development projects at local level allow full involvement of the community, and all the local resources in the statutory and voluntary sectors to be fully deployed. Individuals, and families, also need to recognise that they too have a responsibility to maintain and improve their health. Health care professionals should see their role in a different light, being concerned not only with treating illness but in improving the health of those with whom they come into contact.

There are major inequalities in health in this country, as in others. Almost every investigation in every disease shows this. Many, though not all, are avoidable. To tackle these differences will require commitment, skills and expertise. The knowledge is available; the potential can be realised if there is the courage and leadership to drive the changes through. The quest for better health is also the quest for social justice.

Health of disabled people

The special chapter in this year's Report focuses on the health of disabled people. Disability is common. According to the 1995 Health Survey for England[52], which followed up an extensive survey series by the then Office for Population Censuses and Surveys (OPCS, now part of the Office for National Statistics[ONS])[53,54,55,56,57,58], almost one in five adults has either a moderate or severe disability, with the prevalence increasing to approximately one in two by the age of 75 years; about 5% of children have a disability.

Nevertheless, some disabilities, and the effects of those disabilities, can remain more or less hidden - for example, loss of continence, sexual problems and the impact which disability may have on families and family relationships as relatives become carers; learning disabilities and the disabilities which can result from mental illness also pose difficulties in ascertainment.

All forms of disability pose particular challenges to individuals, carers and providers (whether formal or voluntary) of care and support. There has been progress, but much remains to be done. The Disability Discrimination Act 1995[59] highlights the dual role of the NHS as a service provider and as an employer; the need to work with disabled people to use their expertise gained through living with their disability and to strive for their full participation in society is increasingly recognised; a coherent strategy for public health[1,2] should offer increasing scope to prevent disability and to treat the causes of disability; and the further development of partnerships should not only help to alleviate the impact of disability on individuals and their relatives and carers, but to empower disabled people in regard to their own care and their contributions to society as a whole.

Consent

The principle of consent has been a focus of public and professional concern alike in several areas of practice in recent years.

In general, a patient has the right under common law to give or withhold consent to medical examination or treatment. This is a basic principle of health care. Patients are entitled to receive sufficient information, in a way that they can understand, about proposed treatments, the possible alternatives and any substantial risk or risks which may be special in kind or magnitude or special to the patient, so that they can make a balanced judgment. Those seeking consent must ensure that they are adequately trained for this task, and can supply the necessary information[60]. The Department issued guidance on consent to examination or treatment in 1990[61].

The Court has ruled that a mentally competent patient has an absolute right to refuse to consent to medical treatment for any reason, rational or irrational, or for no reason at all, even where the decision may lead to his or her own death[62].

Decisions involving children are more complex, and will usually involve their parents: however, several reports have drawn attention to the need to involve children in the decision-making process, and properly to assess their competence to make decisions about their own health care[63]. Children or young people who are competent to consent to treatment are entitled to do so[64].

After a series of Court cases in relation to caesarean sections, the Court of Appeal has clarified relevant law and professional practice. It emphasises the right of a mentally competent pregnant woman to refuse treatment, irrespective of risk to an unborn child, and the importance of legal representation of the woman in such proceedings. The Court of Appeal has laid down ten principles of procedure which should be applied in future cases.

A person lacks capacity to give or withold informed consent if some impairment or disturbance of mental functioning renders that person unable to make such a decision. That inability to make a decision will occur when the patient is unable to comprehend and retain the information which is material to the decision, especially as to the likely consequences of having or not having the treatment in question, or is unable to use the information and weigh it in the balance as part of the process of arriving at a decision. If a compulsive disorder or phobia from which the patient suffers stifles belief in the information presented, then the decision may not be a true one. Other temporary factors such as confusion, shock, fatigue, pain or drugs may completely erode capacity, but those concerned in making a decision on whether the patient lacks capacity must be satisfied that such factors are operating to such a degree that the ability to decide is absent.

When a patient is not capable of giving consent, the legal test set out in *Re F* [61,65] was that the intervention should be in his or her best interests. An operation or other treatment will be in a patient's best interests if it is carried out either to save his or her life, or to ensure improvement or to prevent deterioration in the patient's physical or mental health.

Written consent is necessary for the storage or posthumous use of gametes in assisted reproduction[66]. The removal of gametes is subject to the same consent requirements as all other medical interventions. On behalf of the UK Health Ministers, a review of consent procedures for the removal, storage and use of gametes is being conducted by Professor Sheila McLean, Professor of Law and Ethics in Medicine at the University of Glasgow, and a consultation document is expected to be issued in late 1997. Further details of recent Court rulings on surgical intervention in pregnancy and the use of gametes were distributed to the NHS in June[67].

The legal background to possible interventions that may help to save the life of a close relative, but may pose risks to an adult incapable of consent, such as bone-marrow donation, was clarified by a recent Court decision that an application must be made to the Court before bone-marrow harvesting was undertaken. The Court will consider, in the light of the donor's best interests, whether the procedure would be lawful[68].

Advance refusals of treatment, if validly made and applicable in the circumstances, have full legal effect[69], although some doctors may not be aware of the legal position[70]. In 1994, the House of Lords Select Committee on Medical Ethics called for the development of a Code of Practice on advance directives, a recommendation thoughtfully taken up by the British Medical Association (BMA) in 1995[71]. However, an advance directive cannot be used to request an unlawful act, such as euthanasia.

The principle of consent is central to the Council of Europe Convention on Human Rights and Biomedicine[72], which was opened for signature in April 1997. The Convention contains 38 Articles concerning the conditions under which it would be ethically acceptable to undertake a medical intervention, undertake research, or retrieve for transplant regenerative tissue such as bone marrow, where the person concerned is not capable of giving consent. The Convention sets strict safeguards to ensure the protection of such persons.

The issue of consent to the use of personal health information is complex. As well as the long-established common law duty of confidence, there are a number of relevant statutory provisions. DH guidance, *The protection and use of patient information*, issued in 1996[73], emphasises the importance of informing patients about the essential uses of their personal health information - for example, for monitoring and protecting public health. However, some concerns remain that awareness of and compliance with this detailed guidance may be limited. These issues have also been considered in preparations for implementation of the EC Directive on Data Protection by October 1998.

Domestic violence

Domestic violence, a term usually applied to violence inflicted on women by a male partner, does not conventionally include child abuse or elder abuse (both important causes of abuse within the family and home), nor does it include violence inflicted within homosexual relationships (whether male or female) or by women on male partners. Domestic violence is not just physical: it also encompasses mental and emotional abuse. It is a crime.

One in four assaults reported in British crime surveys are domestic, although only a small proportion of such assaults are reported. Up to one in three women report that they have been physically abused by a male partner; one-quarter of these incidents involve former partners. Domestic violence is often repeated, and in some 40% of cases where women are killed in violent incidents, the assailant is a current or former partner.

Factors leading to domestic violence are imperfectly understood, but receiving considerable attention in this country and elsewhere. It is more common, or may start, during pregnancy and in the post-partum period; there are adverse consequences for children who experience domestic violence, and the children of mothers who are subject to domestic violence are also more likely to be abused themselves. Domestic violence has considerable implications for the NHS - particularly in accident and emergency departments, primary care and in specialist settings such as maternity services and child and adolescent mental health services. Health care costs incurred are considerable; personal costs even more so - perhaps especially if not acknowledged or recognised.

During 1995, the DH Social Services Inspectorate hosted two major conferences on domestic violence, reports of which were circulated to all social services departments in 1996[74] to assist in the development of a framework for local inter-agency co-operation and co-ordination, also encouraged by the Home Office circular *Domestic violence - don't stand for it*[75]. Part IV of the Family Law Act 1996[76], related to family homes and domestic violence, comes into effect on 1 October 1997. It provides for a single set of civil remedies to address domestic violence and to provide a regulatory framework for occupation and non-molestation orders; it also extends the categories of people entitled to apply for such orders to all current and previous partners, whether or not married. An occupation order determines who is allowed to live in the home and can direct another party to leave the home; a non-molestation order prevents the respondent from molesting the applicant or a child. DH has responsibility for health and social care aspects of domestic violence.

Effective implementation of the new legislation will require improved recognition of domestic violence; further facilities to help, advise and support women who experience domestic violence; and an effective interface with other agencies, especially social services and the criminal justice system. A number of professional bodies have identified the extent of the problem, and are developing programmes to support their members in working with women who have been subject to domestic violence. The Royal College of Nursing, the Royal College of Obstetricians and Gynaecologists, and primary care, accident and emergency and public health departments are taking matters forward. Such education programmes should be led by professional bodies but be responsive to local needs.

DH will help to ensure that connections are made between various existing initiatives under way; to assist, where appropriate, in informing health care professionals about the nature and extent of the problem; and to co-ordinate effective use of NHS resources in helping those subject to domestic violence.

Air quality and health

Air pollution damages health, as described in a series of reports by DH Advisory Groups and the Committee on the Medical Effects of Air Pollutants (COMEAP) and its predecessor, the Advisory Group on the Medical Aspects of Air Pollution Episodes (MAAPE)[77,78,79]. These reports and those of the Department of the Environment (DoE) and the DH Expert Panel on Air Quality Standards have informed the process of setting air quality standards for the UK. In April 1997, these standards were incorporated into the UK-wide national air quality strategy[80], which sets objectives in air pollution control to be achieved by the year 2005, and probably represents the most striking advance in air quality management since the first Clean Air Act in 1956[81].

The strategy outlines a range of measures which will be taken to improve air quality: some form part of an integrated European approach to air pollution, whereas others highlight the scope for local initiatives. Tighter controls on emissions from motor vehicles, improvements in fuel composition, and a stated need for air pollution to be considered in local planning decisions and the development of transport policy represent an integrated approach; combined with the principle of sustainable development, this should bring about further improvements in air quality.

Progress has been made. Concentrations of some air pollutants have fallen since the 1950s' London smogs, and the reduction in use of coal for domestic heating has been largely responsible for this improvement. Nevertheless, there has been a substantial increase in the use of motor vehicles and a consequent increase in the output of other pollutants; photochemical reactions upon the primary pollutants emitted by motor vehicles also produce ozone and secondary particles[82].

A series of epidemiological studies of the effects of pollutants on health undertaken in European cities, including London, have examined the relations between day-to-day variations in the concentrations of pollutants and measures of effects on health. Mortality rates, rates of admissions to hospital and the prevalence of symptoms of diseases including asthma and other respiratory diseases largely confirm the results of United States (US) studies[83,84]. A surprising finding was that hospital admissions for respiratory diseases in London appear to be related to ozone concentrations. The effect is stronger in the Summer, when ozone concentrations are higher than in Winter; an increase in the 8-hour average daytime concentration of ozone of 29 parts per 1,000 million (ppb) was associated with a relative risk of admission of 1.0483 (CI: 1.0246-1.0725), or nearly a 5% increase in risk[85]. Although ozone concentrations in urban areas tend to be lower than in rural areas, effects may occur even in urban areas and are being further investigated as part of a research initiative on air pollution and health funded by DH, the DoE and the Medical Research Council (MRC). The studies indicate that ultra-fine particles appear to be unexpectedly toxic in animal models, even at very low concentrations[86]; such particles occur in the air in large numbers but, because of their small size, they contribute little to the overall mass of particles present.

Asthma is often linked to air pollution, but although the symptoms of asthma may be made worse by exposure to air pollutants, there is little evidence to support the idea that air pollution causes asthma. UK research indicates that pollutants such as nitrogen dioxide can increase the response of the airways to allergens[87,88], and raised concentrations of nitrogen dioxide and allergen exposure often occur indoors.

Whilst it is widely accepted that air pollution may have an adverse effect on certain cardiovascular and respiratory diseases, until recently it has not been possible to calculate with acceptable accuracy the extent of those effects. Recent epidemiological studies and air pollution data are being reviewed, and the COMEAP intends to publish an estimate of the possible effects of air pollution, in association with data on overall deaths and hospital admissions, in Autumn 1997.

To provide the public with the best possible information on air quality and the possible effects of air pollutants on health, DH and the DoE will review the banding system used to describe air quality and publish a handbook on air pollution and health to set out known effects of air pollutants on health and summarise the results of recent research.

EXECUTIVE SUMMARY

VITAL STATISTICS

Population size

The estimated resident population of England at 30 June 1996 was 49.1 million, an increase of 0.4% compared with 1995 and of 3.7% compared with 1986.

Age and sex structure of the resident population

There has been a sharp rise in the number of young adults aged 25-34 years, with a steep fall in the number of 15-24-year-olds, over the past 10 years. All other age-groups, except those aged 55-64 years, show a rise in numbers over the same period. Very elderly people (aged 85 years and over) still continue to increase in number, and represent a growing proportion of all pensioners.

Fertility statistics

In 1994, 760,400 conceptions occurred to women resident in England, a 2% fall from the figure in 1993, with an overall conception rate of 74.8 per 1,000 women aged 15-44 years. Numbers of conceptions in England and Wales for the quarter ending March 1996 show a 7% increase over conceptions in the quarter ending March 1995. In 1994, there were 8.3 conceptions per 1,000 girls aged 13-15 years in England, compared with 8.0 per 1,000 in 1993 and 8.4 per 1,000 in 1992. During 1996, there were 614,184 live births in England - 0.2% higher than in 1995. In 1995, 147,875 abortions were performed on women resident in England, a fall of 1% compared with 1994.

Trends in reporting congenital anomalies

Appendix Table A.6 shows the number of babies born in England notified with selected congenital anomalies. In 1996, the notification rate for live births with congenital anomalies fell to 80.6 per 10,000 live births, 3% lower than in 1995 and 18% lower than in 1991.

Mortality

Provisional statistics for 1996 in England indicate that 3,696 babies died before the age of one year, compared with 3,739 in 1995. The infant mortality rate fell to 6.0 per 1,000 live births, the lowest ever recorded. Based on provisional statistics, there were 3,345 stillbirths in 1996, compared with 3,403 in 1995; the stillbirth rate per 1,000 total births fell from 5.5 in 1995 to 5.4 in 1996. Deaths registered in England decreased from 529,038 in 1995 to 526,650 in 1996, a fall of 0.5%. For most age-groups, mortality rates fell during the 1980s in males and females, but a 6.3% increase was seen for men aged 15-44 years between 1986 and 1990, but has since remained fairly stable.

Prevalence of disease in the community

Over the period 1993 to 1995, there has been a rise in the proportion of the population prescribed drugs for the treatment of asthma and who had a diagnosis of asthma of 3% among males and 8% in females; a 9% rise in the proportion of the population of women and an 11.5% rise among men aged 15 years and over with a diagnosis of anxiety/depression and who had been prescribed antidepressants; and a 9% rise in the proportion of the population of women and a 7% rise among men aged 35 years and over who had a diagnosis of hypertension and had been treated with antihypertensive drugs. Despite year-to-year fluctuations, the overall trend in self-reported sickness was upwards from 1972 to 1985, but has subsequently appeared to stabilise; in 1995, 31% of males and females reported a long-standing illness.

Trends in cancer incidence and mortality

There was an increase in the age-standardised incidence rate for all malignant neoplasms combined (excluding non-melanoma skin cancer) between 1979 and 1991. The largest percentage increase for any one site was in registrations of malignant melanoma of the skin for males and females.

THE NATION'S HEALTH

Basic sources of information

The Health Survey for England is an annual national survey of those living in private households. In 1996, it covered respiratory disease, accidents and special measures of general health, as well as monitoring Health of the Nation[1] targets on blood pressure and obesity.

Substance misuse

While drug misuse statistics showed a continued rise in the number of individuals presenting for treatment, an independent Task Force confirmed the effectiveness of treatment in reducing the health and social harm of drugs[89]. The Health Education Authority's (HEA's) drug prevention campaign continued.

Following the publication of the report *Sensible drinking*[90], the HEA continued its work on sensible drinking through the 'Think about drink' campaign; there was considerable public concern about drinking by young people.

Nutrition

Several guidelines for good practice in nutrition were published during the year[91,92,93,94], during which there was a particular focus on surveys of infant feeding both in the general population and in the Asian community[95,96].

Health of children

Survival prospects for children showed further progress, with infant mortality falling to 6.0 per 1,000 live births in England and Wales, the lowest recorded level. Progress continued with the Health of the Young Nation initiative.

Health of adolescents

Promotion of young people's health was developed by the Health of the Young Nation initiative. Service issues were addressed in good practice guidance[97,98,99].

Health of women

During the year, the Department of Health (DH) produced new health promotion materials for women and held a conference on gender perspectives in health service provision[100,101].

Health of men

Men's health issues are increasingly important. Particular emphasis has been placed on a wide range of projects and events designed to convey health messages across to men effectively.

Health of black and ethnic minorities

Work by DH and the National Health Service (NHS) to improve the health of people from ethnic minority population groups through improvements in standards of service, provision of better information and by listening to their particular needs continued over the year.

Health in the workplace

The Report for 1994[24] drew attention to occupational health hazards, the importance of workplace risk assessment and the role of occupational health professionals. During 1996, the Health and Safety Executive (HSE) launched the second phase of its campaign 'Good health is good business'.

Health of people in later life

DH continued to promote work on sickness and disability prevention for older people, and services to facilitate independent life in the community.

Mental health

Mental health continues to represent an important focus for the NHS and, although much work is still to be done, some important progress was made during the year.

THE STRATEGY FOR HEALTH

Introduction

The Health of the Nation strategy for England[1] was launched in 1992 and continues to be a key initiative to improve health. With one or two exceptions, progress towards the 27 targets is encouraging. The National Audit Office report on progress[102] identified areas for attention.

Key areas and targets

Coronary heart disease and stroke: The latest data on mortality from CHD and stroke[52] show a downward trend among people aged under 65 years and aged 65-74 years. The strategy for health encompasses activity on various fronts - including physical activity, smoking, and diet - to ensure that progress is maintained.

Cancers: Action continues to tackle smoking among all population groups, particularly teenagers and pregnant women. Screening is the main intervention for reducing breast and cervical cancers; progress is good for both NHS screening programmes, and the cervical cancer target has been met. Work continues on various fronts to reduce the incidence of skin cancer.

Mental health: Technical work advanced on quantification for two of the main strategy for health targets in the mental health key area. A sub-committee was set up to advise on reformulation of these targets in the light of this progress, and a working group on suicide prevention was set up.

HIV/AIDS and sexual health: Work continues to reduce the incidence of HIV and towards the target for sharing equipment among injecting drug users. The conception rates for females aged under 16 years in 1992-94 showed a continuation of the downward trend that began in 1990.

Accidents: Progress continues towards Health of the Nation targets[1], with those in relation to children and young people at or around target levels. Work continued on several new and ongoing DH-funded projects, and three reviews were published on the effectiveness of interventions[103,104,105].

Variations in health

Within England, there are striking differences in life expectancy, morbidity and mortality by social class, sex, region, and ethnic background[27]. Planning and priorities guidance for the NHS emphasise equity, and ask health authorities to identify and act upon variations in health[29]. Work took place nationally to promote the health of women, to encourage health services sensitive to the differing needs of men and women, and to promote the health of ethnic minority groups.

Health of the Young Nation

The Young People's Health Network was launched in June to help organisations that work with young people to share their experiences about health promotion activities.

Consultation on a potential environment key area

DH and the Department of the Environment (DoE) issued a consultation document proposing the environment as a new key area in the strategy for health[106].

Priorities for the NHS

The strategy for health remains a central plank of NHS policy and forms a main context for NHS planning. It provides a strategic approach to improving the health of the population, setting targets to improve health in the five key areas.

Local health alliances

The Health Alliance Awards scheme for 1996/97 attracted 450 entries, a 50% increase on the previous year; this increase was reflected in all NHS regions and in all categories.

Healthy settings

The Workplace Health Advisory Team (WHAT) has been set up to encourage health promotion in small and medium-sized businesses. Work continues in schools on the individual key areas, as well as through the European Network of

Health Promoting Schools. The Prison Service Directorate has been designated a WHO Collaborating Centre and has developed a Health Promoting Prisons Award. The Department continues to develop its links with the 'Healthy cities' network. The 'Health promoting hospitals' initiative is now being run in the NHS regions to establish local and national networks.

Inter-Departmental co-operation

The Health of the Nation strategy relies on cross-Departmental working. Many other Departments have responsibility for crucial aspects of key areas, such as the Department of Transport for road traffic accidents. Co-operative working continues to develop.

HEALTH OF DISABLED PEOPLE

Introduction

Recent years have seen greater recognition of the needs of disabled people and increased action towards meeting them, but much progress has yet to be made. Disability may occur at any time, and is not related to diagnosis in a simple way. Disabilities pose considerable challenges to those who suffer from them; to society as a whole to ensure that disabled people are empowered to take their full part in it; and particular challenges to health, social, educational and employment services, and to the interface between Government Departments and Agencies, local authorities, voluntary agencies, relatives and other carers, and the private sector.

Legislation and civil rights

In 1980, the WHO published a classification of impairments, disabilities and handicaps[107], and in 1981 the United Nations (UN) declared the International Year of Disabled Persons with a theme of "full participation and equality for people with disabilities", which led to a 1983 declaration of standard rules on equal opportunities for persons with disabilities[108]. The Council of Europe's social charter of 1961[109] recommended that all people with physical or mental disabilities should have the right to vocational training, rehabilitation and resettlement, and its 1992 statement[110] consolidated previous recommendations. The Disability Discrimination Act 1995[59] sets out new rights for disabled people in the UK. Under the Act, a disabled person is anyone with "a physical or mental impairment which has a substantial and long-term adverse effect on [the] ability to carry out normal day-to-day activities", and rights may apply in employment;

goods, facilities, services and premises; education; public transport vehicles; and letting or selling land or property.

Epidemiology of disability

Surveys of disability: A major disability survey series conducted by the Office of Population Censuses and Surveys (OPCS, now part of the Office for National Statistics [ONS])[53,54,55,56,57,58] identified the extent of disability in the community to inform planners of health care and social services. In 1995, the Health Survey for England[52] repeated major parts of the 1985 disability surveys.

Prevalence of disability: In the 1995 Health Survey for England[52], 18% of males and females alike aged over 16 years who were living in private households had some degree of disability, either moderate or severe; 4% of men and 5% of women had a serious disability.

Age and gender differences in disability: The prevalence of disabilities increases markedly with age, with about one-quarter of people having a disability by the age of 60 years, and about 50% being disabled by 75 years-of-age. Among people aged 16-54 years, the prevalence of disability is similar among men and women; from 55-74 years-of-age, the prevalence is higher among men; and among those aged 75 years and over, disability is more common among women.

Causes of disability in adults: The most commonly reported cause of disability in the 1995 Health Survey for England[52] was diseases of the musculoskeletal system and connective tissue (34% of those with a disability), followed by diseases of the ear and mastoid process (24%), diseases of the circulatory system (16%), respiratory diseases (10%) and eye disorders (8%). Other conditions that may be disabling, but not directly attributable to an individual disease, include incontinence.

Social and regional differences in disability: The age-standardised prevalence of disability for people in households whose head was in a non-manual occupation was 14% for men and 16% for women, compared with 19% and 21%, respectively, for manual occupations. Age-standardised rates of disability are higher in the North West than in other health regions.

Trends in disability: Between 1976 and 1994 there has been a striking increase in period life expectancies for men and women alike, equivalent to about two months annually; healthy life expectancy rose by some two weeks annually for men and not at all for women.

Use of statistics on disability: When health problems are ranked by the frequency with which they were reported as a cause of disability, relatively few dominate the picture. Eight principal groups of conditions are each reported to cause more than 5% of serious disability, and together account for 87.7% of all reported causes of serious disability and 87.9% of all reported causes of moderate disability. At least six of these eight broad categories include important opportunities for prevention via a coherent strategy for public health[1,2].

Types of disability

Physical disability: Apart from trauma, almost any long-term, severe illness can cause disability; demographic changes mean an increasing number of elderly people who may have disabilities and, at any age, advances in medical care may lead to survival, with disability, where once death would have been the outcome.

Sensory disability: A sensory disability may occur alone or be associated with other sensory, or with physical, learning or mental disability.

Learning disability: Within the general population, approximately four in 1,000 people have severe learning disabilities and 4-6 per 1,000 have mild learning disability. Most who require services are now cared for in the community.

Mental disability: Mental illness is a significant cause of disability[39] and may have a considerable impact on activities of daily living and employment.

Re-ablement

Re-ablement involves a wide range of services to remove or minimise the barriers encountered by disabled people, which may be physical or attitudinal.

Services for disabled people

NHS services: A wide range of services is available to disabled people through the NHS - much from primary and community health care teams but also from hospital or other services.

Social services: Local authority social services departments have a statutory responsibility to provide, or arrange for the provision of, social care and other personal social services to vulnerable individuals and families, and are accountable for the quality of services they provide.

Role of other Government Departments: The Department of Social Security benefits system has a major part to play in the lives of disabled people - not least as a source of income. The Department for Education and Employment (DfEE) has a major role in the provision of education for young disabled people, and of employment opportunities for disabled people, which will be further enhanced by the Disability Discrimination Act 1995[59].

Voluntary sector: Numerous voluntary organisations, large and small, help to meet the information and support needs of disabled people.

Family and informal carers: The family and carers of disabled people frequently know a great deal about the disabled person whom they care for and/or live with, especially in relation to everyday practical needs, and their expertise is often an under-used resource. Carers are entitled to ask for a separate assessment of their needs, and social workers must take into account the ability of the carer to continue caring[111,112]; the provision of respite care can often make a big difference.

Partnerships: Working in partnership underpins many of the principles of community care and good practice. In many cases, several agencies will be involved in the provision of care for disabled people, and solid partnerships must be established between these agencies, the disabled person concerned and his or her carers.

The way ahead

There are many further opportunities for health and social services to influence the causes and to alleviate the consequences of disability. Current initiatives combine three main themes: the need to tackle practical problems so that issues are seen from the perspective of the person with a disability and their carers; the importance of working with disabled people in the furtherance of such facilities and care, as well as with their own carers and other advocates; and the need to work across boundaries to alleviate the impact of disability, and to try to prevent disability, through organised efforts at national, local and individual levels.

HEALTH CARE

Role and function of the National Health Service in England

Purpose: The purpose of the NHS is to secure through the resources available the greatest possible improvement in the physical and mental health of the people of England by: promoting health, preventing ill-health, diagnosing and treating disease and injury, and caring for those with long-term illness and disability. In achieving its purpose, the NHS is required to be universal in its reach, of high quality, available on the basis of clinical need and not a patient's ability to pay, and responsive to the needs and wishes of patients and carers. The NHS aims to judge its results by the criteria of equity, efficiency and responsiveness.

Policies and strategies: In November, the Government set out a strategy for health services in the White Paper *The National Health Service: a service with ambitions*[113]. In response to constructive debate on the future of primary care, the Government issued two White Papers, *Choice and opportunity*[114] and *Primary care: delivering the future*[115], at the end of the year.

Priority setting: In the White Paper *The National Health Service: a service with ambitions*[113], Ministers set out a framework of national priorities and targets for improvement; health authorities and general practitioner (GP) fundholders should assess the needs of the people they serve and decide what treatments and services are required to meet those needs, and individual clinicians should decide the most clinically appropriate treatment and clinical priority for each patient based on their assessment of that patient's needs.

Research and development: The research and development (R&D) strategy has two complementary programmes: the policy research programme, which provides a knowledge base for strategic matters across the Department and provides evidence-based findings which advance Health of the Nation objectives[1]; and the NHS R&D programme, which is priority-led, with a key role in evidence-based health care. New ways to meet the costs which providers of NHS services incur as a result of their involvement in R&D are being introduced.

Role of the NHS in maintaining public health

Public health and the NHS: Public health in England, published in July 1994[116], outlined the public health functions of health authorities. All health authorities are required to make arrangements to involve professionals in the full range of their work.

Health care needs assessment: The assessment of health care needs continues to develop as a core activity of health authorities, and is being extended further to reach more purchasers of health care.

National Casemix Office and NHS Centre for Coding and Classification: Work continues to develop and implement health care terms (from Read Codes), classifications and groupings of patient data to support the exchange of clinical records, resource management and needs assessment.

National Screening Committee: In July, DH set up a National Screening Committee to advise Ministers and the Department on the timeliness and appropriateness for the introduction, review, modification or cessation of national population screening programmes.

Quality of service and effectiveness of care: The delivery of effective health care services must reflect up-to-date knowledge and understanding of current research, as well as local requirements.

Clinical and health outcomes: Multidisciplinary working groups have been set up to develop new outcomes indicators for ten health topics. Analyses of a set of clinical indicators are under way; a survey of existing indicators showed that they were used and valued in the NHS.

Regional epidemiological services for communicable disease: Surveillance, prevention and control of communicable disease remains a fundamental public health task. A national Service Level Agreement between the NHS Executive and the Public Health Laboratory Service (PHLS) came into effect on 1 April.

Primary health care

Organisation of primary care: During 1996, two White Papers[114,115] set out an agenda to improve primary care services for patients, including pilot schemes of novel configurations of service provision, increased funding and various other initiatives focused on quality of care.

Development of emergency services in the community: The report of a review aimed to improve understanding of and to identify ways to develop emergency services outside hospital emphasised the need for better co-ordination, management and communication in emergencies, and better recognition that an emergency had arisen.

'Out of hours' services: The family doctor service has begun to reconfigure the provision of primary health care outside normal working hours.

Prescribing: The continued increase in the cost of NHS prescribing, together with the development of novel drugs and the widening of indications for others, emphasises the need for informed, effective and cost-effective prescribing. DH continues to work with health care professionals, the pharmaceutical industry and patients' organisations alike to provide support, education and information on prescribing issues.

Specialised clinical services

Specialised services: The National Specialist Commissioning Advisory Group took over the functions of the former Supra-Regional Services Advisory Group from 1 April.

Cancer: Further guidance to support the implementation of the new cancer strategy, published in April 1995[117], as well as guidance on breast cancer[118] and palliative care were issued.

National Confidential Enquiry into Perioperative Deaths: The National Confidential Enquiry into Perioperative Deaths published its report for the period 1993/94[119].

Safety and Efficacy Register of New Interventional Procedures: The Safety and Efficacy Register of New Interventional Procedures of the Academy of the medical Royal Colleges (SERNIP) was established in May to oversee the introduction of novel invasive procedures.

Osteoporosis: During the year, DH continued to work to meet the recommendations of the Advisory Group on Osteoporosis.

Transplantation: During the year, 2,279 organ transplants were performed in England. The number of patients who might benefit from transplants continues to rise. The NHS Organ Donor Register, established in 1994, continued to show an increase in registrations.

National renal review: Scientific evidence and purchasing guidelines related to services for patients with renal failure from the national renal review were published in May[120].

Adult intensive care: Guidelines on admission to and discharge from intensive-care and high-dependency units were published in March[121]. A national intensive-care bed register was launched in December[122].

Emergency care services: The strategies explored in the Chief Medical Officer's review of emergency care outside hospital complemented the NHS Executive's initiatives to relieve pressures on the provision of acute care during Winter periods.

Ambulance performance standards review: New ambulance service procedures should help to direct the quickest responses to the most urgent requests.

Mental health

Mental health information systems: Development of clinical information systems continued to progress in NHS mental health services, in parallel with work to revise the mental health minimum data set.

Mental health and primary care: Mental health problems in primary care are common (up to 24% of consultations)[39]. Support for this aspect of the work of primary care teams is being enhanced by a wide range of research, education and development initiatives.

Occupational mental health: Mental health problems such as depression and anxiety are common in the workplace, where they cause high levels of sickness absence. DH is involved in a wide range of activities to promote awareness and education.

Psychological treatment services: Psychological therapies are in high demand, yet knowledge about their effectiveness is poor. An NHS Executive review of psychotherapy services[123] was published in September.

Child and adolescent mental health services: Increased attention given to child and adolescent mental health issues reflects growth in the understanding of the full range of child mental health disorders, including emotional and conduct disorders, substance misuse and depression in children and adolescents.

Confidential Inquiry into Homicides and Suicides by Mentally Ill People: The Confidential Inquiry into Homicides and Suicides by Mentally Ill People produced its first report in 1996[124]. Recommendations included: training in risk assessment and the use of the Mental Health Act 1983[42], clarity about care plans and improved communication.

Emergency psychiatric services: Mental health emergency services were included in the Chief Medical Officer's review of emergency care in the community. Emerging conclusions published for consultation included recommendations to improve accessibility and improve integration of services, and to extend the range of options available.

Services for people with severe mental illness: The *Spectrum of care*[125], published in 1996, provided guidelines to improve the co-ordination of mental health services and to ensure the provision of a full range of services. A review of 24-hour nursed care[126] was published to facilitate the local development of intensive support facilities.

Services for mentally disordered offenders: The High Security Psychiatric Services Commissioning Board was established in April 1996. The Board has been concerned with high security psychiatric services, the development of longer term secure services for those who no longer require high security places, the development of a training and research strategy and ensuring co-ordination of commissioning strategies[127].

Mental health legislation: During the year, important new procedures for the supervised discharge of some patients following detention under the Mental Health Act 1983[42] were introduced[128,129], and guidance provided to professionals on their duties under the Mental Health Act 1983[42] were reviewed.

Maternity and child health services

Implementation of 'Changing Childbirth': The year saw continued progress in promoting greater continuity and choice in maternity services, supported by education and training initiatives.

Confidential Enquiries into Maternal Deaths: The latest report of the Confidential Enquiries into Maternal Deaths in the United Kingdom for the period 1991-93 was published in June[130,131].

Folic acid and prevention of neural tube defects: Encouraging women of child-bearing age to increase folic acid intakes continues to be a priority; general implications of an increase in consumption are being reviewed.

Sudden infant death syndrome: Various publications[132], including the third annual report of the Confidential Enquiry into Stillbirths and Deaths in Infancy[133], confirmed associations between sleeping position, and various environmental factors and the incidence of sudden infant death syndrome.

Prophylaxis of vitamin K deficiency bleeding in infants: This subject was kept under review.

Retinopathy of prematurity: The first phase of a multidisciplinary research project set up to assess and improve the care of infants with retinopathy of prematurity was completed.

Paediatric intensive care: A national Co-ordinating Group was set up in June to draw up a policy framework for paediatric intensive care.

Congenital limb reduction defects: The report of a review into the aetiology of congenital limb reduction defects was published in October[134].

Asthma

In October, DH launched the 'Control your asthma' card, produced jointly with the National Asthma Campaign, to help asthma sufferers to manage their condition.

Complementary medicine

Progress continues towards implementation of the statutory regulation of osteopaths and chiropractors. A pilot study on GP fundholder purchasing of osteopathy and chiropractic services was started.

Prison health care

Mentally disordered offenders who need specific care and treatment should ideally receive it from health and social services rather than in custodial care. Despite an overall increase in admissions to the NHS and the independent sector from prisons, surveys indicate unmet needs within the prison system[135,136].

COMMUNICABLE DISEASES

HIV infection and AIDS

HIV infection and AIDS data showed a similar pattern to previous years, but more new diagnoses of HIV infections were reported during 1996 than in any previous year since reporting began in 1984. This rise was mainly due to reporting delays, but may also reflect an increased demand for HIV testing related to developments in treatment.

Other sexually transmitted diseases

Nearly 405,000 new cases were seen at genito-urinary medicine (GUM) clinics. New cases of gonorrhoea rose by 5% to 39 per 100,000 population in 1995, but the rate was still below the Health of the Nation target of 49 per 100,000[1]. Reported new cases of chlamydial infection also rose.

Immunisation

Progress continues to be reported in immunisation coverage. Striking control of measles has been seen since the measles, rubella immunisation campaign of November 1994.

Viral hepatitis

In 1996, there were 1,024 reported cases of hepatitis A to the Public Health Laboratory Service (PHLS) Communicable Disease Surveillance Centre (CDSC), and 532 cases of hepatitis B.

Influenza

Influenza followed its usual pattern of seasonal winter increases, associated with considerable morbidity and evolving changes in the circulating viruses.

Meningitis

During 1996, the previously reported increase in cases of meningococcal infection continued, and a higher proportion of cases were reported as septicaemia. The Department and the HEA issued information on meningococcal infection.

Tuberculosis

Tuberculosis notifications continued at a level similar to those of the past three years. The first two reports of the Inter-Departmental Working Group on

Tuberculosis, aimed at improving control of tuberculosis in the UK, were published in July[137,138,139]. Following a review of data from the 1993 survey of notifications of tuberculosis, a decision was made to continue routine BCG immunisation of schoolchildren.

Hospital-acquired infection

Guidance on methicillin-resistant *Staphylococcus aureus* in community settings was issued in May[140]; revision of the guidelines for hospitals is under way. The Nosocomial Infection National Surveillance Scheme was established. Communicable disease and infection control was included in the planning and priorities guidance for the NHS[29].

Emerging and re-emerging infectious diseases

International discussion and collaboration continued with the aim of improving the surveillance of, and response to, novel and re-emerging infectious diseases. Two outbreaks of Ebola virus infection occurred in Gabon. The most discussed newly emergent disease during 1996 was 'new variant' Creutzfeldt-Jakob disease (nvCJD), identified in the UK[12].

Travel-related disease

Reported cases of imported malaria increased in 1996, largely due to an increase in cases in travellers to Asia and southern Africa. The spectrum of adverse reactions attributed to the antimalarial drug mefloquine was the subject of considerable media publicity. Doctors were kept informed, and the place of mefloquine as an antimalarial was reviewed; new guidance is expected to be published in 1997.

Microbiological risk assessment

The scientific development of microbiological risk assessment continues to be an important issue. In June, the Advisory Committee on Dangerous Pathogens published *Microbiological risk assessment: an interim report*[141].

ENVIRONMENTAL HEALTH AND FOOD SAFETY

Chemical and physical agents in the environment

Small Area Health Statistics Unit: The Small Area Health Statistics Unit is funded by Government to investigate claims of unusual clusters of disease or ill-health in the vicinity of point sources of pollution from chemicals and/or radiation.

Air pollution: A new subgroup of the Committee on the Medical Effects of Air Pollutants (COMEAP) has been set up to quantify the effects of air pollution on health in the UK, and the effects of indoor air pollutants will be taken into account in a new research programme.

Radiation: The NHS Executive published revised guidance to health authorities and NHS Trusts on emergency planning for accidents involving radioactivity[142].

Environment and health: DH continued to participate nationally and internationally in activities to identify, and protect against, risks to public health from environmental factors. The UK national environmental health action plan (NEHAP) was published in July[143].

Surveillance of diseases possibly due to non-infectious environmental hazards: Work continued to improve the ability to respond to possible health effects of non-infectious hazards in the environment. A national focus for work on response to chemical incidents and surveillance of health effects of chemicals in the environment was established in December.

Food safety

Foodborne and waterborne diseases: Food poisoning notifications made to the ONS rose by 1.5% compared with 1995. The number of laboratory reports of *Salmonella* isolations remained fairly constant, but there were variations within the overall figure. There was a small year-on-year fall in the number of *Campylobacter* isolations, whilst the number of VTEC O157 isolations fell by 16% - although this figure is higher than in 1994. The Advisory Committee on the Microbiological Safety of Food set up a new working group to consider microbial antibiotic resistance in relation to food safety, and the work of the Foodborne Viral Infections Working Group continued.

Food hazard management: The Food Incident Team investigated 144 food incidents and issued 19 Food Hazard Warnings.

Biotechnology and novel foods: The Advisory Committee on Novel Foods and Processes evaluated a wide range of novel foods, many of which were developed by use of genetic modification.

Toxicological food safety: The Committee on Toxicity of Chemicals in Food, Consumer Products and the Environment (COT) continued to provide independent expert advice, including consideration of oestrogenic compounds of both industrial and natural origin. The COT also reviewed the toxicity of various other naturally occurring toxicants. A report on the occurrence of adverse health effects associated with the use of traditional remedies and dietary supplements was published in October[144].

43

Pesticides: A review of existing pesticidal active ingredients is taking place under the European Union (EU) system for authorisation of plant protection products. The Advisory Committee on Pesticides started a review of the approval of pesticides for amateur use. A second edition of *Pesticide poisoning: notes for the guidance of medical practitioners*[145] was published. A survey by the Working Party on Pesticide Residues of organochlorine residues in human milk samples was started.

Veterinary products: The Veterinary Products Committee and its Medical and Scientific Panel both reviewed organophosphate (OP) sheep dips during the year; epidemiological research continues. The Chief Medical Officer expressed support for the establishment by the Royal Colleges of Physicians and Psychiatrists of a Working Group on the management of any health effects attributable to OPs. DH provided advice on human safety aspects of veterinary medicines and materials in animal feedstuffs to various UK and EU statutory bodies and advisory committees.

MEDICAL EDUCATION, TRAINING AND STAFFING

Junior doctors' hours

The 'New Deal' continues to make progress. Reports in September showed 97% compliance with targets for contracted hours and 78.4% compliance with targets for actual working hours. Action on actual hours of work and work intensity remains a priority.

Advisory Group on Medical and Dental Education, Training and Staffing, the Specialist Workforce Advisory Group and the Medical Workforce Standing Advisory Committee

The numbers of medical students entering medical schools has increased ahead of the target dates to levels recommended by the Medical Workforce Standing Advisory Committee. The Specialist Workforce Advisory Group's recommendations for a significant increase in the number of higher specialist trainees were approved by Ministers and announced on 8 March[146]; its annual report for 1995/96 will be published in Summer 1997. The Advisory Group on Medical and Dental Education, Training and Staffing continued to provide an overview of medical and dental staffing and education policies.

Postgraduate and specialist medical education

Considerable progress was made to implement reforms of higher specialist medical training during the year. The European Specialist Medical Qualifications Order 1995[147], which provides the legal framework for the reforms, came into force on 12 January 1996. The new specialist registrar grade, which replaces the career registrar and senior registrar grades, has now been introduced in all specialties in a rolling programme which began with two vanguard specialties (general surgery and diagnostic radiology) in December 1995. There were also important changes to the management and funding arrangements for postgraduate medical and dental education.

Equal opportunities for doctors

Improved arrangements for flexible training have been introduced with the launch of the new specialist registrar grade.

Retention of doctors

Retention of young doctors within the profession appears to be slightly better than a decade ago.

Undergraduate medical and dental education

The fourth report of the Steering Group on Undergraduate Medical and Dental Education and Research, published in March[148], made a number of recommendations to enhance the close co-operation that already exists between the NHS and universities.

Maintaining medical excellence

Progress continued towards implementation of the recommendations of *Maintaining medical excellence*[149,150]. Guidance on the role of medical directors issued by the British Association of Medical Managers reinforced the importance of procedures being put in place to enable concerns about the performance of medical colleagues to be acted on effectively.

OTHER TOPICS OF INTEREST IN 1996

Medicines Control Agency

Role and performance: The role of the Medicines Control Agency (MCA) is to protect public health by ensuring that all medicines for human use meet stringent criteria of safety, quality and efficacy. The MCA met virtually all of its key licensing and safety targets during the year.

Legal reclassification of medicinal products: In 1996, one drug substance was reclassified as a prescription-only medicine, two were reclassified to pharmacy sale and existing exemptions were widened for four substances; six topical products were also reclassified for pharmacy sale.

Drug safety issues: The MCA reviewed new evidence from a meta-analysis of studies on a possible association between oral contraceptives and a small increase in the risk of breast cancer[151], and issued initial advice[152]. It also issued preliminary advice on a small absolute excess risk of venous thromboembolism in association with the use of hormone replacement therapy[153].

Pharmaceutical developments in the European Union: New European Commission proposals to codify existing EU pharmaceutical legislation and to extend coverage to clinical trials, orphan medicines and starting materials were proposed.

Medical Devices Agency

The Medical Devices Agency is an Executive Agency of the Department of Health. Its role is to ensure that all devices and equipment used in health care meet appropriate standards of safety, quality and performance. The Agency achieves this role through the implementation of the EU Medical Devices Directives, a reporting system for device-related adverse incidents, an Evaluation Programme of a wide range of medical devices and by issuing safety and advice publications to the health service.

National Blood Authority

The National Blood Authority implemented the first stages of major reorganisation plans for the blood service. The national user group set up to monitor the service to hospitals held its first meeting. A review of the interim 'Blood donor's charter'[154] began.

National Biological Standards Board

The National Biological Standards Board has a statutory duty to assure the quality of biological substances used in medicine; during the year it commissioned an external review of the standardisation and control of biological medicines.

National Radiological Protection Board

The National Radiological Protection Board has the responsibility to acquire and advance knowledge about the protection of mankind from radiation hazards (for both ionising and non-ionising radiation), and to provide information and advice to support protection from radiation hazards. During 1996, advice was published on limits for important radionuclides in food and environmental materials[155], radon-affected areas in England and Wales[156] and the risks of acute effects from exposure to ionising radiation[157]. The construction of a radon atlas of England from data on 270,000 homes will facilitate the identification of homes above the Government action level for radon.

United Kingdom Transplant Support Service Authority

The UK Transplant Support Service Authority was established in 1991 to facilitate the matching and allocation of organs for transplantation; it maintains the NHS organ donor register.

Public Health Laboratory Service Board

The core purpose of the Public Health Laboratory Service (PHLS) is to protect the population from infection. During 1996, which marked the 50th anniversary of its foundation, the PHLS implemented major organisational changes and responded successfully to several major public health incidents.

Microbiological Research Authority

The Centre for Applied Microbiology and Research undertakes a wide range of projects to meet public health needs.

National Creutzfeldt-Jakob Disease Surveillance Unit

The National Creutzfeldt-Jakob Disease (CJD) Surveillance Unit, established in 1990 to monitor the incidence of CJD and investigate the epidemiology of the disease, identified a previously unrecognised form of CJD in 1996[12]. The Spongiform Encephalopathy Advisory Committee concluded that the most likely explanation was that these cases were linked to exposure to bovine spongiform encephalopathy (BSE) before the introduction of the specified bovine offals ban in 1989.

Bioethics

Research ethics committees: Following consultation, plans were made to implement streamlined ethical approval of multi-centre research studies.

Bioethics in Europe: The Council of Europe Convention on Human Rights and Biomedicine was adopted in November.

Human genetics and the Human Genetics Advisory Commission: The Human Genetics Advisory Commission was established in December.

Advisory Committee on Genetic Testing: The Advisory Committee on Genetic Testing was established in July

Gene Therapy Advisory Committee: The Gene Therapy Advisory Committee met three times during the year, and approved five gene therapy research protocols.

Assisted conception: The maximum statutory storage period for frozen human embryos was extended and a review of legal consent requirements was established.

Protection and use of patient information: Comprehensive guidance will be issued to the NHS in early 1997 on the protection and use of patient information[158]. A group was established to review the uses of patient information.

Complaints

The new NHS complaints procedure was introduced on 1 April, and final guidance on implementing the new procedure was issued to the NHS in March[159].

Research and development

The Department's research and development strategy promotes strong links with the science base, other major research funders in this country, and with EU research and technology programmes.

Use of information technology in clinical care

Development of the infrastructure needed to provide information systems to support clinical care continued, with progress on several fronts. Concerns about the security and confidentiality of personal health information were addressed by three separate working groups.

Dental health

Dental health of the nation: Wide regional variations in the dental health of 5-year-old children continue. The decline in dental caries in this age-group appears to have halted, and those with the disease have more teeth affected.

General dental services: The Government announced a package of reforms designed to improve patient services and to provide stability and security for dentists. A new Access Fund was set up to improve the availability of general dental services where there was unmet demand.

Community dental services: The dental care of those with special needs is an increasing component of community dental service activity, accompanied by a reduction in the provision of routine dental care for children.

Hospital dental services: The number of hospital dentists in England rose by 5.8% between September 1994 and September 1995.

Continuing education and training for dentists: There were 445 trainees in the regionally based vocational training schemes on 1 September 1995.

Dental research: Three workshops were held as part of the NHS national research programme in primary dental care.

INTERNATIONAL HEALTH

England, Europe and health

The UK shares many health challenges with the rest of Europe, and the opportunity to work together on common problems brings substantial benefits. European programmes and initiatives allow countries to pool their experience and knowledge, and to take advantage of the greater resources that international co-operation brings into play.

The European Union: During 1996, the European Community (EC) continued its programme of public health initiatives. The Health Council met in May and November; it adopted conclusions on transmissible spongiform encephalopathies and noted action being taken to develop a global early-warning system and network for communicable diseases. The Advisory Committee on Health met twice, and the Chief Medical Officers of Member States met twice to promote closer collaboration between the EC, the World Health Organization (WHO) and the Council of Europe.

Council of Europe: The Council's European Health Committee took forward work on several fronts and adopted a convention on human rights and biomedicine.

Relations with Central and Eastern Europe: In 1996, the Czech Republic and Slovenia applied to join an enlarged EU; eight other countries have already applied.

The Commonwealth

The Chief Medical Officer led the British delegation to the Commonwealth Health Ministers' meeting on 19 May.

World Health Organization

European Regional Committee: The Chief Medical Officer led the UK delegation to 46th session of the European Regional Committee, which agreed a programme budget for the 1998-99 biennium.

Executive Board: In May, the Chief Medical Officer was elected to the WHO Executive Board.

World Health Assembly: At the 49th World Health Assembly, the UK supported a resolution calling for the prompt payment of contributions from Member States, and for a financial plan to be drawn up to bring expenditure into line with expected income.

References

1. Department of Health. *The Health of the Nation: a strategy for health in England.* London: HMSO, 1992 (Cm. 1986).
2. Department of Health. *Public health strategy launched to tackle root causes of ill-health.* London: Department of Health, 1997 (Press release: 97/157).
3. Department of Health. *On the State of the Public Health: the annual report of the Chief Medical Officer of the Department of Health for the year 1992.* London: HMSO, 1993; 2.
4. Department of Health. *On the State of the Public Health: the annual report of the Chief Medical Officer of the Department of Health for the year 1993.* London: HMSO, 1994; 2.
5. Department of Health. *On the State of the Public Health: the annual report of the Chief Medical Officer of the Department of Health for the year 1994.* London: HMSO, 1995; 2.
6. Department of Health. *On the State of the Public Health: the annual report of the Chief Medical Officer of the Department of Health for the year 1995.* London: HMSO, 1996; 2.
7. World Health Organization. *World health statistics annual 1995.* Geneva: World Health Organization, 1996.
8. Drever F, Whitehead M, Roden M. Current patterns and trends in male mortality by social class (based on occupation). *Population Trends* 1996; **86**: 15-20.
9. Roberts I, Power C. Does the decline in child injury mortality vary by social class? A comparison of class specific mortality in 1981 and 1991. *BMJ* 1996; **313**: 784-6.
10. Office for National Statistics. *Infant and perinatal mortality: social and biological factors, 1995.* London: Office for National Statistics, 1996 (Population and Health Monitor DH3 96/3).
11. Bone MR, Bebbington AC, Jagger C, Morgan K, Nicolaas G. *Health expectancy and its uses.* London: HMSO, 1995.
12. Will RG, Ironside JW, Zeidler M, et al. A new variant of Creutzfeldt-Jakob disease in the UK. *Lancet* 1996; **347**: 921-5.
13. Department of Health. *On the State of the Public Health: the annual report of the Chief Medical Officer of the Department of Health for the year 1995.* London: HMSO, 1996; 3-4, 212-4.

14. Spongiform Encephalopathy Advisory Committee. *Research into the link between BSE and nvCJD: statement by the Spongiform Encephalopathy Advisory Committee (SEAC).* London: Department of Health, 1997.

15. Department of Health. *New variant of Creutzfeldt-Jakob Disease (CJD).* London: Department of Health, 1996 (Professional Letter: PL/CMO(96)5).

16. Department of Health. New variant of Creutzfeldt-Jakob Disease. *CMO's Update* 1997; **15**: 4.

17. Department of Health. *Changing childbirth: part 1: report of the Expert Maternity Group.* London: HMSO, 1993. Chair: Baroness Cumberlege.

18. Department of Health. *Making it happen: the contribution, role and development of nurses, midwives and health visitors: report of the Standing Nursing and Midwifery Advisory Committee.* Wetherby (West Yorkshire): Department of Health, 1995 (Executive Letter: EL(95)58).

19. Bagnall P, Dilloway M. *In a different light: school nurses and their role in meeting the needs of school-aged children.* London: Department of Health, 1996.

20. NHS Executive. *A policy framework for commissioning cancer services: palliative care services.* Wetherby (West Yorkshire): Department of Health, 1996 (Executive Letter: EL(96)85).

21. House of Commons Health Committee. *Inquiry into children's health: Session 1994-95.* London: HMSO, 1995.

22. House of Commons Science and Technology Committee. *Human genetics: the science and its consequences: third report from the Science and Technology Committee: Session 1994-95.* London: HMSO, 1995 (HC 41). Chair: Sir Giles Shaw.

23. House of Commons Science and Technology Committee. *Human genetics: the Government's response to the third report of the House of Commons Select Committee on Science and Technology: Session 1995-96.* London: HMSO, 1996 (HC 231). Chair: Sir Giles Shaw.

24. Department of Health. *On the State of the Public Health: the annual report of the Chief Medical Officer of the Department of Health for the year 1994.* London: HMSO, 1995; 7, 88-127.

25. Department of Health. *On the State of the Public Health: the annual report of the Chief Medical Officer of the Department of Health for the year 1995.* London: HMSO, 1996; 7, 75-6.

26. Department of Health. *On the State of the Public Health: the annual report of the Chief Medical Officer of the Department of Health for the year 1995.* London: HMSO, 1996; 7-8.

27. Department of Health. *Variations in health: what can the Department of Health and the NHS do?* London: Department of Health, 1995.

28. NHS Executive. *Priorities and planning guidance for the NHS: 1996/97.* Leeds: Department of Health, 1995.

29. NHS Executive. *Priorities and planning guidance for the NHS: 1997/98.* Leeds: Department of Health, 1996.

30. Scottish Office Home and Health Department. *Report on the circumstances leading to the 1996 outbreak of infection with E. coli O157 in Central Scotland: the implications for food safety and the lessons to be learned.* Edinburgh: Stationery Office, 1997.

31. Lord President's Office. *Tackling drugs together: a strategy for England 1995-1998.* London: HMSO, 1995 (Cm. 2846).

32. Health Education Authority. *A parent's guide to solvents.* London: Health Education Authority, 1995.

33. Department of Health, Task Force to Review Services for Drug Misusers. *Report of an independent review of drug treatment services in England.* London: Department of Health, 1996.

34. Taylor JC, Norman CL, Bland JM, Ramsey JD, Anderson HR. *Trends in deaths associated with abuse of volatile substances: 1971-1995.* London: St George's Hospital Medical School, 1997 (report no. 10).

35. Home Office. *Ministers take fizz out of under-age alcohol abuse.* London: Home Office, 1997 (Press Release 173/97).

36. Department of Health. *On the State of the Public Health: the annual report of the Chief Medical Officer of the Department of Health for the year 1995.* London: HMSO, 1996; 8-13.

37. Calman K, Royston G. Risk language and dialects. *BMJ* (in press).

38. Advisory Committee on Dangerous Pathogens. *Microbiological risk assessment: an interim report.* London: HMSO, 1996.

39. Department of Health. *On the State of the Public Health: the annual report of the Chief Medical Officer of the Department of Health for the year 1995.* London: HMSO, 1996; 13-4, 95-126.

40. Department of Health. *The patient's charter: mental health services.* London: Stationery Office, 1997.

41. Department of Health. *Developing partnerships in mental health.* London: Stationery Office, 1997 (Cm. 3555).

42. *The Mental Health Act 1983.* London: HMSO, 1983.

43. Health Committee Fourth Report. *Child and adolescent mental health services.* London: HMSO, 1997 (HC26-1).

44. Armstrong E, ed. *The primary mental health care toolkit.* Wetherby (West Yorkshire): Department of Health, 1996.

45. Department of Health. Primary mental health care toolkit. *CMO's Update* 1997; **15:** 4.

46. Department of Health. *On the State of the Public Health: the annual report of the Chief Medical Officer of the Department of Health for the year 1995.* London: HMSO, 1996; 16-7.

47. Department of Health. *On the State of the Public Health: the annual report of the Chief Medical Officer of the Department of Health for the year 1995.* London: HMSO, 1996; 17-8.

48. Hammer SM, Katzenstein DA, Hughes MD, et al. A trial comparing nucleoside monotherapy with combination therapy in HIV-infected adults with CD4 counts from 200 to 500 per cubic millimeter. *N Engl J Med* 1996; **335:** 1081-90.

49. DELTA Co-ordinating Committee. DELTA: a randomised double-blind controlled trial comparing combinations of zidovudine plus didanosine or zalcitabine or zidovudine alone in HIV-infected individuals. *Lancet* 1996; **348:** 283.

50. British HIV Association Guidelines Co-ordinating Committee. British HIV Association guidelines for antiretroviral treatment of HIV-seropositive individuals. *Lancet* 1997; **349:** 1086-92.

51. Calman KC. Equity, poverty and health for all. *BMJ* 1997; **314:** 1187-91.

52. Prescott-Clarke P, Primatesta P, eds. *Health Survey for England 1995: a survey carried out on behalf of the Department of Health (vols 1 and 2).* London: Stationery Office, 1997 (Series HS, no.5).

53. Martin J, Meltzer H, Elliot D. *The prevalence of disability among adults.* London: HMSO, 1988 (OPCS Surveys of Disability in Great Britain: report 1).

54. Martin J, White A. *The financial circumstances of disabled adults living in private households.* London: HMSO, 1988 (OPCS Surveys of Disability in Great Britain: report 2).

55. Bone M, Meltzer H. *The prevalence of disability among children.* London: HMSO, 1988 (OPCS Surveys of Disability in Great Britain: report 3).

56. Martin J, White M, Meltzer H. *Disabled adults: services, transport and employment.* London: HMSO, 1989 (OPCS Surveys of Disability in Great Britain: report 4).

57. Smith M, Robus N. *The financial circumstances of families with disabled children living in private households.* London: HMSO, 1989 (OPCS Surveys of Disability in Great Britain: report 5).

58. Meltzer H, Smith M, Robus N. *Disabled children: services, transport and education.* London: HMSO, 1989 (OPCS Surveys of Disability in Great Britain: report 6).

59. *The Disability Discrimination Act 1995.* London: HMSO, 1995.

60. Richardson N, Jones P, Thomas M. Should house officers obtain consent for operation and anaesthesia? *Health Trends* 1996, **28:** 56-9.

61. Department of Health. *Patient consent to examination or treatment.* London: Department of Health, 1990 (Health Circular: HC(90)22).

62. Sidaway v Bethlem Royal Hospital Governors and others, House of Lords, [1985] 1 AC 871, per Lord Templeman at pages 904-5; Re T (An adult) (Consent to medical treatment), Court of Appeal (Civil Division) [1993] Fam 95, per Lord Donaldson MR at page 102; Re C (Refusal of medical treatment) [1994] 1 AII/ER/819.

63. Alderson P, Montgomery J. *Health care choices: making decisions with children.* London: Institute of Public Policy Research, 1996.

64. *Gillick v West Norfolk and Wisbech Area Health Authority et anor* [1986] 1 AC 112.

65. Re F (Mental patient sterilisation), Court of Appeal (Civil Division) [1990] 2 AC 1, 55E-F.

66. R v Human Fertilisation and Embryology Authority, Ex parte Blood, *The Times,* 7 February 1997.

67. Department of Health. *Consent to treatment: a summary of legal rulings.* London: Department of Health, 1997 (Executive Letter: EL(97)32).

68. Re Y (Mental incapacity: bone marrow transplant) [1996] 2 FLR 787.

69. Re C (Refusal of medical treatment) [1994] 1 FLR 31.

70. Grubb A, Walsh P, Lambe N, Murrells T, Robinson S. *Doctors' views on the management of patients in persistent vegetative state (PVS): a UK study.* London: Centre of Medical Law and Ethics, King's College London, 1997.

71. British Medical Association. *Advance statements about medical treatment.* London: BMJ Publishing, 1995.

72. Council of Europe. *Convention for the protection of human rights and dignity of the human being with regard to the application of biology and medicine.* Strasbourg: Council of Europe, 1996 (ETS 164).

73. Department of Health. *The protection and use of patient information.* London: Department of Health, 1996 (Health Service Guidelines: HSG(96)18, Local Authority Social Services Letter: LASSL(96)5).

74. Ball M. *Domestic violence and social care: a report on two conferences held by the Social Services Inspectorate.* Bristol: Social Services Inspectorate, 1996.

75. Home Office. *Domestic violence: don't stand for it.* London: Home Office, 1994.

76. *The Family Law Act 1996.* London: HMSO, 1996.

77. Department of Health, Advisory Group on the Medical Aspects of Air Pollution Episodes. *First report: ozone.* London: HMSO, 1991. Chair: Professor Stephen Holgate.

78. Department of Health, Committee on the Medical Effects of Air Pollutants. *Non-biological particles and health.* London: HMSO, 1995. Chair: Professor Stephen Holgate.

79. Department of Health, Committee on the Medical Effects of Air Pollutants. *Asthma and outdoor air pollution.* London: HMSO, 1995. Chair: Professor Stephen Holgate.

80. Department of the Environment, Welsh Office, Scottish Office. *The United Kingdom National Air Quality Strategy.* London: Stationery Office, 1997 (Cm. 3587).

81. *The Clean Air Act 1956.* London: HMSO, 1956.

82. Department of the Enviroment. *United Kingdom photochemical oxidants review group: third report: ozone in the United Kingdom: 1993.* London: Department of the Environment, 1994.

83. Walters S, Phupinyokul M, Ayres J. Hospital admission rates for asthma and respiratory disease in the West Midlands: their relationship to air pollution levels. *Thorax* 1995; **50:** 948-54.

84. Katsouyanni K, Touloumi G, Spix C, et al. Short-term effects of ambient sulphur dioxide and particulate matter on mortality in 12 European cities: results from time series data from the APHEA project. *BMJ* 1997; **314:** 1658-63.

85. Ponce de Leon A, Anderson HR, Bland MJ, Strachan DP. Effects of air pollution on daily hospital admissions for respiratory disease in London between 1987-88 and 1991-92. *J Epidemiol Commun Health* 1996; **50 (suppl 1):** 563-70.

86. Gilmour PS, Brown DM, Lindsay TG, Beswick PH, MacNee W, Donaldson K. Adverse health effects of PM_{10} particles: involvement of iron in generation of hydroxyl radical. *Occup Environ Med* 1996, **53:** 817-22.

87. Tunnicliffe WS, Burge PS, Ayres JG. Effects of domestic concentrations of nitrogen dioxide on airway responses to inhaled allergen in asthmatic patients. *Lancet* 1994, **344:** 1733-6.

88. Wang JH, Devalia JL, Duddle JM, Hamilton SA, Davies RJ. Effect of six-hour exposure to nitrogen dioxide on early-phase nasal response to allergen challenge in patients with a history of seasonal allergic rhinitis. *J Allergy Clin Immunol* 1995, **96:** 669-76.

89. Department of Health. *The Task Force to Review Services for Drug Misusers: report of an independent review of drug treatment services in England.* London: Department of Health, 1996.

90. Department of Health. *Sensible drinking: the report of an Inter-Departmental Working Group.* London: Department of Health, 1995.

91. Department of Health. *Guidelines on the nutritional assessment of infant formulas: report of the Working Group on the Nutritional Assessment of Infant Formulas of the Committee on Medical Aspects of Food and Nutrition Policy.* London: Stationery Office, 1996 (Report on Health and Social Subjects no. 47).

92. Department of Health. *Eat Well! 2: a progress report from the Nutrition Task Force on the action plan to achieve the Health of the Nation targets on diet and nutrition.* Wetherby (West Yorkshire): Department of Health, 1996.

93. Department of Health Nutrition Task Force. *Low income, food, nutrition and health: strategies for improvement: a report by the Low Income Project Team for the Nutrition Task Force.* London: Department of Health, 1996.

94. Jackson AA, ed. *Nutrition for medical students: nutrition in the undergraduate medical curriculum.* London: Department of Health, 1996.

95. Thomas M, Avery V. *Infant feeding in Asian families: early feeding practices and growth.* London: Stationery Office (in press).

96. Foster K, Lader D, Cheesborough S. *Infant feeding 1995.* London: Stationery Office (in press).

97. NHS Executive. *Child health in the community: a guide to good practice.* Wetherby (West Yorkshire): Department of Health, 1996.

98. Department for Education and Employment, Department of Health. *Supporting pupils with medical needs in school.* London: Department for Education and Employment, 1996 (DfEE Circular 14/96).

99. Department for Education and Employment, Department of Health. *Supporting pupils with medical needs: a good practice guide.* London: Department for Education and Employment, 1996.

100. Health Education Authority. *Women's health promotion: a resource pack for health care purchasers and providers.* London: Department of Health, 1996.

101. Department of Health. *Well women: today and tomorrow: health tips for the over 35s.* London: Department of Health, 1996.

102. National Audit Office. *The Health of the Nation: a progress report: Session 1995-96.* London: HMSO, 1996 (HC 656).

103. Towner E, Dowswell T, Simpson G, Jarvis S, Meyrick J, Morgan A. *Health promotion in childhood and young adolescence for the prevention of unintentional injuries.* London: Health Education Authority, 1996.

104. Coleman P, Munro J, Nichol J, Harper R, Kent G, Wild D. *The effectiveness of interventions to prevent accidental injury to young persons aged 15-24 years: a review of the evidence.* Sheffield: Medical Care Research Unit, University of Sheffield, 1996.

105. NHS Centre for Reviews and Dissemination. *Effective health care: preventing falls and subsequent injury in older people.* York: University of York, 1996.

106. Department of Health, Department of the Environment. *The environment and health: a consultative document for the environment as a key area in the Health of the Nation strategy.* London: Department of Health, 1996.

107. World Health Organization. *International classification of impairments, disabilities and handicaps.* Geneva: World Health Organization, 1980.

108. United Nations. *Standard rules on the equalization of opportunities for persons with disabilities.* New York: United Nations, 1993 (General Assembly, 48th Session: resolutions adopted on reports of the Third Committee 48/96).

109. Council of Europe. *A social charter.* Strasbourg: Council of Europe Press, 1961.

110. Council of Europe. *A coherent policy for the rehabilitation of people with disabilities.* Strasbourg: Council of Europe Press, 1992 (Recommendation: R(92)6).

111. *The Carers (Recognition and Services) Act 1995.* London: HMSO, 1995.

112. Department of Health. *NHS responsibilities for meeting continuing health care needs.* Wetherby (West Yorkshire): Department of Health, 1995 (Health Service Guidelines: HSG (95)8, Local Authority Circular: LAC(95)5).

113. Department of Health. *The National Health Service: a service with ambitions.* London: HMSO, 1996 (Cm. 3425).

114. Department of Health, Scottish Office Home and Health Department, Welsh Office. *Choice and opportunity: primary care: the future.* London: Stationery Office, 1996 (Cm. 3390).

115. Department of Health. *Primary care: delivering the future.* London: Stationery Office, 1996 (Cm. 3512).

116. Department of Health, NHS Executive. *Public health in England: roles and responsibilities of the Department of Health and the NHS.* London: Department of Health, 1994.

117. Department of Health, Welsh Office. *A policy framework for commissioning cancer services: a report by the Expert Advisory Group on Cancer to the Chief Medical Officers of England and Wales: guidance for purchasers and providers of cancer services.* London: Department of Health, 1995.

118. Department of Health Cancer Guidance Sub-group of the Clinical Outcomes Group. *Guidance for purchasers: improving outcomes in breast cancer (vols 1 and 2).* London: Department of Health, 1996.

119. National Confidential Enquiry into Perioperative Deaths. *The report of the National Confidential Enquiry into Perioperative Deaths 1993/94.* London: National Confidential Enquiry into Perioperative Deaths, 1996. Chair: Professor John Blandy.

120. NHS Executive. *Purchasing renal services.* Wetherby (West Yorkshire): NHS Executive, 1996 (Executive Letter: EL(96)35).

121. NHS Executive. *Guidelines on admission to and discharge from intensive care and high dependency units.* London: Department of Health, 1996.

122. NHS Executive. *Intensive care bed-state register.* Wetherby (West Yorkshire): NHS Executive, 1996 (Executive Letter: EL(96)76).

123. Parry G, Richardson A. *NHS psychotherapy services in England: review of strategic policy.* London: NHS Executive, 1996.

124. Steering Committee on the Confidential Inquiry into Homicides and Suicides by Mentally Ill People. *Report of the Confidential Inquiry into Homicides and Suicides by Mentally Ill People.* London: Royal College of Psychiatrists, 1996.

125. Department of Health. *The spectrum of care: local services for people with mental health problems.* London: Department of Health, 1996.

126. NHS Executive. *24-hour nursed care for people with severe and enduring mental illness.* Leeds: Department of Health, 1996.

127. NHS Executive. *High security psychiatric services: changes in function and organisation.* Leeds: Department of Health, 1995.

128. *The Mental Health (Patients in the Community) Act 1995.* London: HMSO, 1995.

129. Department of Health, Welsh Office. *The Mental Health (Patients in the Community) Act 1995: guidance on supervised discharge (after-care under supervision) and related provisions: supplement to the Code of Practice published August 1993 pursuant to Section 118 of the Mental Health Act 1983.* Wetherby (West Yorkshire): Department of Health, 1996.

130. Department of Health, Welsh Office, Scottish Office Home and Health Department, Department of Health and Social Services Northern Ireland. *Report on Confidential Enquiries into Maternal Deaths in the United Kingdom 1991-1993.* London: HMSO, 1996.

131. Department of Health. *Report of the Confidential Enquiries into Maternal Deaths United Kingdom 1991-1993.* London: Department of Health, 1996 (Professional Letter: PL/CMO(96)4, PL/CNO(96)2).

132. Department of Health. *Reduce the risk of cot death.* London: Department of Health, 1996.

133. Confidential Enquiry into Stillbirths and Deaths in Infancy. *Report of the Confidential Enquiry into Stillbirths and Deaths in Infancy (CESDI).* London: HMSO, 1996.

134. Department of Health Advisory Group on Congenital Limb Reduction Defects. *Report of the Advisory Group on Congenital Limb Reduction Defects.* London: Department of Health, 1995. Chair: Professor Michael Peckham.

135. Brook D, Taylor C, Gunn J, Maden A. Point prevalence of mental disorder in unconvicted male prisoners in England and Wales. *BMJ* 1996; **313:** 1524-7.

136. Birmingham L, Mason D, Grubin D. Prevalence of mental disorder in remand prisoners: consecutive case study. *BMJ* 1996; **313:** 1521-4.

137. Inter-Departmental Working Group on Tuberculosis. *The prevention and control of tuberculosis at local level.* London: Department of Health, Welsh Office, 1996.

138. Inter-Departmental Working Group on Tuberculosis. *Tuberculosis and homeless people.* London: Department of Health, Welsh Office, 1996.

139. Department of Health. *Tuberculosis: two reports of the Inter-Departmental Working Group on Tuberculosis.* Leeds: Department of Health, 1996 (Executive Letter: EL(96)51).

140. Department of Health. *Methicillin-resistant Staphylococcus aureus in community settings.* London: Department of Health, 1996 (Professional Letter: PL/CMO(96)3, PL/CNO(96)1, CI(96)12).

141. Advisory Committee on Dangerous Pathogens. *Microbiological risk assessment: an interim report.* London: HMSO, 1996.

142. NHS Executive. *Emergency planning in the NHS: health services arrangements for dealing with major accidents.* Wetherby (West Yorkshire): Department of Health, 1996 (Executive Letter: EL(96)79).

143. Department of the Environment, Department of Health. *United Kingdom national environmental health action plan.* London: HMSO, 1996.

144. Ministry of Agriculture, Fisheries and Food. *Traditional remedies and dietary supplements.* London: Ministry of Agriculture, Fisheries and Food, 1996 (Food Surveillance Information Sheet no. 94).

145. Proudfoot A. *Pesticide poisoning: notes for the guidance of medical practitioners (2nd edn).* London: HMSO, 1996.

146. NHS Executive. *Specialist Workforce Advisory Group recommendations: higher specialist training numbers 1996/97.* Leeds: Department of Health, 1996 (Executive Letter: EL(96)18).

147. *The European Specialist Medical Qualifications Order 1995.* London: HMSO, 1995 (Statutory Instrument: SI 1995 no. 3208).

148. Department of Health Steering Group on Undergraduate Medical and Dental Education and Research. *Undergraduate medical and dental education and research: fourth report of the Steering Group.* Wetherby (West Yorkshire): Department of Health, 1996.

149. Department of Health. *Maintaining medical excellence: review of guidance on doctors' performance: final report.* Leeds: Department of Health, 1995.

150. Department of Health. *Maintaining medical excellence.* London: Department of Health, 1996 (Miscellaneous Circular: MISC(96)67).

151. Collaborative Group on Hormonal Factors in Breast Cancer. Breast cancer and hormonal contraceptives: reanalysis of individual data on 53,297 with breast cancer and 100,239 women without breast cancer from 54 epidemiological studies. *Lancet* 1996; **347:** 1713-27.

152. Department of Health. *Oral contraceptives and breast cancer.* London: Department of Health, 1996 (Cascade Electronic Message: CEM/CMO(96)7).

153. Committee on Safety of Medicines. Information on the risk of blood clots for women taking hormone replacement therapy (HRT). *Curr Probl Pharmacovigilance* 1996; **22:** 9-10.

154. Department of Health. *The patients' charter: blood donors: interim charter*. London: Department of Health, 1995.

155. National Radiological Protection Board. *Generalised derived limits for radioisotopes of strontium, ruthenium, iodine, caesium, plutonium, americium and curium*. Oxford: National Radiological Protection Board, 1996 (Doc. NRPB 7, no. 1).

156. National Radiological Protection Board. *Radon affected areas: England and Wales*. Oxford: National Radiological Protection Board, 1996 (Doc. NRPB 7, no. 2).

157. National Radiological Protection Board. *Risk from deterministic effects of ionising radiation*. Oxford: National Radiological Protection Board, 1996 (Doc. NRPB 7, no. 3).

158. Department of Health. *Working together to secure the privacy of personal health information in the NHS*. London: Department of Health (in press) (Miscellaneous Circular: MISC(97)1).

159. NHS Executive. *Complaints: listening...acting...improving: guidance on implementing the NHS complaints procedure*. Wetherby (West Yorkshire): Department of Health, 1996 (Executive Letter: EL(96)19).

Communications from the Chief Medical Officer to the medical profession and others during 1996

Copies of CMO letters and *CMO's Updates* can be obtained from: Department of Health Mailings, Two Ten Communications Ltd, Building 150 Thorp Arch Trading Estate, Wetherby, West Yorkshire LS23 7EH.

CMO Letters

Implementing the reforms of specialist medical training: commissioning the specialist registrar grade (Professional Letter PL/CMO(96)1) (6 March).

Methicillin resistant Staphylococcus aureus in community settings (Professional Letter PL/CMO(96)3, PL/CNO(96)1, CI(96)12) (14 May).

Report of the Confidential Enquiries into Maternal Deaths, United Kingdom 1991-1993 (Professional Letter PL/CMO(96)4, PL/CNO(96)2 (5 June).

New variant of Creutzfeldt-Jakob disease (CJD) (Professional Letter PL/CMO(96)5 (1 July).

Change to the routine pre-school booster immunisation programme (Professional Letter PL/CMO(96)6) (16 July).

Influenza immunisation (Professional Letter PL/CMO(96)7) (20 September).

CMO's Update

CMO's Update 9 (February). Includes: Air pollution and health; Building bridges for severely mentally ill people; Aftermath of the Gulf War; Diphtheria in the former Soviet Union; Interferon beta; Regional epidemiology; Sensible drinking; Health variations; Epidemiological overview on health-related behaviours.

CMO's Update 10 (May). Includes: Combined Hib/DTP vaccines; Safe use of lasers; National Poisons Information Service; Shellfish toxins; Pesticide poisoning; Ultraviolet radiation and skin cancer; New guidelines on cervical screening; Good health is good business; Mefloquine for malaria prophylaxis; Continuing NHS health care; Brachial plexus neuropathy after radiotherapy for breast cancer; Mental health services; National Confidential Enquiry into Peri-operative Deaths; Influenza immunisation; Protection and use of patient information; Occupational exposure to HIV and use of zidovudine.

CMO's Update 11 (July). Includes: The Health of the Nation: four years on; Safety and efficacy register of new interventional procedures; Breast cancer outcomes; Honey and infant botulism; Independent review of drug treatment services; New variant of Creutzfeldt-Jakob disease; Tuberculosis and BCG immunisation; Confidential Inquiry into Suicides and Homicides; Patient partnership; Confidential Enquiries into Maternal Deaths 1991-1993.

CMO's Update 12 (October). Includes: On the State of the Public Health; Influenza information leaflets for patients; Intensive care national bed-state register; Pregnancy and avoidance of infection from food and from contact with animals; Breast cancer screening; Burdens of disease; Death certification and referral to the coroner; New variant of Creutzfeldt-Jakob disease; Wheelchair initiatives; Adverse reactions to latex medical devices; Choice and opportunity in primary care; Asthma patient card; Health Survey for England.

Public Health Link

Copies of Public Health Link Communications can be obtained from: The Chief Medical Officer, Richmond House, 79 Whitehall, London SW1A 2NS.

Electronic cascade messages

A new variant of CJD (CEM/CMO(96)1) (20 March).
BSE/CJD update (CEM/CMO(96)2) (25 March).
False negative results - Abbott ImX anti-HIV-1/HIV-2, 3rd generation plus assay (CEM/CMO(96)3) (10 April).
Safety of pharmaceutical products (CEM/CMO(96)4) (19 April).
Phthalates in infant formula feeds (CEM/CMO(96)5) (28 May).
Multidrug resistant tuberculosis at a London hospital (CEM/CMO(96)6) (14 June).
Oral contraceptives and breast cancer (CEM/CMO(96)7) (15 June).
Phytoestrogens in soya infant formula milk (CEM/CMO(96)8) (17 July).

CHAPTER 1

VITAL STATISTICS

(a)   Population size

The estimated resident population of England at 30 June 1996 was 49.1 million, an increase of 0.4% compared with 1995 and of 3.7% compared with 1986.

(b)   Age and sex structure of the resident population

Figure 1.1 shows the change in the age structure of England between 1985 and 1995, in particular striking increases in the 25-34 years and 45-54 years age-groups, reflecting the post-war and mid-1960s 'baby booms'. There is also a steep fall in the number of 15-24-year-olds over the past 10 years as the 'baby boomers' born in the mid-1960s move into the older age-group, combined with a fall in fertility rates in the late 1970s. Similar factors explain the drop in the number of 55-64-year-olds between 1985 and 1995, as those born in the peak after World War 1 move into the 65-74 years age-group, combined with low fertility rates in the 1930s. The very elderly (aged 85 years and over) still continue to increase in number (see Appendix Table A.1), as do other age-groups.

Figure 1.1: *The changing age structure in England, 1985 and 1995*

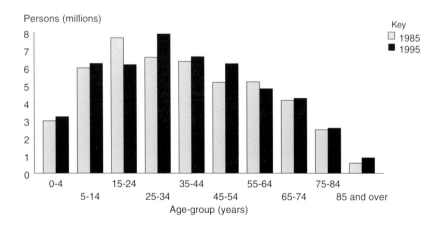

Source: ONS

Figure 1.2: *Conceptions, England and Wales, 1993/94-1995/96*

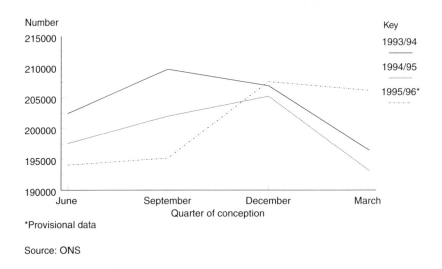

*Provisional data

Source: ONS

(c)   Fertility statistics

Conceptions

Data on conceptions relate to pregnancies that led to a maternity or to a legal termination under the Abortion Act 1967[1,2]; they exclude spontaneous and illegal abortions. In 1994, 760,400 conceptions occurred to women resident in England, a 2% fall from the figure in 1993 (776,800), with an overall conception rate of 74.8 per 1,000 women aged 15-44 years (a 2% fall compared with the rate in 1993).

Whilst the general trend in conceptions has been downward, there appears to have been an upwards shift away from this trend in numbers of conceptions from December 1995. Quarterly conceptions plotted for the period April 1995 to March 1996 show a 7% increase in numbers of conceptions for the quarter ending March 1996 compared with the quarter ending March 1995 (see Figure 1.2). This increase may reflect the impact of the announcement, on 18 October 1995 by the Committee on Safety of Medicines[3,4], of evidence pointing to an increased risk of thromboembolism in association with contraceptive pills that contain gestodene or desogestrel.

Table 1.1: *Live births and proportion of live births outside marriage, crude birth rate, general and total period fertility rates, and sex ratio, England, 1986, 1995 and 1996*

Year of birth	Live births	Crude birth rate*	General fertility rate†	Total period fertility rate (TPFR)	Percentage of live births outside marriage	Sex ratio
1986	623609	13.2	62.5	1.77	21.4	105.1
1995	613257	12.5	60.4	1.71	33.7	105.1
1996	614184	12.6‡	60.6‡	1.74‡	35.5	105.5

* Births per 1,000 population of all ages.
† Births per 1,000 females aged 15-44 years.
‡ Provisional (based on 1995 population figures).
Note: Sex ratio represents number of male births per 100 female births.

Source: ONS

Conceptions to girls aged under 16 years

In 1994, there were 8.3 conceptions per 1,000 girls aged 13-15 years in England, compared with 8.0 per 1,000 in 1993 and 8.4 per 1,000 in 1992.

Total live births

In 1996, there were 614,184 live births in England - 0.2% higher than in 1995, (see Table 1.1). In England, the total period fertility rate (TPFR), which measures the average number of children that would be born per woman if current age-specific fertility rates continued throughout her childbearing years was 1.74 in 1996, compared with 1.71 in 1995. The TPFR for England has now remained below 2.1, the level that would give long-term 'natural' replacement of the population, since 1972.

The proportion of live births occurring outside marriage increased from 12% of all live births in England and Wales in 1980 to 36% in 1996; most of this rise can be attributed to a growing number of births outside marriage registered by both parents. Figure 1.3 illustrates the trends in births outside marriage by type of registration over the past decade. Births outside marriage that were solely registered remained relatively stable, at 7-8% of all births; however, the proportion of births outside marriage that were registered by both parents rose from 14% of all births in 1986 to 28% in 1996. Three-quarters of these births were registered by parents living at the same address, and presumably cohabiting.

Figure 1.3: *Live births outside marriage as percentage of all live births, England and Wales, 1986-96*

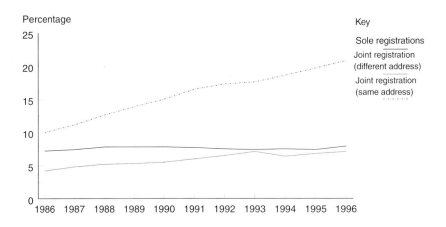

Source: ONS

Figure 1.4: *Live births per 1,000 women aged 40-44 years and total period fertility rate (TPFR), England and Wales, 1938-96*

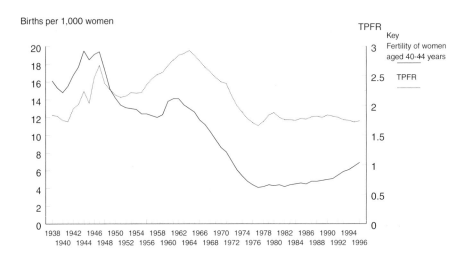

Source: ONS

Figure 1.5: *Quarterly moving average abortion rates per 1,000 women aged 14-49 years, England, 1986-96*

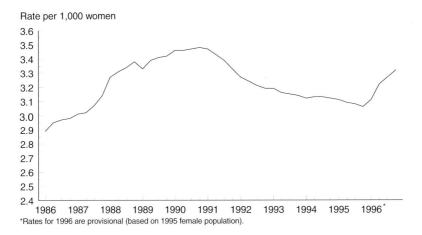

Rate per 1,000 women

*Rates for 1996 are provisional (based on 1995 female population).

Source: ONS

Fertility of women aged 40 years and over

Although overall total fertility is declining slowly (indicated by the TPFR), the trend over recent years to delay childbearing has led to an increase from 4.5 births per 1,000 women in 1986 to 6.9 in 1996 for women aged 40-44 years in England and Wales (see Figure 1.4).

Abortions

In 1995, 147,875 abortions were performed under the Abortion Act 1967[1,2] for women who were resident in England, a fall of 1% compared with 1994. In each year between 1990 to 1995, the highest quarterly abortion rate has been recorded in the March quarter and, since 1989, the lowest quarterly abortion rate has been recorded in the December quarter. Use of quarterly moving averages to smooth out variations shows an increase which starts between the March and June 1996 quarters and continued to increase between the June and September quarters (see Figure 1.5).

References

1. *The Abortion Act 1967.* London: HMSO, 1967.
2. *The Abortion Act 1967 (as amended by Statutory Instrument: SI 480c.10).* London: HMSO, 1991.
3. Committee on Safety of Medicines. *Combined oral contraceptives and thromboembolism.* London: Committee on Safety of Medicines, 1995.
4. Department of Health. *On the State of the Public Health: the annual report of the Chief Medical Officer of the Department of Health for the year 1995.* London: HMSO, 1996; 9-10, 204.

(d)   Trends in reporting congenital anomalies

Appendix Table A.6 shows the number of babies born in England notified with
selected congenital anomalies. In 1996, the notification rate for live births with
congenital anomalies fell to 80.6 per 10,000 live births, 3% lower than in 1995
and 18% lower than in 1991.

An exclusion list was introduced in January 1990 to identify minor anomalies
which should no longer be notified. As a result, the total number of notifications
received fell by 4,058 (34%) between 1989 and 1990. This fall was accounted
for entirely by a decrease in notifications of live births with anomalies. Four
groups shown in the table were affected by the exclusion list: ear and eye
anomalies, cardiovascular anomalies, hypospadias and talipes. For these groups
the comments in the following paragraphs are restricted to the changes that took
place between 1991 and 1996; for the remainder, the comments refer to the
changes between 1986 and 1996.

Since 1986, there has been a reduction in the rate of central nervous system
anomalies for live births (from 7.7 to 2.5 per 10,000 live births) and stillbirths
(from 1.3 to 0.8 per 10,000 total births). Conditions such as hydrocephalus and
anencephaly, which are within the group most likely to be detected prenatally by
diagnostic ultrasound or alphafetoprotein screening, have shown the largest fall.
A similar decrease has been reported in other countries.

Figure 1.6: *Stillbirths and infant mortality rates, England, 1986-96*

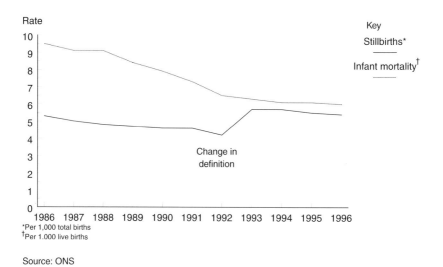

*Per 1,000 total births
†Per 1.000 live births

Source: ONS

Between 1986 and 1996, the rate (per 10,000 live births) for cleft lip/palate anomalies has fallen from 12.7 to 8.4. Since 1991, the rate (per 10,000 live births) for ear and eye anomalies has fallen from 4.4 to 3.1, for hypospadias/epispadias has fallen from 10.5 to 7.9 and for talipes has fallen from 13.0 to 8.9.

(e)   Mortality

(i)   *Infant and perinatal mortality*

Provisional statistics for 1996 in England indicate that 3,696 babies died before the age of one year, compared with 3,739 in 1995. The infant mortality rate fell to 6.0 per 1,000 live births, the lowest ever recorded.

Based on provisional statistics, there were 3,345 stillbirths in England during 1996 compared with 3,403 in 1995. The stillbirth rate fell from 5.5 to 5.4 per 1,000 total births between 1995 and 1996 (see Figure 1.6).

(ii)   *Childhood mortality*

Provisional statistics for 1996 in England indicate that 1,630 children died between the ages of 1 and 15 years (inclusive), compared with 1,755 in 1995, continuing a downward trend in these figures since 1980.

(iii)   *Adult mortality*

Deaths registered in England decreased from 529,038 in 1995 to 526,650 in 1996, a fall of 0.5%. For most age-groups, mortality rates fell during the late 1980s among males and females alike; a 6.3% increase was seen for men aged 15-44 years between 1986 and 1990, but has since remained fairly stable (see Figures 1.7 and 1.8).

Mortality among young adults aged 15-44 years

Although deaths in young adults aged 15-44 years account for only 3% of total deaths in England and Wales, many may be preventable, many may have profound effects on their families, and economically they account for a large number of years of 'working life' lost. Mortality among males in this age-group increased between 1993 and 1995 (108.9 to 111.2 per 100,000), but fell slightly in 1996 to 109.7 per 100,000 (see Figure 1.9) . Female mortality in this age-group remained relatively constant between 1993 and 1995 (59.4 to 59.5 per 100,000), but rose slightly in 1996 (to 60.5 per 100,000) (see Figure 1.10). Between 1986 and 1996, mortality in males aged 25-39 years increased, whereas

Figure 1.7: *Percentage change in age-specific mortality rates, males, England, 1986-96 (1986 = 100)*

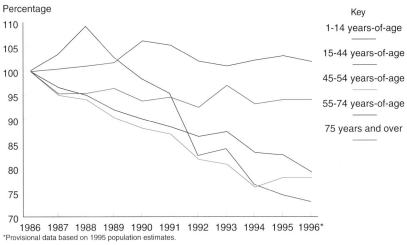

*Provisional data based on 1995 population estimates.

Notes: Deaths for England represent the number of deaths registered in each year
except for 1993-95, which represent the number of deaths occurring in each year.
Deaths of infants under 1 year-of-age have been excluded.

Source: ONS

Figure 1.8: *Percentage change in age-specific mortality rates, females, England, 1986-96 (1986 = 100)*

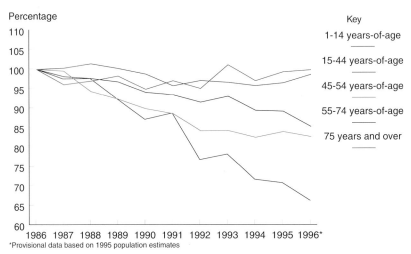

*Provisional data based on 1995 population estimates

Notes: Deaths for England represent the number of deaths registered in each year
except for 1993-95, which represent the number of deaths occurring in each year.
Deaths of infants under 1 year-of-age have been excluded.

Source: ONS

among those aged 15-24 and 40-44 years, deaths have decreased (see Figure 1.9). Among females, only the 25-29 years age-group has shown increased mortality between 1986 and 1996, but there has been an increase in mortality between 1994 and 1996 for those aged 15-19 years (see Figure 1.10).

Comparison of the percentage differences between the expected number of deaths based on 1989-91 death rates with the actual numbers for 1994-96 for males indicates that, although deaths due to accidents (-21%) and heart disease (-16%) have decreased, deaths from infectious disease (excluding HIV infection) (+38%), respiratory disease (+24%) and HIV infection (+22%) have all increased. The overall numbers of deaths are lower than expected by 2%.

A similar exercise for females indicates that whilst deaths from accidents (-13%), cancer of the cervix (-37%) and cancer of the breast (-11%) have decreased, deaths due to infectious disease (excluding HIV infection) (+34%), heart disease (+14%), respiratory disease (+15%), diseases of the digestive system (+12%) and HIV infection (+71%) have all increased. The overall numbers of deaths are lower than expected by 2%.

Trends in death rates from drug misuse and accidental poisoning show a steady increase in deaths since 1986 with a 109% increase (2.24 to 4.69 per 100,000) among 15-19-year-old males and a 472% increase (0.76 to 4.35 per 100,000) in males aged 40-44 years; the highest mortality rate in males aged 15-44 years occurs among the 25-29-year-old age-group (11.42 per 100,000) (see Figure 1.11). Mortality rates among females aged 15-44 years from drug misuse and accidental poisoning are much lower than for males, and experienced lower percentage increases in each age-group between 1986 and 1996. There has been an 87% increase in deaths (0.94 to 1.77 per 100,000) among females aged 15-19 years, and a 140% increase (0.57 to 1.38 per 100,000) in 40-44-year-old females since 1986. The mortality rate for females aged 25-29 years rose sharply between 1995 and 1996 to 2.40 per 100,000, giving this age-group the highest age-specific rate among females for 1996 (see Figure 1.12).

(f)   Prevalence of disease in the community

General Practice Research Database

The General Practice Research Database (GPRD) provides data on over three million patients on consultations, prescriptions and referrals.

Over the period 1993 to 1995, there has been a rise in the proportion of the population prescribed asthma drugs and who had a diagnosis of asthma of 3% among males and 8% in females (see Table 1.2). Over the same period, there has

Figure 1.9: *Percentage change in age-specific mortality rates, males aged 15-44 years, England and Wales, 1986-96 (1986 = 100)*

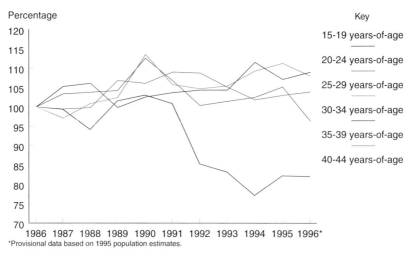

*Provisional data based on 1995 population estimates.

Notes: Deaths for England and Wales in 1986-92 represent the number of deaths registered in each year; since 1993, figures represent the numbers of deaths occurring in each year.

Source: ONS

Figure 1.10: *Percentage change in age-specific mortality rates, females aged 15-44 years, England and Wales, 1986-96 (1986 = 100)*

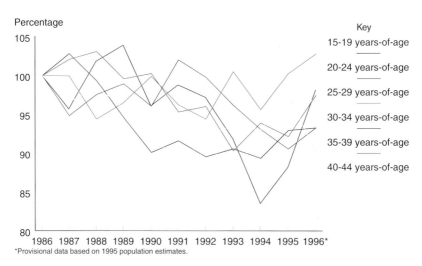

*Provisional data based on 1995 population estimates.

Notes: Deaths for England and Wales in 1986-92 represent the number of deaths registered in each year; since 1993, figures represent the numbers of deaths occurring in each year.

Source: ONS

Figure 1.11: *Age-specific mortality rates from drug misuse and accidental poisoning for males aged 15-44 years, England and Wales, 1986-96*

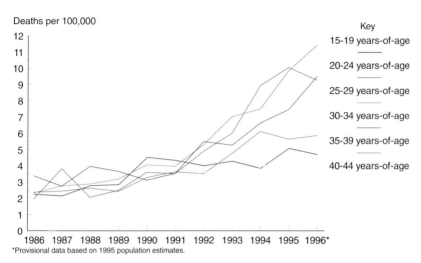

Deaths per 100,000

Key
15-19 years-of-age
20-24 years-of-age
25-29 years-of-age
30-34 years-of-age
35-39 years-of-age
40-44 years-of-age

*Provisional data based on 1995 population estimates.

Notes: Deaths for England and Wales represent the number of deaths registered in each year except 1993 and 1994, which represent the number of deaths occurring in each year.

Source: ONS

Figure 1.12: *Age-specific mortality rates from drug misuse and accidental poisoning for females aged 15-44 years, England and Wales, 1986-96*

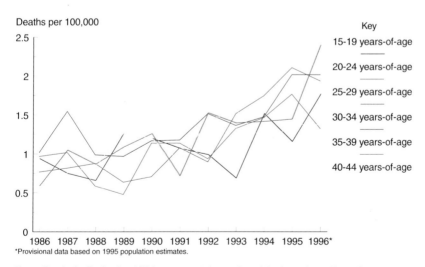

Deaths per 100,000

Key
15-19 years-of-age
20-24 years-of-age
25-29 years-of-age
30-34 years-of-age
35-39 years-of-age
40-44 years-of-age

*Provisional data based on 1995 population estimates.

Notes: Deaths for England and Wales represent the number of deaths registered in each year except 1993 and 1994, which represent the number of deaths occurring in each year.

Source: ONS

Table 1.2: *Time trends in the prevalence per 1,000 population of treated asthma, anxiety/depression and hypertension, England and Wales, 1993-95**

| | 1993 | | 1994 | | 1995 | |
	Males	Females	Males	Females	Males	Females
Asthma	63.0	60.7	64.5	63.9	64.7	65.6
Anxiety/depression†	39.3	94.6	41.3	98.2	43.8	103.1
Hypertension‡	90.2	115.3	93.0	120.2	96.7	125.8

* Age-standardised to 1993.

† 15 years-of-age and over.

‡ 35-years-of-age and over.

been a 9% rise in the proportion of the population of women and an 11.5% rise among men aged 15 years and over with a diagnosis of anxiety/depression and who had been prescribed antidepressants. There has also been a 9% rise in the proportion of the population of women and a 7% rise among men aged 35 years and over who had a diagnosis of hypertension and had been treated with antihypertensive drugs.

Chronic sickness

The General Household Survey (GHS)[1,2] is a continuous survey collecting information about 18,000 adults and 5,000 children in Great Britain each year. It provides two measures of self-reported sickness; chronic sickness is defined as a long-standing illness, disability or infirmity, while acute illness is defined as the restriction of normal activities, as a result of illness or injury, during the two weeks before interview. Respondents who report a long-standing illness are also asked if this limits their activities in any way. Between 1972 and 1995, despite year-to-year fluctuations, the overall trend in self-reported sickness has been upwards, but since the mid-1980s the proportion of the population reporting both chronic and acute illness has stabilised. In 1995, 31% of males and females reported a long-standing illness compared with 29% of males and 31% of females in 1985, and 20% of males and 21% of females in 1972.

Between 1994 and 1995, there was no significant change in the prevalence of self-reported sickness. For example, rates for limiting long-standing illness remained at 18% for males and 20% for females, while the proportion reporting an acute illness which restricted their activity in the previous 14 days was 13% and 15%, respectively, compared with 12% and 15%, respectively, in 1994.

References

1. Office of Population Censuses and Surveys. *Living in Britain: results from the 1994 General Household Survey* . London: HMSO, 1996 (Series GHS no. 25).
2. Office for National Statistics. *Living in Britain: results from the 1995 General Household Survey.* London: Stationery Office, 1997 (Series GHS no. 26) (in press).

(g) Trends in cancer incidence and mortality

Data from the 1988 and 1989 GHSs[1,2] show that 1% of adults reported cancer as a cause for long-standing illness, and a similar figure is indicated by the Office for National Statistics (ONS) Longitudinal Study, which is discussed in the report of the 1990 review of the cancer registration system[3]. A full description of the cancer registration system, with appendices that contain guidance notes and definitions, and a discussion of some factors relevant to the interpretation of cancer registration data, will be published early in 1997[4].

The latest totals of cancer registrations for England and Wales relate to 1991 (see Appendix Tables A.7 and A.8). The age-standardised incidence rates for all malignant neoplasms combined (excluding non-melanoma skin cancer) rose by nearly 10% among males and by nearly 20% in females between 1979 and 1991. The largest percentage increase for any one site was in registrations of malignant melanoma of the skin for males and females. Figures 1.13 and 1.14 show the percentage change in the directly age-standardised incidence rates in England and Wales for the major sites of cancer, between 1979 and 1991, among males and females, respectively.

Among males, lung cancer, the most common cancer (24% of all malignancies in 1991), has declined steadily over the past 12 years and the rate is now 20% below that at its peak in the late 1970s. As the survival for lung cancer is very short, this trend closely follows that for mortality. While there has been only a small increase in colorectal cancer, prostate cancer has increased by around 40% since 1979; if these trends continue, prostate cancer will take over from colorectal cancer as the second most common cancer in men (currently, both make up 13% of all malignancies). Bladder cancer increased during the 1980s, but the rate has stabilised at around 20% above that in 1979. Although the decline in stomach cancer since 1979 has been closely similar to that for lung cancer, there has been a downward trend since at least the early 1970s; mortality shows a parallel downward trend since the early part of this century.

Among females, breast cancer is by far the most common cancer (28% of registrations in 1991); up to 1988, the rate rose on average by about 2% annually.

Figure 1.13: *Percentage change in directly age-standardised cancer incidence rates for major cancers, males, England and Wales, 1979-91 (1979 = 100)*

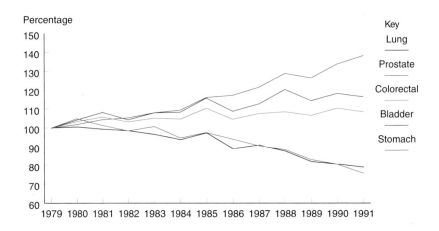

Source: ONS

Figure 1.14: *Percentage change in directly age-standardised cancer incidence rates for major cancers, females, England and Wales, 1979-91 (1979 = 100)*

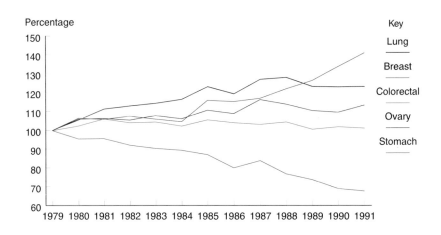

Source: ONS

The subsequent sharper increase appears to be partly accounted for by the introduction of the national breast screening programme: rates in women aged 50-64 years (the screened age-group) in 1991 were some 30% higher than would have been expected had the pre-screening trend continued. There has been little change in the rate of colorectal cancer among females - as in males, the second most common cancer. By the late 1980s, lung cancer (the third most common cancer in women) had risen by almost 30%, but has since levelled off. The rate of ovarian cancer rose during the mid-1980s, but has since been fairly stable. The striking fall in the rate of stomach cancer among women is similar to that in men, as is the long-term downward trend in mortality.

References

1. Office of Population Censuses and Surveys. *General Household Survey 1988.* London: HMSO, 1990 (Series GHS no. 19).
2. Office of Population Censuses and Surveys. *General Household Survey 1989.* London: HMSO, 1991 (Series GHS no. 20).
3. Office of Population Censuses and Surveys. *Review of the national cancer registration system: report of the Working Group of the Registrar General's Medical Advisory Committee.* London: HMSO, 1990 (Series MB1 no. 17).
4. Office for National Statistics. *Cancer statistics: registrations 1990.* London: Stationery Office (Series MBI no. 23) (in press).

CHAPTER 2

THE NATION'S HEALTH

(a)   Basic sources of information

Statistics on morbidity complement standard mortality data. Some are derived from routine sources (eg, data on hospital admissions or general practitioner [GP] consultations), but health surveys also provide essential information about the health of the population because they can cover individuals who are not in contact with health or social care services, address a wide range of aspects of health and facilitate the collection of data in a standardised fashion[1,2].

Health Survey for England

The Health Survey for England, an annual national survey of a representative sample of the population living in private households, focused on cardiovascular disease and its main risk-factors from 1991-94. Since 1993, these Surveys have had a sample size in excess of 15,000, which makes it possible to provide prevalence estimates at regional level. Data derived from the report of the 1994 Survey, published early in 1996[3], can readily be used to monitor the effects of public health policies[4].

During 1995, the Survey included information on other topics (respiratory disease, accidents and disability), in addition to core data on socio-demographic variables and the monitoring of Health of the Nation targets on obesity and blood pressure[5]. Also, for the first time, children aged 2-15 years were included. Preliminary analyses indicate, for example, that 11% of adults and 20% of children had at some time been diagnosed by a doctor as suffering from asthma, and that 21% of adult men and 15% of adult women had had an accident which led to a medical consultation in the previous year, although the severity of such accidents varied greatly. The full report of the 1995 Survey will be published early in 1997[6]. The 1996 Survey covered respiratory disease, accidents and particular measures of general health in addition to the core data; the 1997 Survey will also focus on children and young people in line with the Health of the Young Nation initiative.

The Health Survey for England is part of a wider Departmental health survey programme which includes, for example, the National Survey of Psychiatric Morbidity and the Dietary and Nutritional Surveys.

References

1. Department of Health. *On the State of the Public Health: the annual report of the Chief Medical Officer of the Department of Health for the year 1995.* London: HMSO, 1996; 65-6.

2. Gupta S. Health surveys as a tool for government: the Health Survey for England as a paradigm case. *Arch Publ Health* 1994; **52:** 99-113.

3. Colhoun H, Prescott-Clarke P, eds. *Health Survey for England 1994: a survey carried out on behalf of the Department of Health (vols 1 and 2).* London: HMSO, 1996 (Series HS; no. 4).

4. Gupta S. Health trends in *Health Trends. Health Trends* 1996; **28**: 43-4.

5. Department of Health. *The Health of the Nation: a strategy for health in England.* London: HMSO, 1992 (Cm. 1986).

6. Prescott-Clarke P, Primatesta P, eds. *Health Survey for England 1995: a survey carried out on behalf of the Department of Health (vols 1 and 2).* London: Stationery Office (in press) (Series HS; no. 5).

(b)   Substance misuse

Drug misuse

The Government continued with the implementation of the second year of the three-year anti-drugs strategy 'Tackling Drugs Together'[1]. Two *Drug misuse statistics* bulletins were published for the six-month periods ending March and September 1995[2,3]; during the period April to September 1995, the number of individual drug misusers presenting to services in England for problem drug misuse for the first time (or for the first time in six months) was 22,848 - a rise of 10% compared with the previous six months.

In May, the Task Force set up to review the effectiveness of services for drug misusers published an independent review of drug treatment services in England[4]. It found that, although there were no simple solutions to drug dependence, treatment options existed which were effective in improving the life and health of drug misusers and in reducing the cost to society of the consequences which arise from drug misuse. The Department of Health (DH) consulted on draft guidance to purchasers of drug services, based on the findings of the Task Force's work. A national treatment outcomes research study (NTORS) continued to track 1,100 drug misusers to evaluate the long-term health and social impact of treatment on drug misusers.

The Department continued its contract with the Health Education Authority (HEA) for a drug and solvents prevention campaign, which focused on informing young people and parents about the health risks of drug and solvent misuse, particularly ecstasy (methylenedioxymethamphetamine or MDMA), lysergic acid diethylamide (LSD), amphetamines, psilocybin mushrooms and certain volatile substances. The Department continued its contract with Network Scotland to provide a continuous, free and confidential drugs helpline service offering information and advice.

75

Alcohol

Patterns of alcohol consumption and drinking behaviour reported in the 1994 General Household Survey (GHS)[5] showed that, in Great Britain, among those aged 18 years and over, 27% of men and 13% of women were drinking above the then recommended sensible drinking levels (21 units a week for men and 14 units weekly for women). The percentage for men was unchanged since the 1992 GHS[6], while the proportion for women had risen 2% since 1992.

The report *Sensible drinking*[7], published in December 1995, revised the Government's advice on sensible levels of alcohol consumption, based on the most up-to-date scientific and medical evidence of the effects of alcohol on health. In the light of the new advice, the HEA developed a revised health promotion campaign. From October 1996, 'Think about drink' leaflets for the general public have been distributed through local health promotion organisers. The HEA have been awarded a further contract to extend the campaign during 1997.

Considerable public concern was expressed during the year about young people's drinking habits; some evidence indicated an increase in alcohol consumption, and the wider availability of various new drinks containing alcohol which might particularly appeal to younger age-groups was noted. The latest comprehensive survey of teenagers' drinking habits in Great Britain took place in November and December; the results will be available during 1997. The most recent national data available (from the equivalent Teenage Drinking Survey in 1994) showed that 17% of 11-15-year-olds in England (up from 13% in 1990) drank alcohol at least once a week; the proportion who said in 1994 that they never drank alcohol (about 40%) was unchanged since 1990.

References

1. Lord President's Office. *Tackling drugs together: a strategy for England: 1995-1998.* London: HMSO, 1995 (Cm. 2846).

2. Department of Health. *Drug misuse statistics.* London: Department of Health, 1996 (Statistical Bulletin 96/7).

3. Department of Health. *Drug misuse statistics.* London: Department of Health, 1996 (Statistical Bulletin 96/24).

4. Department of Health. *The Task Force to Review Services for Drug Misusers: report of an independent review of drug treatment services in England.* London: Department of Health, 1996.

5. Office for National Statistics. *Living in Britain: results from the 1994 General Household Survey.* London: HMSO, 1996 (Series GHS no. 25).

6. Office of Population Censuses and Surveys. *General Household Survey 1992.* London: HMSO, 1994 (Series GHS no. 23).

7. Department of Health. *Sensible drinking: the report of an Inter-Departmental Working Group.* London: Department of Health, 1995.

(c) Nutrition

In October, the Committee on Medical Aspects of Food and Nutrition Policy (COMA) published *Guidelines on the nutritional assessment of infant formulas*[1], which set out principles for the nutritional evaluation of newly developed manufactured products. Two expert groups continued their work on diet and cancer and on the nutritional status of the population. The COMA took part in consultation conducted by the Ministry of Agriculture, Fisheries and Food (MAFF) on functional foods and health claims. The COMA Panel on Child Nutrition enlarged its remit to include the nutrition of pregnant and lactating women, and was renamed the Panel on Child and Maternal Nutrition. This Panel was unable to endorse the addition of very-long-chain polyunsaturated fatty acids, which are manufactured as novel foods, to infant feeds. Guidance to implement the Infant Formula and Follow-on Formula Regulations 1995[2] on educational and informational materials was developed by several consultation processes.

Eat Well! 2[3], the final report of the Nutrition Task Force, was published in April together with a Government response. Several projects were completed, including publication of *Low income, food, nutrition and health: strategies for improvement*[4]; *Nutrition for medical students: nutrition in the undergraduate medical curriculum*[5]; and a checklist for audit to accompany the *Nutrition guidelines for hospital catering*[6].

Data collection and analysis of three diet and nutrition surveys continued during 1996 in preparation for publication of the reports in 1997[7,8,9]. One of these surveys focused on Asian infants; circulating concentrations of vitamin D and haemoglobin have now been measured in some 1,000 two-year-olds from this ethnic group, with results to be reported during 1997. Pilot work for the National Diet and Nutrition Survey of people aged 4-18 years was concluded, and field work will begin in January 1997. A call for proposals under the £1.5-million phase 2 DH/Medical Research Council (MRC) Nutrition Research Programme received 158 bids; commissioning will take place in 1997. An annual report[10] of the work of the COMA will be published in Summer 1997.

References

1. Department of Health. *Guidelines on the nutritional assessment of infant formulas: report of the Working Group on the Nutritional Assessment of Infant Formulas of the Committee on Medical Aspects of Food and Nutrition Policy.* London: Stationery Office, 1996 (Report on Health and Social Subjects no. 47).
2. *Food: the Infant Formula and Follow-on Formula Regulations 1995.* London: HMSO, 1995 (Statutory Instrument: SI 1995 no. 77).
3. Department of Health. *Eat Well! 2: a progress report from the Nutrition Task Force on the action plan to achieve the Health of the Nation targets on diet and nutrition.* Wetherby (West Yorkshire): Department of Health, 1996.

4. Department of Health Nutrition Task Force. *Low income, food, nutrition and health: strategies for improvement: a report by the Low Income Project Team for the Nutrition Task Force.* London: Department of Health, 1996.

5. Jackson AA, ed. *Nutrition for medical students: nutrition in the undergraduate medical curriculum.* London: Department of Health, 1996.

6. Department of Health. *Nutrition guidelines for hospital catering.* London: Department of Health, 1995.

7. Thomas M, Avery V. *Infant feeding in Asian families: early feeding practices and growth.* London: Stationery Office (in press).

8. Foster K, Lader D, Cheesborough S. *Infant feeding 1995.* London: Stationery Office (in press).

9. Finch S, Lowe C, Doyle W et al. *National Diet and Nutrition Survey: people aged 65 years or over.* London: Stationery Office (in press).

10. Department of Health. *Committee on Medical Aspects of Food and Nutrition Policy: annual report 1995.* London: Department of Health, 1996.

(d)   Health of children

Survival prospects for children have continued to improve. In 1996, infant mortality fell to 6.0 per 1,000 live births in England and Wales, the lowest recorded level (see page 65).

The July 1995 launch of the Health of the Young Nation initiative within the Health of the Nation strategy[1] helped to provide better understanding of the particular health needs of children and a fuller recognition of the lasting consequences of those factors that influence health and health-related behaviour among children. This initiative provides a focus on young people's health, and aims to ensure that they are equipped to make responsible and informed choices about their health and lifestyle. Alliances are a key to progress in this area, and cover a wide range of Government bodies (such as the Department for Education and Employment [DfEE] and the Health Education Authority [HEA]), as well as many local initiatives. The importance of schools as a healthy setting was increasingly recognised (see page 101).

The NHS Executive's draft consultation document, *Child health in the community: a guide to good practice*[2], issued in March 1995, met a keen response with many valuable comments, and guidance to assist those in the NHS, local authorities and voluntary bodies who have responsibilities for purchasing and providing health services for children outside hospital was issued in September 1996[3].

In July 1995, the House of Commons Health Committee announced that it would conduct an inquiry into children's health[4]. The deliberations of the Committee included consideration of various factors, including service provision, which may influence the health of children; it will report in Spring 1997.

References

1. Department of Health. *The Health of the Nation: a strategy for health in Engl*c
    HMSO, 1992 (Cm. 1986).
2. Department of Health. *Child health in the community: a guide to good prac*
    Department of Health, 1995.
3. Department of Health. *Child health in the community: a guide to good practice.* Wetherby
    (West Yorkshire): Department of Health, 1996.
4. House of Commons Health Committee. *Inquiry into children's health: Session 1994-95.*
    London: HMSO, 1995.

(e)   Health of adolescents

During 1996, activities to promote the health of young people were developed as part of the Health of the Young Nation initiative (see page 97), which was launched in July 1995[1]. Health of the Nation key area activities also included projects aimed at young people, particularly in schools (see page 101).

In March, the second of two DH-funded conferences on adolescent care in practice, organised by the Royal College of General Practitioners, was held in Hull.

In September, the NHS Executive issued *Child health in the community: a guide to good practice*[2] (see page 78). This guide included a chapter on general aspects of adolescent health as well as chapters on the specialised areas of child and adolescent mental health and school health. Medical needs of young people in school were also addressed through a joint DfEE and DH circular[3] and by *Supporting pupils with medical needs*[4], a guide to good practice that was published in October.

Throughout the year, planning continued for the 1997 Health Survey for England, which will include a boosted sample of children and young people to provide up-to-date information on young people's health, and baseline data against which future trends may be interpreted.

During 1996, the House of Commons Health Committee took evidence related to the health needs of adolescents as part of its inquiry into children's health; it is expected to report early in 1997.

References

1. Department of Health. *On the State of the Public Health: the annual report of the Chief Medical Officer of the Department of Health for the year 1995.* London: HMSO, 1996; 3, 79-80.
2. NHS Executive. *Child health in the community: a guide to good practice.* Wetherby (West Yorkshire): Department of Health, 1996.

3.	Department for Education and Employment, Department of Health. *Supporting pupils with medical needs in school.* London: Department for Education and Employment, 1996 (DfEE Circular 14/96).

4.	Department for Education and Employment, Department of Health. *Supporting pupils with medical needs: a good practice guide.* London: Department for Education and Employment, 1996.

## (f)	Health of women

As part of its work to "mainstream a gender perspective into all policies and programmes" - following the commitment made by the United Kingdom (UK) Government at the Fourth United Nations (UN) World Conference on Women, held in Beijing, China, in September 1995 - DH held a conference in September 1996 entitled 'Making gender matter in health care and health promotion'. The conference explored the importance of 'gender perspectives' with NHS purchasers and providers of health care, and considered cost-effective ways to make health services more sensitive to the differing needs of men and women.

At this conference, Baroness Cumberlege, Parliamentary Under Secretary of State for Health in the House of Lords, launched a new resource pack[1] on women's health promotion, developed by the HEA with DH funding. The pack is aimed at all engaged in purchasing or providing health promotion services for women, whether in the NHS, local authorities or the voluntary sector.

DH continues to develop health promotion materials aimed specifically at women. A new free booklet, *Well women: today and tomorrow: health tips for the over 35s*[2], was launched in June. Aimed particularly at women in the lower socio-economic groups, this booklet contains practical health advice for women before, during and after the menopause; some 600,000 copies had been distributed by the end of the year.

During 1996, the Department also funded a joint women's health initiative with the HEA and the British Broadcasting Corporation (BBC) to mark the fiftieth anniversary of *Woman's Hour*. The initiative, called 'Best of health', focused attention on women's health over six months of broadcasts and other activities, including a touring exhibition bus.

References

1.	Health Education Authority. *Women's health promotion: a resource pack for health care purchasers and providers.* London: Department of Health, 1996.

2.	Department of Health. *Well women: today and tomorrow: health tips for the over 35s.* London: Department of Health, 1996.

(g)   Health of men

Since men's health was highlighted in the 1992 Report[1], increased interest and attention have been paid to this topic. In general, men's health continues to improve. Average male life expectancy was 74.3 years in 1995, and is projected to rise to 75.5 years by 2001-2002, compared with 71.6 years in 1983.

The key areas identified in the Health of the Nation initiative[2] have a major effect on men's health. Work carried out within the strategy during 1996 will help further to improve men's health and should influence mortality and morbidity statistics alike. Gender variations were featured in the report of the Variations Sub-Group of the Chief Medical Officer's Health of the Nation Working Group[3]. The Department will commission an extensive £2.4 million research programme on variations in health during 1997 (see page 96).

In September, the NHS Executive's conference, 'Making gender matter in health care and health promotion', considered cost-effective ways for NHS purchasers and providers of care to make services more sensitive to the particular needs of men and women (see page 80)[4]. North Derbyshire Health Authority produced a videotape *Clued up about cancer*[5] for use by men in the workplace, which was launched at the conference. This project was funded by DH in support of the 'Europe Against Cancer' programme. The workplace provides an important setting to communicate health promotion messages to men. The work of the Health of the Nation Workplace Taskforce and the Workplace Health Advisory Team (see page 101) will facilitate this work.

A two-year research project 'Men's health ducking the targets', funded by DH, undertaken by Community Health UK and due to report in 1997, is examining the impact of health messages for men among the intended audience.

Men's health was also the focus of initiatives outside the Department. For example, the Royal College of Nursing Men's Health Forum published a review of recent research and literature[6] in July, and is continuing its activities to promote men's health.

A new DH publicity programme for men's health, aimed at men aged 40-60 years, should be launched in 1997.

References

1.   Department of Health. *On the State of the Public Health: the annual report of the Chief Medical Officer of the Department of Health for the year 1992.* London: HMSO, 1993; 5, 79-106.
2.   Department of Health. *The Health of the Nation: a strategy for health in England.* London: HMSO, 1992 (Cm. 1986).

3.   Department of Health. *Variations in health: what can the Department of Health and the NHS do?* London: Department of Health, 1995.

4   NHS Executive. *Making gender matter in health care and health promotion: report of a conference at the Forum Hotel, 23 September 1996.* London: Department of Health, 1996.

5.   North Derbyshire Health Authority. *Clued up about cancer.* Derby: North Derbyshire Health Authority, 1996.

6.   Royal College of Nursing Men's Health Forum, Lloyd T. *Men's health review: prepared on behalf of the men's health forum.* London: Royal College of Nursing, 1996.

(h)   Health of black and ethnic minorities

The Department remains committed to improving the health and well-being of people from black and ethnic population groups, and has concentrated its efforts on work to improve access to services and to address the different patterns of disease among the various population groups. It continues to support and to fund further development of links with ethnic minority communities through voluntary groups, medical and nursing Royal Colleges and other educational establishments and the NHS over a wide range of issues that will assist in the improvement of health among ethnic minority communities.

Several recent publications that focus on related issues have recently been produced and have been well received by health professionals and ethnic minority communities alike. For example, a symposium held with the Cancer Research Campaign (CRC) which addressed the health needs of ethnic minorities in relation to cancer was followed up with the joint publication of *Cancer and minority ethnic groups*[1]; further collaboration with the CRC is planned.

The Department funded the Office for Public Management and the King's Fund to produce *Responding to diversity*[2] and *Facing up to difference*[3], which will help purchasers and providers of care in the NHS to tackle ethnic minority health with greater confidence and help them to provide more culturally competent services. Another publication[4] that highlights the importance of using bilingual workers in the health service gives examples of good practice.

A *Directory of ethnic minority initiatives*[5], which sets out many of the projects that the Department has funded, has proved to be a popular and useful reference guide for health authorities and ethnic minority groups.

The NHS Ethnic Health Unit continued to fund projects to improve access to services and to improve the confidence of NHS managers in addressing the health needs of their ethnic minority populations. On the international front, the Department is building links with health professionals in the United States of America who have experience in dealing with ethnic health issues; these links will be developed and closer relations for further co-operation and exchange of information is planned.

References

1. King J, Bahl V, Selby P, eds. The proceedings of the Cancer Research Campaign/Department of Health symposium on cancer and minority ethnic groups held at Regent's Park College, London, 4 May 1995. *Br J Cancer* 1996; **74 (Suppl XXIX):** S1-80.

2. Office for Public Management. *Responding to diversity.* London: Office for Public Management, 1996

3. Chandra J. *Facing up to difference: a toolkit for creating culturally competent health services for black and minority ethnic communities.* London: King's Fund, 1996.

4. Baxter C, Baylav A, Fuller J, Marr A, Sanders M. *The case for the provision of bilingual services with the NHS.* London: Department of Health, 1996.

5. Department of Health. *Directory of ethnic minority initiatives.* London: Department of Health, 1996.

(i)   Health in the workplace

The special chapter on health in the workplace in the Report for 1994[1] set out the background to the development of occupational health practice in the UK, described the main occupational health hazards and illnesses, and identified some future developments. It emphasised the importance of risk assessment and management and pointed to the role that occupational health professionals can play to improve health at work.

The Health and Safety Executive (HSE) launched the second phase of its campaign, 'Good health is good business', during the European Week of Health and Safety in October. The campaign aims to raise awareness of occupational health risks and to improve management competence in controlling them[2]. The second phase focuses on work-related dermatitis and occupational cancers including those linked to asbestos.

To help to raise awareness of work-related ill-health, the Department and the HSE facilitated the production of a distance-learning package on occupational health for general practitioners (GPs), which should be available in Autumn 1997. Medical practitioners made a major contribution during the year to a self-reported work-related illness survey by validating subjects' reported diagnoses and offering an opinion on their relation with work. This survey has been commissioned by the HSE and builds on earlier work[3]. The preliminary findings and a comparison with the 1990 survey should also be published in Autumn 1997.

The Health of the Nation strategy included the setting up of a Workplace Health Advisory Team (see page 101). A National Audit Office report on health and safety in the acute hospital sector of the NHS was published in November[4]; it identified areas for improvement, and will be subject to a Public Accounts Committee hearing in February 1997.

Progress with the 'Health at work in the NHS' campaign was made during 1996, with the development of an organisational stress management tool for use in the NHS working environment. During pilot studies in three NHS Trusts - involving the acute, mental health and community sectors - it proved useful and successful, and is being further developed by the HEA.

The HSE published guidance documents during the year[5,6,7,8], contributed to inter-Departmental guidance on alcohol misuse at work[9] and published several research reports[10,11,12]. The Advisory Committee on Dangerous Pathogens published an interim report on microbiological risk assessment[13].

References

1. Department of Health. *On the State of the Public Health: the annual report of the Chief Medical Officer for the Department of Health for the year 1994.* London: HMSO, 1995; 7, 88-127.
2. Health and Safety Executive. *Health risk management: a practical guide for managers in small and medium size enterprises.* Sudbury (Suffolk): HSE Books, 1995.
3. Hodgson JT, Jones JR. *Self-reported work-related illness.* Sudbury (Suffolk): HSE Books, 1996 (HSE research paper 33).
4. National Audit Office. *Health and safety in NHS acute hospital Trusts in England: Session 1996-97.* London: Stationery Office, 1996 (HC 82).
5. Health and Safety Executive. *In the driving seat: advice to employers on reducing back pains in drivers and machinery operators.* Sudbury (Suffolk): HSE Books, 1996.
6. Health and Safety Executive. *Managing asbestos in workplace buildings.* Sudbury (Suffolk): HSE Books, 1996.
7. Health and Safety Executive. *Preventing dermatitis at work: advice for employers and employees.* Sudbury (Suffolk): HSE Books, 1996.
8. Health and Safety Executive. *Violence at work: a guide for employers.* Sudbury: (Suffolk): HSE Books, 1996.
9. Health and Safety Executive. *Don't mix it! A guide for employers on alcohol at work.* Sudbury (Suffolk): HSE Books, 1996.
10. Honey S, Hillage J. *Health surveillance in Great Britain.* London: Health and Safety Executive, 1996 (Contract Research Report 121/1996).
11. Health and Safety Executive. *Evaluation of the Display Screen Equipment Regulations 1992.* London: Health and Safety Executive, 1996 (Contract Research Report 130).
12. Health and Safety Executive. *The costs and benefits of the Noise at Work Regulations 1989.* London: Health and Safety Executive, 1996 (Contract Research Report 116).
13. Advisory Committee on Dangerous Pathogens. *Microbiological risk assessment: an interim report.* London: HMSO, 1996.

(j)   Health of people in later life

The Department continues to promote services for older people to facilitate their independent life in the community. Further improvements in community health services and falling lengths of hospital stay have been mirrored by the growth of local authority provision in domiciliary services predominantly used by older people. In reviewing its priorities for the NHS, DH has placed emphasis on the need for sensitive hospital discharge practices, and high quality community and rehabilitation services. Particular priority has been given to the need for individual assessment, early detection of problems, and the development of more integrated patterns of service for older people through joint working between all relevant agencies. However, the challenges of this approach are recognised, and aspects of disability in particular are the topic of this year's special chapter (see page 104); the health of people in later life has been discussed in previous reports[1,2].

DH continued to promote work on sickness and disability prevention for older people; an expert working group has been set up to look further at available measures of health state and possible future developments in data collection. DH has also supported the development of health mentoring projects and other initiatives using older volunteers, and of advice to GPs on health promotion for older people.

Guidance on NHS responsibilities for meeting continuing health care needs, issued in February 1995[3], confirmed and clarified the NHS's responsibilities for meeting a range of continuing health care needs, many of which will be found among elderly people. Following local consultation, health authorities put policies and criteria for continuing health care into operation on 1 April 1996.

References

1. Department of Health. *On the State of the Public Health: the annual report of the Chief Medical Officer of the Department of Health for the year 1990.* London: HMSO, 1991; 68-95.
2. Department of Health. *On the State of the Public Health: the annual report of the Chief Medical Officer of the Department of Health for the year 1995.* London: HMSO, 1996; 78.
3. Department of Health. *NHS responsibilities for meeting continuing health care needs.* Wetherby (West Yorkshire): Department of Health, 1995 (Health Service Guidelines: HSG(95)8, Local Authority Circular: LAC(95)5).

(k)   Mental health

Mental health continues to represent an important focus for the NHS; up to one-quarter of consultations in primary care settings concern a mental health problem[1]. NHS strategy aims to promote good mental health firstly by reduction in the distress associated with mental illness and by prevention of suicide; and secondly to promote the development of a spectrum of care[2], sensitive to patients' needs and wishes for those suffering from a wide range of morbidity associated with mental health issues.

During the year, the Confidential Inquiry into Homicides and Suicides produced its first report[3] and work to develop understanding of the relations between mental illness, homicide and suicide will be based on a firm foundation for future audit in this important area. Emergency services were reviewed; work was done to develop further the spectrum of care initiative[2]; a review of 24-hour nursed accommodation was undertaken; solutions to the problems and challenges posed by inter-Agency working were outlined[4]; and services for mentally disordered offenders were addressed by the High Security Psychiatric Services Commissioning Board, and supervised discharge procedures introduced[5].

But the needs of those with severe mental illness, although they represent (and will continue to represent) a priority for the NHS, are only one feature of a service which addresses the needs of all those with mental health problems. For example, the mental health of children and young people received attention in a House of Commons Health Committee inquiry. Work also continues to improve information to professionals and patients concerned with health and social care services, and to develop mental health care which is firmly rooted in evidence about effectiveness. In October 1996, the NHS Executive published the report of its review of psychotherapy services in England[6].

References

1.   Department of Health. *On the State of the Public Health: the annual report of the Chief Medical Officer of the Department of Health for the year 1995.* London: HMSO, 1996; 13-4, 95-126.
2.   Department of Health. *The spectrum of care: local services for people with mental health problems.* Wetherby (West Yorkshire): Department of Health, 1996.
3.   Steering Committee of the Confidential Inquiry into Homicides and Suicides by Mentally Ill People. *Report of the Confidential Inquiry into Homicides and Suicides by Mentally Ill People.* London: Royal College of Psychiatrists, 1996.
4.   Department of Health. *Developing partnerships in mental health.* London: Stationery Office (in press).
5.   Department of Health, Welsh Office. *Mental Health (Patients in the Community) Act 1995: guidance on supervised discharge (after-care under supervision) and related provisions: supplement to the 1993 Code of Practice pursuant to Section 118 of the Mental Health Act 1983.* London: HMSO, 1996.
6.   NHS Executive. *Review of psychotherapy services: review of strategic policy.* Wetherby (West Yorkshire): Department of Health, 1996.

CHAPTER 3

THE STRATEGY FOR HEALTH

(a)   Introduction

The Health of the Nation White Paper[1], which set out a strategy for health in England, was launched in July 1992. It identified five key areas responsible for much of the premature death and avoidable ill-health in this country, and for which there were known effective interventions. The strategy also emphasised the roles of other Government Departments, not just the Department of Health (DH), in influencing health, and of organisations other than the National Health Service (NHS) that work to improve health. It set out a series of settings where health promotion might most profitably be targeted, and it argued strongly for the benefits of joint working at all levels.

The Health of the Nation initiative includes 27 specific targets within the five key areas. One of the criteria against which each key area was judged for inclusion was that it should be possible to set and monitor quantified targets. Where exceptions were made to this rule - notably in the mental health key area - targets were nonetheless set, and work was immediately started to devise ways to monitor them.

The results of subsequent regular monitoring show encouraging progress for most of the targets where data are available. However, three targets show trends in the wrong direction: those for teenage cigarette smoking; obesity; and alcohol consumption among women. Such information helps to highlight where effort needs to be concentrated.

A National Audit Office study[2] of the Health of the Nation initiative, published in October, concluded that DH should continue to address:

- those areas where progress is good and to consider whether the targets might profitably be revised in those areas;

- areas where progress is slow or negative to see what further action should be taken; *and*

- the need to improve data quality, especially for mental health targets.

This report went to a hearing of the Public Accounts Committee in November; their response is expected in Spring 1997.

The original Health of the Nation White Paper[1] made clear that it was not to be considered the final word on the strategy for health, but rather the start of a developing process. In November 1996, DH and the Department of the Environment (DoE) jointly launched a consultation document[3] on a new environment key area for the strategy; consultation on this proposal is due to end in February 1997.

Partnerships to promote health continue to be forged. The Chief Medical Officer's 'Challenge' has been developed for wider use and it has been welcomed in the private sector, particularly by supermarket chains - Sainsbury's, Waitrose, Safeway and Somerfield have all successfully applied to use the 'Meeting the challenge' logo for promotions to encourage healthy eating.

References

1. Department of Health. *The Health of the Nation: a strategy for health in England.* London: HMSO, 1992 (Cm. 1986).
2. National Audit Office. *The Health of the Nation: a progress report: Session 1995-96.* London: HMSO, 1996 (HC 656).
3. Department of Health, Department of the Environment. *The environment and health: a consultative document for the environment as a key area in the Health of the Nation strategy.* London: Department of Health, 1996.

(b)   Key areas and targets

(i)   *Coronary heart disease and stroke*

Between the 1990 health strategy baseline and 1994-96, death rates from coronary heart disease (CHD) had fallen by an estimated 24% among people aged under 65 years and by about 18% among people aged 65-74 years. Over the same period, stroke mortality rates fell by an estimated 10% for people aged under 65 years and by 17% for people aged 65-74 years.

Action to achieve the CHD/stroke targets (of a fall in death rates by at least 40% for both CHD and stroke in people aged under 65 years and a fall in death rate for CHD by at least 30% and of stroke by at least 40% among people aged 65-74 years by the year 2000)[1] has focused on the principal risk-factors: physical inactivity; diet and obesity; smoking (see page 90); alcohol; and hypertension.

Physical activity

Following the successful completion of the work of the Physical Activity Task Force in January, the Government issued a *Strategy statement on physical activity*[2] in March to coincide with the launch of the Health Education Authority's (HEA's) major new physical activity campaign, 'Active for life'. This campaign will run for three years and is intended to influence the public's knowledge, attitudes and behaviour in relation to physical activity, and will encourage people to include 30 minutes of moderate physical activity, such as walking and cycling, as part of their everyday routine.

Blood pressure

The Health of the Nation blood pressure target is to reduce mean systolic blood pressure by at least 5 mmHg by the year 2005. The latest figures from the Health Survey for England[3] show that mean systolic blood pressure in adults has fallen by 2 mmHg between 1991/92 and 1995, and that 61% of those with high blood pressure were on treatment - of whom 67% had normal blood pressure. These figures were a considerable improvement on the 1991 data, which found that 52% of all hypertensive adults were on treatment, 61% of whom were normotensive.

Some social class variations in hypertension, a key risk-factor in stroke, persist according to preliminary analyses from the 1995 Survey[3]: people in social class V were more likely to have high blood pressure than those in social class I, and those living in northern regions had a higher mean systolic blood pressure than those in the south. Some of these variations in blood pressure may be explained in part by the prevalence of other risk-factors such as obesity. Health promotion and treatment both have future important contributions to make to the effective control of blood pressure in the population[4].

Alcohol

Following the publication of *Sensible drinking*[5] in December 1995, a review of the Health of the Nation alcohol targets[1] began during 1996, with a view to develop new targets to take account of this report's revised sensible drinking messages - particularly the shift from recommended weekly sensible levels to recommended daily levels, and the increased emphasis on wider issues of alcohol-related harm, including the dangers of being drunk.

Obesity

Latest figures indicate that the prevalence of obesity in the adult population continues to increase[3]. Obesity reflects imbalance between energy intake and expenditure, and strategies to combat obesity must therefore take into account physical activity as well as diet. Action to reduce the prevalence of obesity among adults is being taken forward through the Nutrition Task Force programme to reduce the fat content of the diet and through the HEA's 'Active for life' campaign to increase moderate regular physical activity in the population. Research into effective interventions in the prevention and treatment of obesity has been commissioned.

(ii)   Cancers

Lung cancer

Smoking remains the single most important cause of preventable disease and premature death in this country and is associated with some 121,000 deaths annually; lung cancer alone is responsible for over 31,000 of these. Adult levels of cigarette smoking continue to fall, but this progress is not being shown for teenage smoking[6].

Adults

General Household Survey (GHS) data for England in 1994[7] show that the prevalence of cigarette smoking has continued to fall for men and women alike. Between 1990 and 1994, the proportion of men who smoked fell from 31% to 28%, and that for women fell from 28% to 25%.

The biggest ever national anti-smoking campaign was launched in December 1994; run by the HEA, this £18 million, 4-year campaign is particularly aimed at smokers in social classes IIIM, IV and V and at parents (because children whose parents both smoke are twice as likely to smoke cigarettes themselves than children whose parents do not smoke).

Teenagers

The 12% prevalence level of regular cigarette smoking found among teenagers in 1994[6] shows that the Health of the Nation target[1] of 6% was missed. Efforts will continue to reach this target and, on 8 July, a new teenage anti-smoking campaign was launched. Up to £1 million annually will be spent over three years on this programme to counter the 'positive' images of cigarette smoking currently held by some teenagers.

Sources of cigarette supply are also important, and the campaign will offer help and support to retailers, and remind them of their statutory responsibilities in this area.

Tobacco consumption

Figures for the year to June 1996 indicate that cigarettes released for home consumption in the United Kingdom (UK) fell to 81,200 million compared with 83,200 million in the previous 12 months, representing an annual reduction of roughly 2.9% from the 1990 baseline of 98,000 million, against a target of 59,000 million by the year 2000.

Price is widely recognised as a very important factor in cigarette smoking; a 10% rise in price generally leads to a fall in consumption of 3-6%. The 1993 Budget contained a commitment to raise tobacco duties on average by at least 3% in real terms each year. The rise in the 1996 Budget was 5%; in real terms, cigarettes are more than 50% more expensive than they were in 1979.

Smoking in pregnancy

The campaign to reduce cigarette smoking among pregnant mothers now continues as part of the general adult smoking education campaign; it includes resources and training in smoking cessation advice for midwives. Progress is being measured by the Infant Feeding Survey (IFS). The 1990 IFS[8] showed that the percentage of smokers in Great Britain who did give up during pregnancy increased from 24% in 1985 to 27% in 1990, against a target of 33% in the year 2000; results of the 1995 IFS survey will be available in mid-1997.

Breast cancer

The Health of the Nation target[1] is to cut breast cancer deaths in the population invited for screening by at least 25% by the year 2000 - from 93.4 per 100,000 (in 1990) to no more than 70.1 per 100,000[9,10]. The latest data (for the period 1994-96) show a rate of 81.4 per 100,000 (a reduction of almost 13%)[9].

The key intervention to reduce mortality from breast cancer is early detection through screening, to enable the provision of effective treatment at an earlier stage. Proxy indicators remain good: women are still taking up breast screening invitations and screening targets (take-up, cancer detection, and biopsy rates) are being met. In 1995/96, 1.1 million women were screened within the programme, and overall 76% of women aged 50-64 years who were invited for screening took up their invitation. Although slightly below the 1994/95 figure of 77%, this proportion still represents a considerable increase over previous years and is substantially above the 70% target. At 31 March 1996, 65% of women aged 50-64 years resident in England had been screened at least once in the previous three years, and in only seven of 105 health districts was coverage less than 50%; 5,569 new cancers were detected, a rate of 5.3 per 1,000 women screened.

Cervical cancer

The Health of the Nation target is to reduce the incidence of invasive cervical cancer by at least 20% by the year 2000 from a 1986 baseline (ie, to 12.8 new cases per 100,000 women)[10]. Latest figures (from 1993) show that incidence rates have fallen to 11.2 per 100,000 women, and have been below the target rate since 1991. In addition, cervical cancer deaths fell by over 30% between 1988 and 1995.

As with breast cancer, screening is the main intervention to reduce the incidence of cervical cancer by detection of early changes to the cervix which may lead to cancer, so enabling preventive treatment. In 1995/96, 3.9 million women were screened. At 31 March 1996, 84.7% of women aged 25-64 years resident in England had been screened at least once within the previous five years. Increasing uptake over recent years has been a striking achievement of the NHS cervical screening programme. The priority now is to obtain further improvements in screening quality; new quality assurance guidelines were published by the NHS cervical screening programme in March[10].

Skin cancer

The Health of the Nation White Paper[1] includes a target to halt the year-on-year increase in the incidence of skin cancer by the year 2005. To achieve this target, work has been concentrated on increasing public awareness of the dangers of over-exposing the skin to harmful ultraviolet (UV) radiation from the sun. The Chief Medical Officer's 'Sun challenge', issued in February 1995, sought assistance and support from the private sector and local authorities to get the messages about safety in the sun over to the public.

The Department has continued to fund the HEA's 'Sun know how' campaign, which is intended to inform the public of the risk of skin cancer and to forge health alliances with the media, high street retailers and a network of local organisers. The campaign will continue in 1997 with the theme of 'travels'. DH also continues to fund the production of sunburn forecasts by the Meteorological Office for use by weather forecast presenters.

The Chief Medical Officer launched a pilot Internet site 'Xtreme' on 2 September. The site, which aims to increase the awareness of skin cancer, will operate until 31 March 1997 when its effectiveness will be evaluated before a decision is taken on whether it should be continued. The Health Information Service provides freephone advice (tel: 0800 665544) about precautions that should be taken in the sun.

A three-year, £1.8-million research programme has been commissioned to examine risk-factors, public health interventions and measurement of progress towards the target for skin cancer.

During 1996, the 'Europe against cancer' programme focused on skin cancer, with distribution of posters and leaflets within all European Union (EU) countries. Sunfile[11], a guide to health promotion resources available to those working on skin cancer prevention, was produced by the UK.

(iii)   Mental health

Further progress was made during the year towards measurement of two specific Health of the Nation[1] targets. For the target "to improve significantly the health and social functioning of mentally ill people", the new Health of the Nation Outcome Scale (HoNOS)[12] was adopted by the Committee for Regulation of Information Requirements, and formally launched by the Research Unit of the Royal College of Psychiatrists at a conference in October. Work on the development of a similar instrument for child and adolescent mental health care progressed well and should be completed during 1997.

Work on the target "to reduce the suicide rate of severely mentally ill people by at least 33% by the year 2000" included a pilot study of data collection in five health districts. Departments of public health collaborated with coroners to gather all information available from primary care, specialist care and police sources. Local panels were set up to judge whether suicide victims appeared to have been severely mentally ill. The Chief Medical Officer's Health of the Nation Working Group set up a sub-committee to prepare recommendations to assess the two targets.

A sub-group of the Wider Health Working Group, chaired by Baroness Cumberlege, Parliamentary Under Secretary of State for Health in the House of Lords, was set up to investigate ways to reduce the numbers of suicides. It reported in November, and supported a six-strand approach: to educate health and social care professionals about the assessment and management of depression; to improve services for severely mentally ill people; to provide advice and support to high-risk occupational groups; to reduce access to means of suicide, where practicable; to improve public understanding of mental health generally, and knowledge on where to seek help; and to learn lessons about prevention through audit of suicide.

(iv)   HIV/AIDS and sexual health

The Health of the Nation objectives for HIV/AIDS and sexual health are to reduce the incidence of HIV infection and other sexually transmitted diseases (STDs) and to reduce unwanted pregnancies, and to ensure effective provision of means to achieve these ends[1].

In 1996/97, the Department allocated £185.7 million to health authorities in England toward HIV treatment costs, and £51.3 million to prevent the spread of HIV by public education, protecting the blood supply, provision of testing facilities and staff training. Also in 1996/97, £13.7 million were allocated to local authorities, £1.63 million to voluntary organisations and £5.25 million to health promotion contractors, including the HEA, and the National AIDS/Drugs Helpline.

The year saw a number of initiatives towards the Health of the Nation objective[1] to reduce unwanted pregnancies and improve effective family planning services to those that want them:

- the Contraceptive Education Service, delivered via contract by the Family Planning Association and the HEA, is developing new initiatives to raise awareness and understanding of contraceptive methods and family planning services among professionals and public alike;

- a second round of publicity for the 'Sexwise' helpline, in Trent and the North East regions ('Sexwise' offers young people a free, confidential phoneline and the opportunity to talk to a trained adviser about sex and personal relationships; the line has received over one million calls since it was launched in London and the North West in March 1995);

- the HEA ran a publicity campaign to raise awareness of emergency contraception and also produced a compendium of young people's services to facilitate the exchange of information between professionals and to contribute to the development of services; *and*

- grants were provided to various voluntary organisations to produce information, training and other resources.

Family planning services are increasingly responsive to the needs of young people. The conception rates for females aged under 16 years in 1992-94, published in September 1996, showed a continuation of the downward trend that began in 1990 (see page 60), although preliminary data from 1995 and 1996 indicate a very small rise.

Existing indicators suggest that the target for 1997 of a fall from 20% in 1990 to 10% of injecting drug users who report sharing injecting equipment in the previous four weeks is likely to be met; however, concern remains that hidden populations, such as those not in contact with services, may have higher rates of needle sharing and consequently greater risk from HIV, hepatitis B and hepatitis C.

(v)   Accidents

Encouraging progress continues to be made towards the Health of the Nation targets for reductions in accident mortality[1]. Over the four years since the health strategy baselines were set, death rates from accidents have fallen by 34% among children aged under 15 years, and by about 26% in those aged 15-24 years. Among those aged over 65 years, a smaller fall of some 6% has been seen, although changes in the assignment of deaths from osteoporosis may have led to underestimation of this fall.

The Accident Prevention Task Force was disbanded in 1996 on completion of its work. It was responsible for several research reports on accident prevention. Three effectiveness reviews[13,14,15] were published during the year, each covering one of the target age-groups; these reports outline published research on accident prevention interventions, their effectiveness and areas for further research.

The DH Public Health Information Strategy (PHIS) team published its second report[16] in July, which outlined the opportunities for linking and sharing accident data between existing sources and set standards for future developments.

The Child Accident Prevention Trust continued to run its successful 'Child safety week' campaign; DH funded an evaluation of the 1995 week.

DH, along with other Government departments, has funded two projects undertaken by the Royal Society for the Prevention of Accidents (RoSPA). 'Step forward', a video training package to develop child pedestrian safety skills was launched in December; and 'Together safely', a comprehensive document to help schools develop a holistic approach to health and safety was launched in September. DH also funded the RoSPA to study the impact of accident prevention training in a primary care setting; a report is due in Summer 1997.

References

1. Department of Health. *The Health of the Nation: a strategy for health in England.* London: HMSO, 1992 (Cm. 1986).
2. Department of Health. *Active for life campaign launched: physical activity strategy statement published.* London: Department of Health, 1996 (Press Release: 96/80).
3. Prescott-Clarke P, Primatesta P, eds. *Health Survey for England 1995: a survey carried out on behalf of the Department of Health (vols 1 and 2).* London: Stationery Office (in press) (series HS no. 5).
4. Gupta S. Health trends in *Health Trends. Health Trends* 1996; **28**: 43-4.
5. Department of Health. *Sensible drinking: the report of an Inter-Departmental Working Group.* London: Department of Health, 1995.
6. Office of Population Censuses and Surveys, Diamond A, Goddard E. *Smoking among secondary school children in 1994.* London: HMSO, 1995.
7. Office for National Statistics. *Living in Britain: results from the 1994 General Household Survey.* London: HMSO, 1996 (series GHS no. 25).
8. White A, Freeth S, O'Brien M. *Infant feeding 1990.* London: HMSO, 1992.
9. Office for National Statistics. *Deaths registered in 1995 by cause and by area of residence.* London, Office for National Statistics, 1996 (*ONS Monitor* no. DH2 96/2).
10. Department of Health. *The Health of the Nation technical supplement.* London: Department of Health, 1996.

11. Boys P, ed. *The sunfile catalogue: Europe against cancer: resources on sun awareness and the prevention of cancer.* London: United Kingdom Co-ordinating Committee on Cancer Research, 1996.

12. Department of Health. HoNOS: a psychiatric thermometer. *CMO's Update* 1994; **4**: 7.

13. Towner E, Dowswell T, Simpson G, Jarvis S, Meyrick J, Morgan A. *Health promotion in childhood and young adolescence for the prevention of unintentional injuries.* London: Health Education Authority, 1996.

14. Coleman P, Munro J, Nichol J, Harper R, Kent G, Wild D. *The effectiveness of interventions to prevent accidental injury to young persons aged 15-24 years: a review of the evidence.* Sheffield: Medical Care Research Unit, University of Sheffield, 1996.

15. NHS Centre for Reviews and Dissemination. *Effective health care: preventing falls and subsequent injury in older people.* York: University of York, 1996.

16. Department of Health. *Agreeing an accident information structure.* London: Department of Health, 1996 (Public Health Information Strategy; Implementation Project no. 19B).

(c)   Variations in health

Within England, as in other developed countries, there are striking differences in life expectancy, morbidity, and mortality in relation to social class, sex, region and ethnic background. A Chief Medical Officer Working Group report[1], published in October 1995, gave the following explanation for such differences: "It is likely that cumulative differential lifetime exposure to health damaging or health promoting physical and social environments is the main explanation for observed variations in health and life expectancy, with health related social mobility, health damaging or health promoting behaviours, use of health services, and genetic or biological factors also contributing. Their importance will vary according to the variation considered, the health indicator used, and the setting. Socio-economic and cultural factors underpin all the explanations for observed differences".

At a national level, a range of activities took place during 1996 to encourage action to identify and act upon the causes of some of these differences. Priorities and planning guidance for the NHS[2] emphasises the importance of equity, described as "improving the health of the population as a whole and reducing variations in health status by targeting resources where needs are greatest". Health authorities are asked in the guidance to pay particular attention to variations in health status when planning how to use the resources directly available to them, and through collaborating with others. Progress is monitored through a performance management framework, introduced in 1996 to help to structure the way in which health authorities and the NHS Executive assess past performance and future objectives in taking forward the Health of the Nation strategy[3], including the needs of vulnerable groups. A major research initiative on variations in health will be launched in early 1997.

Work to promote the health of women, and to make health services more sensitive to the differing needs of men and women is described on page 80, and work to promote the health of minority ethnic groups on page 82.

96

References

1. Department of Health. *Variations in health: what can the Department of Health and the NHS do?* London: Department of Health, 1995.
2. NHS Executive. *Priorities and planning guidance for the NHS: 1997/98.* Wetherby (West Yorkshire): Department of Health, 1996.
3. Department of Health. *The Health of the Nation: a strategy for health in England.* London: HMSO, 1992 (Cm. 1986).

(d)   Health of the Young Nation

As noted in last year's Report[1], the strategy for health developed a new focus, the Health of the Young Nation, launched in July 1995 at a conference to mark the third anniversary of the launch of the Health of the Nation initiative[2]; this followed interest generated by the special chapter on the health of adolescents in the 1993 Report[3].

A three-year contract to develop a national Young People's Health Network was awarded to the HEA with effect from April 1996. The Network is central to the Health of the Young Nation initiative and its development is steered jointly by DH and the Department for Education and Employment (DfEE). Additional direction is provided by an advisory group, mainly comprising representatives of relevant voluntary organisations. The Young People's Health Network will help organisations that work with young people to share experiences related to health promotion activities. The Network will provide information about current research into health promotion aimed at young people, and evaluate health promotion initiatives and strategies for involving and consulting young people in project development.

The Network was launched in June. The launch included a presentation of research on the health needs and concerns of young people by the Institute of Education of the University of London. The first edition of the Network newsletter, which focused on mental health, was distributed in October[4]. Through this newsletter, the HEA advertised for tenders for two Network projects - to identify models and develop training materials on evaluation of health promotion initiatives, and to investigate ways to consult young people - to be commissioned in 1997.

In June, DH officials met with a group of columnists from teenage magazines who offer sympathetic advice to readers on their personal problems (so-called 'agony aunts'); they provided valuable insight into the problems faced by young people, and are represented on the advisory group for the Young People's Health Network. Schools are also a major setting for Health of the Young Nation activities (see page 101).

References

1. Department of Health. *On the State of the Public Health: the annual report of the Chief Medical Officer of the Department of Health for the year 1995.* London HMSO, 1996; 3, 79-80.
2. Department of Health. *The Health of the Nation: a strategy for health in England.* London: HMSO, 1992 (Cm. 1986).
3. Department of Health. *On the State of the Public Health: the annual report of the Chief Medical Officer of the Department of Health for the year 1993.* London: HMSO, 1994: 5, 74-112.
4. Health Education Authority. *Young People's Health Network: newsletter 1.* London: Health Education Authority, 1996.

(e)   Consultation on a potential environment key area

On 11 November, DH and the DoE issued a joint consultation document, *The environment and health*[1], which sought comments on whether the environment should be included as a new key area in the Health of the Nation strategy[2].

Environment and health is the first new key area to be proposed for inclusion in the strategy for health since its launch in 1992. The document sets out initial proposals for suitable targets, objectives and partnerships to implement them. The proposed target areas are outdoor air quality, indoor air quality, radon, noise and lead in drinking water; these are derived from targets within the Government's Sustainable Development Strategy[3], which recognises that existing environmental targets can deliver benefits to health.

By proposing the environment as a key area, the Government hopes to extend the Health of the Nation concept of alliances and to encourage individuals and organisations to improve the environment and so benefit health, to complement other work at local level - such as 'Local Agenda 21', by which local authorities carry forward their own programmes of work on sustainable development, and the 'Healthy Cities' initiatives (see page 101).

The consultation document was widely distributed to local authorities, health authorities, professional organisations, voluntary and interest groups, business co-ordinators and others, and requested views on the appropriateness of including the environment as a new key area in the strategy for health. It also sought views and additional ideas on the proposed targets and effective partnerships to deliver them. The consultation exercise closes on 11 February 1997, when the adoption and final format of the potential key area will be considered in the light of comments received.

References

1. Department of Health, Department of the Environment. *The environment and health: a consultative document for the environment as a key area in the Health of the Nation strategy.* London: Department of Health, 1996.
2. Department of Health. *The Health of the Nation: a strategy for health in England.* London: HMSO, 1992 (Cm. 1986).
3. Department of the Environment. *Sustainable development: the UK strategy.* London: HMSO, 1994 (Cm. 2426).

(f)   Priorities for the NHS

The Health of the Nation initiative[1] has been a key strategic goal for the NHS since its launch in 1992[2] and has been highlighted in successive *Priorities and planning guidance*[3,4,5]. It is now a central plank of Government policy for the NHS, setting the context for NHS planning and making public health central to the work of the NHS[6]. The strategy has had an increasing influence on health authorities' plans to purchase services and to meet the health care needs of the local people. It has also encouraged the formation of health alliances with various local organisations to improve health. Most directors of public health (DsPH) now feature the Health of the Nation initiative prominently in their annual reports on the health of their local populations.

The NHS Executive's role is to facilitate, co-ordinate, support and involve the NHS in the further development of work to contribute to the strategy for health and to encourage local initiatives. A project steering board, which reports to the Chief Executive's Health of the Nation Working Group, co-ordinates, supports and develops implementation of the strategy for health under the three main project headings of purchasing, providing and primary care, with supporting work across normal Departmental boundaries on education and training, research and development, information and communications.

A performance management framework for the Health of the Nation initiative was developed as part of the purchasing project, and was distributed to all health authorities and Regional Offices at the end of September. This framework will help to integrate the strategy for health more closely into the general management of health services. The NHS has greatly contributed to this development work and will use the framework for routine audit and for a more formal review of progress with Regional Offices.

An NHS Trust project to support Trusts in tackling the prevalence of obesity in the general population - one key area target - has enlisted a number of pilot NHS Trusts committed to equip their staff with accurate and up-to-date information about healthy weight management and to create an organisational infrastructure to enable staff to act on this knowledge.

The primary care project is concentrating on targets in two other areas - accident prevention in people aged over 75 years and mental health care interventions in general practice.

References

1. Department of Health. *The Health of the Nation: a strategy for health in England*. London: HMSO, 1992 (Cm. 1986).
2. NHS Management Executive. *First steps for the NHS: recommendations of the Health of the Nation focus groups*. London: Department of Health, 1992.
3. NHS Executive. *Priorities and planning guidance for the NHS 1994/95*. Leeds: Department of Health, 1993 (Executive Letter: EL(93)54).
4. NHS Executive. *Priorities and planning guidance for the NHS 1995/96*. Leeds: Department of Health, 1994 (Executive Letter EL(94)55).
5. NHS Executive. *Priorities and planning guidance for the NHS 1996/97*. Leeds: Department of Health, 1995 (Executive Letter: EL(95)68).
6. NHS Executive. *NHS priorities and planning guidance 1997/98*. Leeds: Department of Health, 1996 (Executive Letter: EL(96)45).

(g)   Local health alliances

The Health of the Nation initiative[1] emphasises the advantages of health alliances to work at all levels to help to deliver improvements in health. The second year of the Health Alliance Awards Scheme culminated in a national awards ceremony in April. This scheme operates at regional and national levels to encourage and reward effective local alliances working in each of the five key areas, and 1996 awards also included a special category for the Health of the Young Nation initiative with prizes sponsored by Persil Funfit. Johnson & Johnson have also entered a partnership with the Department to sponsor the Health Alliance Awards, starting with the national prizes in 1996 (except Health of the Young Nation).

The Health Alliance Awards Scheme brought many imaginative and effective local partnerships to national notice, which are then widely promulgated - for instance in the *Target* newsletter. The 1996 winners also generated considerable local press interest: winning alliances included 'Topic of cancer', which aimed to raise children's awareness of the issues surrounding cancer, and 'Best foot forward', a project led by the National Federation of Women's Institutes to encourage their members to walk regularly.

The closing date for entries for the 1997 Awards was 31 October 1996. More than 450 entries were received, an increase of 50%, with increases in all categories and in all regions.

Reference

1. Department of Health. *The Health of the Nation: a strategy for health in England*. London: HMSO, 1992 (Cm. 1986).

(h)   Healthy settings

Proposals for further progress in the settings of homes and the environment are discussed in the section on consultation on a potential environment key area (see page 98).

The Workplace Health Advisory Team (WHAT) is a two-year project being run by the HEA on behalf of the Department to encourage the formation of alliances between and involving small and medium-sized businesses, so that they can undertake health promotion activities for their workforces which they would not be able to do on their own. The WHAT will develop a variety of different models for such alliances, undertake pilot studies, and expand these nationally during 1997, with the aim to establish 40 self-sustaining alliances by the time the project ends in 1998.

Sir John Chalstrey, Lord Mayor of London for 1995-96, chose 'Good health to the City and the Nation' as the theme for his year of office. This issue linked with several of the healthy settings, including the workplace, and DH supplied a secondee to help the Lord Mayor to develop his theme.

In 1996, DH and the DfEE continued to fund the HEA to co-ordinate activity for the European Network of Health Promoting Schools (ENHPS) within the UK. Data collection from a three-year research project by the National Foundation for Educational Research, under the aegis of the ENHPS, was completed at the end of 1996; a report will be published in Summer 1997.

Work on individual key areas[1] continues in schools. From April, DH funded a peer education project by Youth Clubs UK. Also in April, the children's mental health charity Young Minds published a guide on mental health for schools which was funded by DH[2]. In September, the RoSPA published *Together safely: a whole school approach to health and safety*[3], for which development was funded jointly by DH, the DfEE, the Health and Safety Executive (HSE), the Department of Transport (DoT) and the Scottish Office.

Drugs education in schools had a particularly high profile in 1996. In July, the DfEE held a major national conference to highlight the work of the innovative drug education project funded by grants for Education Support and Training.

The Prison Service Directorate of the Home Office has been designated a World Health Organization (WHO) Collaborating Centre. To encourage health promotion activities in prisons, the Directorate has developed a Health Promoting Prisons Award Scheme. All prisons have been invited to apply for the Award, which is a standard-setting rather than a competitive exercise; judging will take place in February 1997.

The Department continues to develop its links with the 'Healthy cities' network. The UK 'Health for all network' was developed from the WHO 'Healthy cities project' and has been supported with funding from the Department. The Network is the lead organisation in the UK in national and international liaison on the WHO's 'Health for all by the year 2000' strategy and on healthy cities work. The Department has been able to visit several of the individual sites and is working to disseminate information and good practice.

The Health of the Nation White Paper[1] provided a commitment to develop health promotion in hospitals, recognising the unique opportunities that hospitals can offer for general health promotion for patients, staff and all who come into contact with them. The NHS Executive consulted the NHS widely through workshops and questionnaires on how to take forward this initiative, and an NHS working group published the guidance document *Health promoting hospitals*[4] in September 1994; this guidance and five factsheets with good practice information have been widely distributed. In addition, the NHS Executive funded a central database and a part-time consultant for two years (1994-96) to encourage networking and to identify and disseminate good practice. Regions took over the initiative from April 1996 to facilitate the establishment of local and national networks.

References

1. Department of Health. *The Health of the Nation: a strategy for health in England.* London: HMSO, 1992 (Cm. 1986).
2. Young Minds. *Mental health in your school: a guide for teachers and others working in schools.* London: Jessica Kingsley, 1996.
3. Aucott S. *Together safely: developing a whole school approach to health and safety.* London: Royal Society for the Prevention of Accidents, 1996.
4. NHS Executive. *Health promoting hospitals.* Leeds: Department of Health, 1994.

(i)   Inter-Departmental co-operation

Much of the work on healthy settings relies on co-operative work with other Government Departments. The work with schools requires collaboration with the DfEE, which has agreed to help to produce and distribute a special schools' edition of *Target* as an insert to the Spring 1997 edition of *Schools Update*. DH is a member of the Home Office Steering Group which has developed the Health Promoting Prisons Award Scheme, and will continue to be involved through the judging and review process. It has also worked closely with the DoE to produce the consultation paper[1] on the potential environment key area for the Health of the Nation initiative[2]. Both departments will continue to collaborate to analyse the results of the consultation and to take forward any recommendations. Work has continued with Ministry of Agriculture, Fisheries and Food on nutrition and on rural suicides, with the DoT on accidents and on strategies to encourage walking and cycling, and with the HSE on the work of the WHAT.

In virtually any aspect of the Health of the Nation strategy it is possible to identify some cross-Departmental working. Working relations do take some time to become established, but effective co-operation continues to be led by the Cabinet sub-Committee which oversees the Health of the Nation strategy. The theme of cross-Departmental working is echoed in all of the relevant committees, including the Chief Medical Officer's Working Group and other related groups such as the Inter-Departmental Group on Public Health.

References

1.   Department of Health, Department of the Environment. *The environment and health: a consultative document for the environment as a key area in the Health of the Nation strategy.* London: Department of Health, 1996.
2.   Department of Health. *The Health of the Nation: a strategy for health in England.* London: HMSO, 1992 (Cm. 1986).

CHAPTER 4

HEALTH OF DISABLED PEOPLE

(a)   Introduction

Recent years have seen greater recognition of the needs of disabled people, and increased action to reduce the barriers that have for so many years restricted their ability to be involved in the community and in their own care. But much progress has yet to be made, not just in the provision of appropriate facilities in people's homes and local environments, but also in achieving further changes in the general perception of disability - not just among policy-makers and employers, but in the public as a whole - and in identifying the challenges that disabled people face.

The high prevalence of physical disability was shown by a major survey series conducted by the then Office of Population Censuses and Surveys (OPCS, now part of the Office for National Statistics [ONS]) in 1985[1,2,3,4,5,6]; this has now been followed up in the 1995 Health Survey for England[7] (see page 108). These data are supplemented by an extensive survey of psychiatric morbidity[8,9,10,11,12,13,14,15], as described in the special chapter of last year's Report[16], and by other studies by the Department of Social Security in relation to the Family Resource Survey (unpublished) and the General Household (GHS) and Benefits Surveys.

But what is disability? Disability may occur at any time - from birth, as a result of accident or illness of any kind, or in association with old age; it incorporates learning disabilities, the disabilities which can arise from mental illness, physical disability and sensory impairment, and combinations thereof. Disability is not related to diagnosis in a simple way; for example, impairment after stroke can be mild or very severe. When thinking about disability, the World Health Organization (WHO) classification of related terms may be helpful[17]:

- *impairment:* the loss or abnormality of psychological, physiological or anatomical structure or function;

- *disability:* any restriction or lack (resulting from an impairment) of ability to perform an activity in the manner or within the range considered normal for a human being; *and*

- *handicap:* a disadvantage for a given individual, resulting from an impairment or disability that limits or prevents fulfilment of a social role that is normal (depending upon age, sex, social and cultural factors) for that individual.

Disabilities pose considerable challenges to those who suffer from them, and to society as a whole to ensure that disabled people are empowered to take their full part within it.

More specifically, people with disabilities pose challenges to health, social, educational and employment services, and to the interface between these services and between Government Departments and Agencies, local authorities, voluntary agencies, relatives and other carers, and the private sector; these challenges should be met to ensure that individuals with disability can meet their own, more personal and more demanding, challenges.

References

1. Martin J, Meltzer H, Elliot D. *The prevalence of disability among adults.* London: HMSO, 1988 (OPCS Surveys of Disability in Great Britain: report 1).
2. Martin J, White A. *The financial circumstances of disabled adults living in private households.* London: HMSO, 1988 (OPCS Surveys of Disability in Great Britain: report 2).
3. Bone M, Meltzer H. *The prevalence of disability among children.* London: HMSO, 1988 (OPCS Surveys of Disability in Great Britain: report 3).
4. Martin J, White M, Meltzer M. *Disabled adults: services, transport and employment.* London: HMSO, 1989 (OPCS Surveys of Disability in Great Britain: report 4).
5. Smith M, Robus N. *The financial circumstances of families with disabled children living in private households.* London: HMSO, 1989 (OPCS Surveys of Disability in Great Britain: report 5).
6. Meltzer H, Smith M, Robus N. *Disabled children: services, transport and education.* London: HMSO, 1989 (OPCS Surveys of Disability in Great Britain: report 6).
7. Prescott-Clarke P, Primatesta P, eds. *Health Survey for England 1995: a survey carried out on behalf of the Department of Health (vols 1 and 2).* London: Stationery Office (in press) (Series HS no. 5).
8. Meltzer H, Gill B, Petticrew M, Hinds K. *The prevalence of psychiatric morbidity among adults living in private households.* London: HMSO, 1995 (OPCS Surveys of Psychiatric Morbidity in Great Britain: report 1).
9. Meltzer H, Gill B, Petticrew M, Hinds K. *Physical complaints, service use and treatment of adults with psychiatric disorders.* London: HMSO, 1995 (OPCS Surveys of Psychiatric Morbidity in Great Britain: report 2).
10. Meltzer H, Gill B, Petticrew M, Hinds K. *Economic activity and social functioning of adults with psychiatric disorders.* London: HMSO, 1995 (OPCS Surveys of Psychiatric Morbidity in Great Britain: report 3).
11. Meltzer H, Gill B, Petticrew M, Hinds K. *The prevalence of psychiatric morbidity among adults living in institutions.* London: HMSO, 1996 (OPCS Surveys of Psychiatric Morbidity in Great Britain: report 4).
12. Meltzer H, Gill B, Petticrew M, Hinds K. *Physical complaints, service use and treatment of residents with psychiatric disorders.* London: HMSO, 1996 (OPCS Surveys of Psychiatric Morbidity in Great Britain: report 5).
13. Meltzer H, Gill B, Petticrew M, Hinds K. *The economic activity and social functioning of residents with psychiatric disorders.* London: HMSO, 1996 (OPCS Surveys of Psychiatric Morbidity in Great Britain: report 6).
14. Meltzer H, Gill B, Petticrew M, Hinds K. *Psychiatric morbidity among homeless people.* London: HMSO, 1996 (OPCS Surveys of Psychiatric Morbidity in Great Britain: report 7).
15. Foster K, Meltzer H, Gill B, Petticrew M, Hinds K. *Adults with a psychotic disorder: living in the community.* London: HMSO, 1996 (OPCS Surveys of Psychiatric Morbidity in Great Britain: report 8).

16. Department of Health. *On the State of the Public Health: the annual report of the Chief Medical Officer of the Department of Health for the year 1995*. London: HMSO, 1996; 13-4, 95-126.

17. World Health Organization. *International classification of impairments, disabilities and handicaps*. Geneva: World Health Organization, 1980.

(b) Legislation and civil rights

Societies have always recognised the special needs of those unable to support themselves or dependents because of illness, disability or age - although their responses, over the course of history, have varied greatly.

In recent times, the Tomlinson report in 1943[1] recognised that rehabilitation did not just mean returning people to their previous work (which might be impossible), but should incorporate training for alternative work and aim at "restoring the patient's mental and physical capacity at the earliest possible date and to the fullest possible extent", but did not explicitly consider other aspects and challenges of disability.

The Piercy Committee of 1956[2] no longer saw rehabilitation primarily as restoring working capacity, but as making the patient "able as early as possible to resume a normal life ... of work and leisure" and commented on the "change of focus [from] employment of the disabled person ... to consider him [or her] more broadly as a human being and a social unit". The Committee found it impossible to investigate the costs of rehabilitation and any potential savings, but concluded that "the value in terms of enablement to take a full part in ordinary life or to contribute to it economically often bears no relation to the cash expenditure involved".

In 1972, the Tunbridge report[3] on National Health Service (NHS) rehabilitation services noted that demographic change had greatly altered the needs for hospital rehabilitation, with two-thirds of the demand coming from elderly or mentally ill patients rather than the young, physically disabled patients treated as a result of war or industrial injuries.

The WHO published its classification of impairments, disabilities and handicaps in 1980[4]. In 1981, the United Nations (UN) declared the International Year of Disabled Persons with a theme of "full participation and equality for people with disabilities", which led to a 1983 declaration of standard rules on equal opportunities for persons with disabilities[5].

The Council of Europe's social charter of 1961[6] recommended that all people with physical or mental disabilities should have the right to vocational training, rehabilitation and resettlement, and its 1992 statement[7], consolidating previous recommendations, advocates "a system where the emphasis is placed on giving [disabled people] the greatest possible independence and which arises from the full recognition of the right to be different. It is the duty of society to adapt itself to the particular needs of people with disabilities".

The Disability Discrimination Act 1995[8] sets out new rights for disabled people in the United Kingdom (UK). Under the Act, a disabled person is anyone with "a physical or mental impairment which has a substantial and long-term adverse effect on [the] ability to carry out normal day-to-day activities". The impairment may be physical (including sensory deficits) or mental (including learning disabilities). Guidance on the definition of disability[9] defines 'substantial' as a limitation beyond the normal differences in ability which may exist among people, and 'long-term' means that the effects have lasted at least 12 months; are likely to last at least 12 months; or are likely to last for the rest of the life of the person affected, although specific provisions may apply in certain conditions.

An impairment is held to affect normal day-to-day activities if it affects one of: mobility; manual dexterity; physical co-ordination; continence; ability to lift, carry or otherwise move everyday objects; speech, hearing or eyesight; memory or ability to concentrate, learn or understand; or perception of the risk of physical danger.

Under the Act[8], rights may apply in employment; goods, facilities, services and premises; education; public transport vehicles; and letting or selling land or property.

References

1. Inter-Departmental Committee on the Rehabilitation and Resettlement of Disabled Persons. *Report of the Inter-Departmental Committee on the Rehabilitation and Resettlement of Disabled Persons.* London: HMSO, 1943 (Cm. 6415).
2. Ministry of Labour and National Service. *Report of the Committee of Inquiry on the Rehabilitation, Training and Resettlement of Disabled Persons.* London: HMSO, 1956 (Cm. 9883).
3. Department of Health and Social Security, Welsh Office. *Rehabilitation: report of a sub-Committee of the Standing Medical Advisory Committee.* London: HMSO, 1972.
4. World Health Organization. *International classification of impairments, disabilities and handicaps.* Geneva: World Health Organization, 1980.
5. United Nations. *Standard rules on the equalization of opportunities for persons with disabilities.* New York: United Nations, 1993 (General Assembly, 48th Session: resolutions adopted on reports of the Third Committee 48/96).
6. Council of Europe. *A social charter.* Strasbourg: Council of Europe Press, 1961.
7. Council of Europe. *A coherent policy for the rehabilitation of people with disabilities.* Strasbourg: Council of Europe Press, 1992 (Recommendation: R(92)6).
8. *The Disability Discrimination Act 1995.* London: HMSO, 1995.
9. Department for Education and Employment. *Guidance on matters to be taken into account in determining questions relating to the definition of disability.* London: HMSO, 1996.

(c)   Epidemiology of disability

(i)   Surveys of disability

In 1985, a series of major disability surveys was conducted by the then Office of Population Censuses and Surveys (OPCS, now part of the Office for National Statistics [ONS])[1,2,3,4,5,6]. This survey identified the extent of disability in the community to inform planners of health care and social services, and contributed to a society-wide trend towards increased awareness of the needs of disabled people. Recent years have seen many improvements in access for wheelchair users (eg, ramps and disabled lavatories), hearing loops and signed performances for hearing impaired people, and design for visually impaired people (eg, contrasting surfaces and larger high-contrast signing). Voluntary bodies have contributed greatly, but local and central Government have also been active in fields as varied as education and rehabilitation, and with the Disability Discrimination Act 1995[7].

In 1995, ten years on, the Health Survey for England[8] repeated major parts of the 1985 disability survey series, and used the same questions recommended by the WHO to determine levels of disability; preliminary data from this survey first became available in 1996.

Some differences in methodology and sampling make it difficult directly to compare results from the 1995 Health Survey with those from the disability survey series ten years earlier. Disability is a continuum, and prevalence estimates vary depending upon the exact definitions used, and the subjective judgment by disabled people as to whether their particular condition falls within a particular definition - such as being able to walk 200 metres. In 1985, a postal screening survey was used which may not have identified some people with moderate disabilities; no such screening survey was used in 1995. In 1995, minor changes were made to make the Health Survey for England more compatible with WHO recommendations. In future, it is planned to repeat disability surveys every five years, and the 1995 Health Survey data will provide a valuable baseline to monitor change, and to compare levels of disability between countries.

(ii)   Prevalence of disability

Figure 4.1 shows the extent of disability found in the 1995 Health Survey for England[8]; it includes incontinence problems sufficiently serious to be categorised as disabilities. Eighteen per cent of males and females alike aged over 16 years who were living in private households had some degree of disability, either moderate or serious; 4% of men and 5% of women had a serious disability.

Figure 4.1: *Overall prevalence of disability among adults aged 16 years and over living in private households, England, 1995*

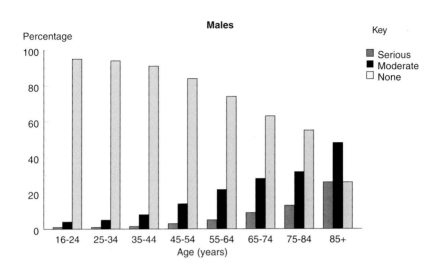

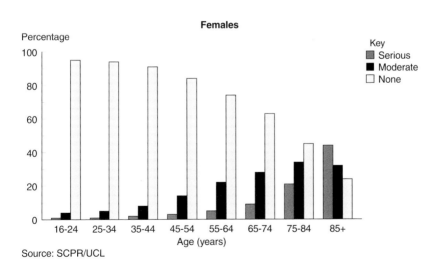

Source: SCPR/UCL

Table 4.1: *Prevalence of disability (including incontinence disabilities),*
England, 1995

Age (years)	Males				Females			
	None	Any disability	Serious disability	Moderate disability	None	Any disability	Serious disability	Moderate disability
16-24	95	5	1	4	94	5	0	5
25-34	94	6	1	5	93	7	1	6
35-44	91	10	2	8	90	10	2	8
45-54	84	16	2	14	86	15	3	12
55-64	74	27	5	22	78	21	5	16
65-74	63	37	9	28	69	31	8	23
75-84	55	45	13	32	46	54	18	36
85+	27	73	25	48	25	75	41	34

Note: Totals may not add up to 100 due to rounding.
Source: SCPR/UCL

(iii) Age and gender differences in disability

The prevalence of disabilities increases markedly with age, with about one-quarter of people being disabled by the age of 65 years, and about 50% being disabled after 75 years of age; three-quarters of people aged 85 years and older are disabled (see Table 4.1). When these data are applied to the 1995 population, and including the results of disability questions asked to children aged 10-15 years, it appears that some 7.3 million people aged 10 years and older consider themselves to be disabled, of whom 47% are aged 65 years and older, 33% aged

Table 4.2: *Percentage with no, one or more different types of disability*
(locomotion, personal care, sight, hearing and communication),
England, males and females aged 16 years and older

Age (years)	Males						Females					
	0	1	2	3	4	5	0	1	2	3	4	5
16-24	95	4	1				94	5	1			
25-34	94	4	1				93	5	2			
35-44	91	6	3				90	6	3			
45-54	84	11	4	1			86	9	5	1		
55-64	74	15	8	3	1		78	13	6	2		
65-74	63	24	9	3	1		69	19	9	3		
75-84	55	28	12	4	2		46	29	16	7	2	
85+	27	40	16	10	7	1	25	33	24	13	5	1

Note: Totals may not add up to 100 due to rounding.
Source: SCPR/UCL

Figure 4.2: *Prevalence of disability (including incontinence disabilities), England, 1995*

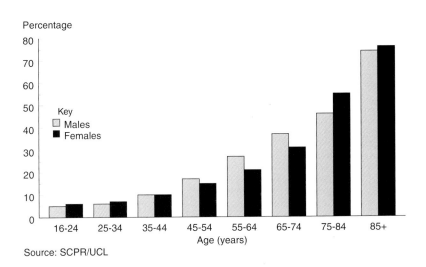

Source: SCPR/UCL

45-64 years and 20% aged 10-44 years. Some disabilities experienced by younger people, such as back problems, may eventually improve; older people more often have long-term disabilities, although interventions such as joint replacement are increasingly able to help.

Among younger people, the prevalence of disability is similar among men and women (see Figure 4.2). However, the prevalence of disability is higher among men in people aged 55-74 years (middle-aged men were more likely to report hearing disabilities), and higher among women in those aged 75 years and older (older women were more likely to report locomotor disabilities).

The Health Survey categorised disabilities into five broad types: locomotor, personal care, sight, hearing and communication. More than one category of disability was reported by 6% of men and 7% of women (see Figure 4.3, and Table 4.2); the proportion who had two or more types of disability increased markedly with age. Personal care disabilities (such as problems with dressing and feeding) were almost invariably associated with severe locomotor disabilities.

Children aged 10-15 years were asked questions on disability, though not questions about bladder problems in the 1995 Health Survey for England[8]. Only 72 children in the Survey were disabled. Data indicate that, overall, 5% of boys and girls alike have at least one disability; about 1% had a serious disability.

Figure 4.3: *Number of different types of disability, all adults aged 16 years and over, England, 1995*

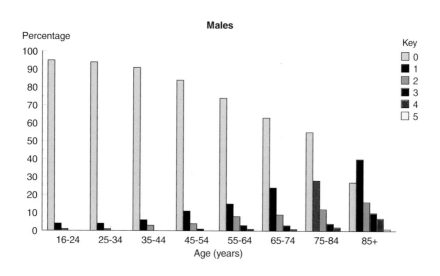

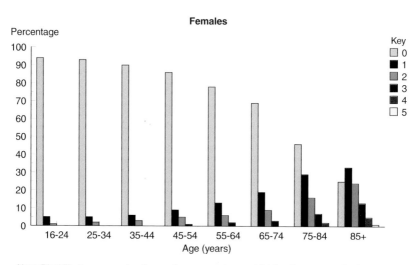

Note: Disability types comprise: locomotion, personal care, sight, hearing, communication.

Source: SCPR/UCL

Table 4.3: *Percentage of boys and girls, aged 10-11, 12-13, and 14-15 years, by type of disability, England, 1995*

Age	Boys 10-11	12-13	14-15	Girls 10-11	12-13	14-15
Locomotor disability						
Moderate disability	1	1	2	-	1	3
Serious disability	-	-	-	-	-	-
Personal care disability						
Moderate disability	-	-	-	-	-	1
Serious disability	1	1	-	-	-	-
Sight disability						
Moderate disability	1	-	1	-	1	1
Serious disability	-	-	-	-	-	-
Hearing disability						
Moderate disability	2	2	1	2	3	3
Serious disability	-	-	-	-	-	-
Communication disability						
Moderate disability	-	1	2	1	-	1
Serious disability	-	1	-	-	-	-

Source: SCPR/UCL

Table 4.3 shows the types of disability reported: hearing and locomotor disabilities were more common than personal care or sight disabilities. Table 4.4 sets out reported causes of disability in this age-group; the most commonly reported causes of disability were ear and eye disorders, respiratory diseases and mental disorders.

Table 4.4: *Health conditions reported as causes of disability, children aged 10-15 years, England, 1995*

Health condition	Total (%)
Diseases of the ear and mastoid process	40
Diseases of the respiratory system	18
Eye disorders	13
Mental disorders	11
Diseases of the musculoskeletal system and connective tissue	6
Diseases of the nervous system	5
Infectious and parasitic diseases	2
Diseases of the digestive system	1
Diseases of blood and blood-forming organs	1

Source: SCPR/UCL

(iv)   Causes of disability in adults

Table 4.5 shows the health conditions that informants reported as the cause of their disability in 1995. The most commonly reported cause of disability (34% of those with a disability) was disease of the musculoskeletal system and connective tissue; study of detailed answers from the Survey shows the chief cause to be osteoarthritis, particularly among older people. Nearly one-quarter of disabilities were caused by disease of the ear and mastoid process (chiefly causing deafness); 16% were caused by disease of the circulatory system; 10% by respiratory disease; and 8% by eye disorders. Serious disabilities were most likely to be caused by arthritis and rheumatism, disease of the nervous system (particularly Parkinson's disease and multiple sclerosis) and circulatory disease (particularly stroke). People with moderate disabilities were more likely to report back and neck problems and deafness as causes of their disability.

Table 4.6 and Figure 4.4 show disabilities where an accident was considered to be the cause of disability. Accidents are a particularly important cause of disability among younger people, but are not considered to cause more than 25% of disabilities in any age or sex group[9].

Informants aged 16 years and older were asked about bladder problems, using the broad definition adopted by the Oxford survey of incontinence[10]. About 7% of men and 11% of women were found to have some bladder problem, with 5% of men and 7% of women having a problem at least once a week. Figure 4.5 shows that the proportion of adults with a bladder problem increases with age, and affects one-quarter of men and women aged 85 years or older. Under the age of 75 years, problems were more common among women; among older people, men reported problems more often than women. Table 4.7 shows an age-related increase in the proportion of affected people who use aids for incontinence; 34% of women and 9% of men aged 75 years and older used incontinence pads. Table 4.8 shows the health care professionals who had been consulted about bladder problems: 32% of men and 39% of women had not consulted anyone; among those who had sought help, almost all had seen their general practitioner (GP), although many had seen a hospital doctor. Only 5% of men and 12% of women reported that they had seen a continence advisor or physiotherapist, although it is possible that some people mistake these health professionals for medical staff.

Because some bladder problems were mild, someone with a 'moderate incontinence disability' was defined as having a bladder problem at least once a month but less than once a week, and using incontinence aids other than sanitary towels. Someone with a 'serious incontinence disability' was defined as having a bladder problem at least once a week and using incontinence aids other than

Figure 4.4: *Percentage of adults with at least one disability caused by an accident, England, 1995*

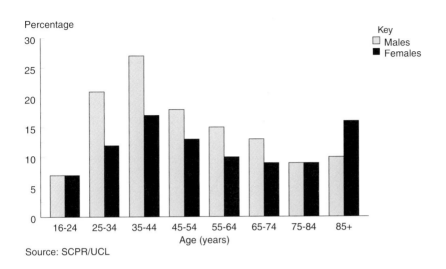

Source: SCPR/UCL

Figure 4.5: *Percentage of adults with a bladder problem, England, 1995*

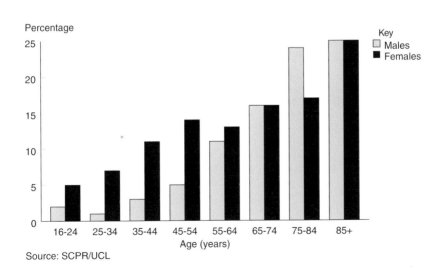

Source: SCPR/UCL

Table 4.5: *Reported causes of disability among adults aged 16 years and over, by level of disability, England, 1995*

Health complaint	All disabilities %	Moderate disability %	Serious disability %
Infectious and parasitic diseases	*1*	*1*	*1*
Neoplasms	*2*	*2*	*2*
Endocrine, nutritional and metabolic diseases			
and immunity disorders	*3*	*3*	*3*
Diabetes mellitus	2	1	2
Osteomalacia/rickets/vitamin D deficiency	0	0	0
Other endocrine and metabolic	2	2	1
Diseases of blood and blood-forming organs	*0*	*0*	*0*
Mental disorders	*2*	*2*	*3*
Senile dementia	0	0	0
Schizophrenia	0	0	0
Anxiety and phobias	1	1	1
Depression	1	0	1
Other mental illness	0	0	1
Mental retardation	0	0	0
Mental disorders not classified above	1	1	0
Diseases of the nervous system			
(other than eye or ear)	*5*	*3*	*10*
Hemiplegia	0	0	0
Parkinson's disease	1	0	2
Multiple sclerosis	1	0	2
Cerebral palsy (infantile)	0	0	0
Paraplegia, quadriplegia etc	0	0	1
Epilepsy	0	0	1
Migraine	0	0	0
Other diseases of the nervous system	3	2	4
Eye disorders	*8*	*8*	*9*
Cataract	1	2	1
Glaucoma	1	1	1
Retinal disorders	0	0	1
Congenital blindness	0	0	0
Other eye complaints	6	5	6
Diseases of the ear and mastoid processes	*24*	*28*	*12*
Vertiginous syndromes	0	0	1
Tinnitus	1	1	1
Deafness	20	24	10
Other ear complaints	2	3	1
Diseases of the circulatory system	*16*	*14*	*21*
Valve disease	0	0	1
Hypertensive disease	2	2	2
Other heart problems	2	2	3
Coronary artery disease	6	6	5
Cerebrovascular disease	3	1	7
Other arterial and embolic diseases	2	2	1
Diseases of veins and lymphatics, and			
other diseases of the circulatory system	1	1	1
Other diseases of the circulatory system	1	1	0

(Continued)

Table 4.5 (continued): *Reported causes of disability among adults aged 16 years and over, by level of disability, England, 1995*

Health complaint	All disabilities %	Moderate disability %	Serious disability %
Diseases of the respiratory system	*10*	*10*	*11*
Bronchitis and emphysema	2	1	3
Asthma	5	5	4
Sinusitis	0	0	0
Lung disease due to external agents	1	1	1
Other respiratory disease	2	3	2
Diseases of the digestive system	*2*	*1*	*2*
Disease of the oesophagus, stomach and duodenum	1	0	1
Hernia of abdominal cavity	1	1	0
Other digestive system disease	0	0	0
Diseases of the genito-urinary system	*1*	*0*	*1*
Kidney and urinary system problems	0	0	1
Disease/disorders of male and female genital organs/ breast/female pelvic organs	0	0	0
Other diseases of the genito-urinary system	0	0	0
Diseases of the skin and subcutaneous tissue	*1*	*1*	*1*
Diseases of the musculoskeletal system and connective tissue	*34*	*32*	*40*
Rheumatoid arthritis	2	1	3
Osteoarthritis and allied disorders	2	2	3
Other arthritis and rheumatism	17	16	20
Knee problems	1	1	1
Back and neck problems	7	7	5
Other joint problems	1	1	1
Acquired deformities	2	2	3
Other musculoskeletal	2	2	4
Injury and poisoning	*4*	*3*	*5*
Head injuries	0	0	0
Loss of limb or extremity	0	0	0
All other injury/poisoning	3	3	5
Congenital anomalies	*0*	*0*	*0*
Old age problems not included in other categories	*5*	*4*	*6*
Insufficient data to classify response	*4*	*4*	*3*
Bases	*2797*	*2099*	*698*

Note: Totals may not add up to 100 due to rounding and multiple disabilities.

Source: SCPR/UCL

Table 4.6: *Percentage of adults with disabilities where at least one disability was caused by an accident, England, 1995*

Age (years)	Males	Females
16-24	7	7
25-34	21	12
35-44	27	17
45-54	18	13
55-64	15	10
65-74	13	9
75-84	9	9
85+	10	16

Source: SCPR/UCL

Table 4.7 *Aids used by adults with a bladder problem, England, 1995*

(Expressed as percentages of adults with a bladder problem)

	Age (years)				
	16-44	45-54	55-64	65-74	75+
Males					
No aid	89	94	89	91	81
Sanitary towel/panty liner	-	-	-	1	2
Incontinence pad	-	-	2	6	9
Protective bed pad	4	-	2	1	2
Penile sheath	4	-	1	1	-
Intermittent catheter	1	-	-	-	2
Indwelling urethral catheter	1	-	2	-	5
Suprapubic catheter	-	-	-	-	-
Other unspecified	-	6	6	2	2
Females					
No aid	65	54	54	52	43
Sanitary towel/panty liner	32	40	36	34	25
Incontinence pad	2	4	9	11	34
Protective bed pad	1	1	4	4	12
Intermittent catheter	1	1	-	1	-
Indwelling urethral catheter	-	-	1	3	1
Suprapubic catheter	-	-	-	-	-
Other unspecified	2	1	4	1	2

Source: SCPR/UCL

Table 4.8: *Health professionals consulted by adults with a bladder problem, England, 1995 (percentages shown may total more than 100% because of multiple consultation)*

	Age (years)				
	16-44	45-54	55-64	65-74	75+
Males					
Continence advisor	4	2	2	5	2
Health visitor	2	2	2	1	1
District nurse	4	2	5	2	5
Other nurse	1	4	3	5	1
General practitioner	47	68	63	70	59
Hospital doctor or specialist	31	41	41	44	35
Physiotherapist	4	-	2	1	-
Pharmacist	4	-	4	-	-
Other health professional	3	2	6	1	1
None of the above	46	31	33	25	32
Females					
Continence advisor	4	9	5	6	10
Health visitor	6	2	2	6	9
District nurse	3	1	9	12	17
Other nurse	8	4	3	5	5
General practitioner	42	51	54	59	58
Hospital doctor or specialist	20	28	34	28	20
Physiotherapist	6	8	8	5	3
Pharmacist	4	3	3	2	3
Other health professional	3	1	2	1	1
None of the above	46	39	37	33	34

Source: SCPR/UCL

sanitary towels. If such incontinence disabilities are added to other categories of disability, they increase the overall prevalence of disability only for people aged 75 years and older; in men, the prevalence of serious disability is increased by 1%, and among women the prevalence of serious disability is increased by 3%. The relatively small effect of including incontinence problems in overall disability figures reflects other concurrent disabilities in people with bladder problems: 7% of those who had no other disabilities had a bladder problem, whereas over 30% of those with a locomotor or personal care disability also had a bladder problem.

119

(v)   Social and regional differences in disability

Table 4.9 shows age-standardised data on disability in different socio-economic groups, defined by the occupation of the head of the household. The age-standardised prevalence of disability for people in households whose head was in a non-manual occupation (I, II, IIINM) was 14% for men and 16% for women; for manual occupations (IIIM, IV, V), the prevalence was 19% for men and 21% for women.

Age-standardised data on disability by region are shown in Table 4.10. There is evidence of increased disability in the north of England; age-standardised rates of disability were significantly higher in the North West than in other regions (20% for men and 22% for women) and significantly lower in Anglia and Oxford (12% for men and 16% for women).

Table 4.11 and Figure 4.6 show the proportion of disabled people of working age (16-64 years for men, 16-59 years for women) who were in paid employment. Among men of working age, 47% of those with a disability and 27% of those with a serious disability were in paid employment; among women, the corresponding figures were 40% and 19%, respectively. Among men, 35% of those with a disability and 56% of those with a serious disability were permanently unable to work; among women, the corresponding figures were 23% and 53%, respectively.

(vi)   Trends in disability

As mentioned above, when comparing disability surveys great care must be taken to ensure that exactly similar questions were asked, and that population samples were approached in a similar way - for example, whether an initial screening questionnaire is administered or whether all subjects were interviewed. Such

Table 4.9: *Age-standardised prevalence of disability by social class, adults aged 16 years and older, England, 1995*

% disabled	Socio-economic group of head of household					
	I	II	IIINM	IIIM	IV	V
Males						
Disabled	9	14	16	19	18	26
Moderate disability	7	12	13	15	14	18
Serious disability	3	2	3	4	4	7
Females						
Disabled	14	15	19	20	22	27
Moderate disability	10	11	15	13	15	21
Serious disability	4	4	4	6	6	6

Source: SCPR/UCL

120

Table 4.10: *Age-standardised prevalence of disability (%) by region, adults aged 16 years and older, England, 1995*

Region	Northern & Yorkshire	North West	Trent	West Midlands	Anglia & Oxford	North Thames	South Thames	South & West
Males								
Disabled	17	20	18	16	12	15	17	15
Moderate disability	12	16	14	13	9	12	13	13
Serious disability	5	4	5	3	2	3	4	2
Females								
Disabled	20	22	19	20	16	17	17	17
Moderate disability	14	15	15	14	12	13	13	12
Serious disability	7	7	4	5	4	4	5	5

Source: SCPR/UCL

121

Table 4.11: *Employment status of disabled people of working age (%), England, 1995*

Age (years)	In paid employment	Looking for work	Permanently unable to work	Other
Males				
16-34	61	13	13	13
35-44	61	4	22	13
45-54	57	5	34	4
55-64	27	3	53	17
Females				
16-34	41	6	7	46
35-44	45	1	25	29
45-54	46	3	28	23
55-59	21	2	35	42

Source: SCPR/UCL

issues are crucial in the estimation of health expectancy as a single measure that combines mortality and morbidity. Whereas life expectancy is the total number of years a person may expect to remain alive, health expectancy measures adjust such data to reflect departures from good health.

Table 4.12: *Proportion (%) of males and females aged 65 years and older unable to perform four activities of independent daily living (bathing, getting in and out of bed, feeding, getting to the toilet), England, 1976, 1980, 1985, 1991*

Age (years)	Males				Females			
	1976	1980	1985	1991	1976	1980	1985	1991
65-69	4	4	4	2	6	4	3	3
70-74	8	6	4	3	15	8	6	3
75-79	18	8	11	5	22	10	9	6
80-84	25	18	15	9	36	13	19	7
85+	43	31	23	20	54	36	33	21

Source: ONS

Figure 4.6: *Employment status of disabled people of working age, males and females, England, 1995*

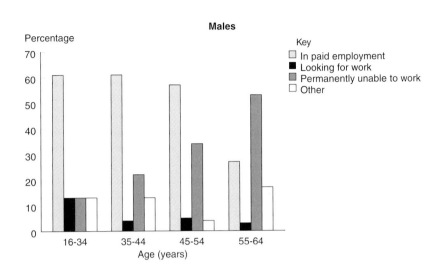

Males

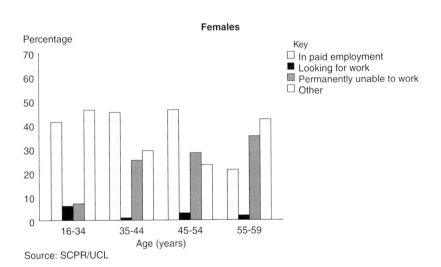

Females

Source: SCPR/UCL

Table 4.13: *Reported causes of disability among adults aged 16 years and over, by level of disability, England, 1995*

Reported cause of disability	All disabilities (%)	Moderate disability (%)	Serious disability (%)
Diseases of the musculoskeletal system	34	32	40
Diseases of the circulatory system	16	14	21
Diseases of the ear and mastoid processes	24	28	12
Diseases of the respiratory system	10	10	11
Diseases of the nervous system	5	3	10
Eye disorders	8	8	9
Old age problems not included in other categories	5	4	6
Injury and poisoning	4	3	5
Endocrine, nutritional and metabolic disease	3	3	3
Mental disorders	2	2	3
Insufficient data to classify response	4	4	3
Neoplasms	2	2	2
Diseases of the digestive system	2	1	2
Infectious and parasitic diseases	1	1	1
Disease of the genito-urinary system	0	0	1
Diseases of the skin and subcutaneous tissue	1	1	1
Diseases of the blood and blood-forming organs	0	0	0
Congenital anomalies	0	0	0
Total	*121*	*116*	*130*

Note: Totals do not add up to 100 because of rounding and multiple disability.
Source: SCPR/UCL

Different estimates of health expectancy are obtained depending upon the definition of morbidity that is adopted. It is possible, for example, to consider self-reported limiting long-standing illness, as asked in the General Household Survey (GHS), or more specific measures of disability - such as the ability to perform specific activities of daily living. The GHS question on limiting long-standing illness includes limitations, however minor, on activities of any kind, which will include some comparatively mild conditions, and there may also be differences between the generations as to how health problems are perceived by individuals. Among people aged under 70 years, limiting long-standing illness reported in the GHS exceeds disability estimated by surveys based on standardised questions. In 1985, the GHS[11] showed that 20% of people aged 16 years and older who lived in private households reported a limiting long-standing illness, but only 13% were identified to have a disability according to the 1985 OPCS disability surveys[1,2,3,4,5,6]. Among people aged over 75 years, levels of limiting long-standing illness from the GHS were lower than disability detected by the disability survey, with a tendency for older people to attribute disabilities to 'old age' rather than ill-health.

Health expectancy and its uses[12] examined trends in England and Wales from 1976 to 1992; subsequently, this analysis has been extended to include 1994 data. Limiting long-standing illness was estimated from GHS data from private households, supplemented by Census data from communal establishments. In 1994, life expectancy for men was estimated to be 74.2 years, with 15 years of limiting long-standing illness, while women could expect to live 79.6 years, with 17.4 years of limiting long-standing illness. Between 1976 and 1994, there was a striking increase in period life expectancies for men and women alike, equivalent to just over two months annually. By contrast, healthy life expectancy rose by some two weeks annually for men, and not at all for women. However, when health expectancy at age 65 years was estimated not only in terms of limiting long-standing illness but also in terms of three more specific disability measures - the ability to walk up and down stairs without help, the ability to go outdoors without help, and independence in four activities of daily living (bathing, transfer, eating, and getting to the toilet) - health expectancy improved between 1980 and 1994 with respect to each of these measures. The expectation of years free of disability for activities for daily living among men aged 65 years and over improved from 11.6 years in 1980 to 13.3 years in 1994; for women aged 65 years and over this expectation rose from 14.4 years in 1980 to 15.6 years in 1994 (see Table 4.12)

(vii)   Use of statistics on disability

The 1995 Health Survey for England[8] gathered information on causes of disability among the large number of people surveyed. These data help to address perhaps the crucial question on disability, the potential to prevent disability given existing medical knowledge.

When health problems are ranked by the frequency with which they were reported as causes of serious disability, relatively few problems dominate the picture, and a broadly similar pattern emerges for moderate or serious disability alike (see Table 4.13). Causes of disability were self-reported in the Survey, rather than obtained from medical records, and some degree of interpretation is therefore needed: for example, osteoarthritis was not recorded as a cause of disability unless it was specifically mentioned by the interviewee, so that most cases appear as 'Other arthritis and rheumatism' rather than 'Osteoarthritis and allied disorders'. However, further analysis of detailed answers (the Health Survey team kindly made some of these available in anonymised form) indicates that osteoarthritis is the dominant cause in the more general category.

Eight principal groups of conditions are each reported to cause 5% or more in respect of prevalence of serious disability (see Table 4.13), and together account for almost 90% of all reported causes of serious and moderate disability. At least six of these eight broad categories include important opportunities for prevention initiatives. The extent of disability from osteoarthritis may be reduced by tackling obesity, and by more effective prevention of accidental injuries. A large proportion of coronary heart disease (CHD) may be potentially preventable, and its incidence has been declining in England since the 1970s; stroke incidence may also be further reduced by better control of known hypertension, by primary prevention of hypertension (through reductions in obesity and salt intake), and by further reduction of cigarette smoking. The category 'Diseases of the ear and mastoid process' is dominated by deafness: of those who report deafness, detailed Survey answers indicate that 27% reported significant exposure to noise in military or occupational settings - again an important prevention opportunity. Among registrations for blindness and partial sight among people aged 16-64 years in England and Wales in 1990-91, a substantial proportion may have been potentially preventable: of those attributed to diabetes mellitus, it has been suggested that with improved screening and treatment over 80% of such cases could be avoided[13,14,15]. Reductions in cigarette smoking should lead to reduced disability from respiratory disease and certain cancers; and many accidental injuries have potentially preventable causes, and safety measures can minimise the physical harm that results from accidents.

A coherent strategy for health[16,17] will tackle many of the risk-factors that lead to disability, as well as reducing mortality.

References

1. Martin J, Meltzer H, Elliot D. *The prevalence of disability among adults.* London: HMSO, 1988 (OPCS Surveys of Disability in Great Britain: report 1).
2. Martin J, White A. *The financial circumstances of disabled adults living in private households.* London: HMSO, 1988 (OPCS Surveys of Disability in Great Britain: report 2).
3. Bone M, Meltzer H. *The prevalence of disability among children.* London: HMSO, 1988 (OPCS Surveys of Disability in Great Britain: report 3).
4. Martin J, White M, Meltzer H. *Disabled adults: services, transport and employment.* London: HMSO, 1989 (OPCS Surveys of Disability in Great Britain: report 4).
5. Smith M, Robus N. *The financial circumstances of families with disabled children living in private households.* London: HMSO, 1989 (OPCS Surveys of Disability in Great Britain: report 5).
6. Meltzer H, Smith M, Robus N. *Disabled children: services, transport and education.* London: HMSO, 1989 (OPCS Surveys of Disability in Great Britain: report 6).
7. *The Disability Discrimination Act 1995.* London: HMSO, 1995.
8. Prescott-Clarke P, Primatesta P, eds. *Health Survey for England 1995: a survey carried out on behalf of the Department of Health (vols 1 and 2).* London: HMSO (in press) (Series HS no. 5).
9. Department of Health. *Agreeing an accident information structure.* London: Department of Health, 1996 (Public Health Information Strategy; Implementation Project no. 19B).
10. Roe B, Wilson K, Doll H, Brooks P. *An evaluation of health interventions by primary care teams and continence advisory services on patient outcomes related to incontinence (vol 1).* Oxford: Health Services Research Unit, Department of Public Health and Primary Care, University of Oxford, 1996.

11. Office of Population Censuses and Surveys. *General Household Survey 1985*. London: HMSO, 1987 (Series GHS no. 16).

12. Bone MR, Bebbington AC, Jagger C, Morgan K, Nicolaas G. *Health expectancy and its uses*. London: HMSO, 1995.

13. Burns Cox CJ. Prevention of blindness: a lost opportunity. *J Med Screening* 1996; **3**: 169.

14. Evans J, Rooney C, Ashwood F, Dattani N, Wormald R. Blindness and partial sight in England and Wales: April 1990 - March 1991. *Health Trends* 1996; **28**: 5-12.

15. Evans JR. *Causes of blindness and partial sight in England and Wales 1990-1991*. London: HMSO, 1995 (Studies on Medical and Population Subjects no. 57).

16. Department of Health. *The Health of the Nation: a strategy for health in England*. London: HMSO, 1992 (Cm. 1986).

17. Department of Health. *Public health strategy launched to tackle root causes of ill-health*. London: Department of Health, 1997 (Press release: 97/157).

(d)   Types of disability

Any consideration of the causes of (and services for) disability within the space available in this Report must of necessity be brief and incomplete, and cannot fully reflect the approach of the Department of Health (DH) and of other Government Departments and Agencies, nor of the voluntary sector and individual carers, across the whole range of disabilities. In this and subsequent sections, any omission does not imply that such causes and contributions are being overlooked.

(i)   *Physical disability*

Apart from trauma caused as a result of accident or war (perhaps the most obvious cause of physical disability and historically, as noted above, a major stimulus to early initiatives on disability), almost any long-term, severe illness can cause disability. Demographic changes, as noted on page 59, also mean an increasing number of older people who may have disabilities; at any age, advances in medical care may lead to survival, with disability, where once death would have been the outcome. Such extra challenges must be recognised and taken into account not just by the individuals concerned but by health, social and other care services and by society as a whole.

Among the many factors that may lead to physical disability are genetic and congenital disorders; serious infectious diseases (including those in the mother during pregnancy); accidents, trauma and poisoning; occupational diseases; nutrition and metabolic disorders; endocrine disorders; gastro-intestinal disease; cardiovascular disease; respiratory disorders; joint, connective tissue and bone disorders; renal and genito-urinary disease; haematological disorders; skin diseases; muscle disorders; neurological diseases; and neoplasms (see Table 4.5).

(ii)   Sensory disability

A sensory disability may occur alone, or be associated with other sensory, or with physical, learning or mental disability.

Visual impairment

Figures for the numbers of blind and partially sighted people in the UK have been compiled by the Royal National Institute for the Blind (RNIB), based on Census returns and local authority returns. The RNIB estimates for 1994 indicate that in England over 865,000 people were blind and partially sighted, of whom 265,373 were registered. Age breakdowns reveal that the greatest numbers of people who are visually impaired are aged 65 years and over, and of these most are aged over 75 years[1].

Local authority returns tend to under-represent the true number of people with a visual impairment. Some register with their local authority and receive certain benefits; others do not register, perhaps because they consider their sight deterioration part of the ageing process; and some people choose not to be placed on the local authority register as they do not want to be 'labelled'.

Although registration with local authorities is not mandatory, registration is a prerequisite for the receipt of certain benefits and concessions. Blind and partially sighted people can ask to be added to the register following the completion of a BD8 Form by a consultant ophthalmologist, who certifies that the person meets with the statutory definition of blindness or the non-statutory definition of partial sight.

Hearing and dual sensory impairment

The Royal National Institute for the Deaf (RNID) estimates that there are 8.4 million deaf and hard-of-hearing adults in the UK; there are wide variations in estimates of the number of deaf-blind people, although the charity SENSE have estimated the number at 21,000. Among the problems in estimating the numbers of people with both a hearing and a visual loss is that many sufferers are over 75 years-of-age and may consider such loss a part of the normal ageing process.

Draft guidelines, *Think dual sensory: good practice guidelines for older people with dual sensory loss*[2], met with widespread support, including from the Association of Directors of Social Services. A final version following pilot studies will be published in Summer 1997. It will set out guidelines for social and health care services in relation to older people for whom the normal ageing process is further complicated by a significant degree of dual sensory loss. It will also explain the background to the initiative and identify initial steps that can help local authorities to plan improved services for older deaf-blind people, and ways to improve access to sensory services.

Speech impairment

Speech impairment is usually associated with other sensory and/or physical disabilities, and is most common at the time of speech and language development or in old age (see page 136).

(iii)   Learning disability

Within the general population, approximately four in 1,000 people (children and adults) have severe learning disabilities and 4-6 per 1,000 have mild learning disability. Many of the more able of this latter group function adequately in society and are not receiving services. These figures indicate that there are approximately 160,000 adults and 30,000 children with severe learning disabilities. The prevalence is increasing slightly because of increased life expectancy and improved neonatal intensive care, which has increased survival among extremely-low-birthweight babies, a high proportion of whom have severe handicapping conditions[3].

The needs for services have increased because the 1960s birth cohort, which is relatively large in line with demographic changes, has now reached adulthood, and those with learning disability often have complex needs. Life expectancy has increased, but mortality rates are still higher than in the general population. People with complex needs have a shorter life expectancy than the population as a whole, although there are now increasing numbers of older people with learning disabilities, who may also require specialised services[4].

A higher number of people with mild learning disabilities tend to come from deprived socio-economic backgrounds, whereas people with more severe learning disability come from a range of backgrounds (although there may also be a higher prevalence from deprived backgrounds). The prevalence of severe learning disability in the Asian community has been reported to be up to three times greater than in the general population. Services must take into account the particular needs of ethnic groups and be delivered appropriately[5].

Many people with learning disability have other disabilities - particularly physical disability (20-30%), epilepsy (15-30%), sensory impairments (30-40%) and mental health problems (6-60%), including severe challenging behaviour (6%). Severe challenging behaviour, once established, may persist - particularly among those who are less intellectually able and who have poor communication skills.

Most people with learning disability are now cared for in the community and it is estimated that fewer than 3,000 people remain in long-stay hospitals (at the peak of hospital care there were about 60,000). The importance of appropriate and cost-effective support in the community is widely recognised and the health service, working with local authorities and the voluntary sector, continues to have an important part to play in the provision of primary care and a range of specialist services, often organised by community learning disability teams. With appropriate help, people with severe and complex needs can often be supported in their family homes or in mainstream learning disability services, avoiding admission to hospital. Specialist learning disability hospital services continue to be needed, particularly for the care of people with associated mental illness, and a range of service provision has been developed.

The need to ensure that people with learning disability can also gain access to the full range of health services is being addressed as part of a review of the NHS role in provision of such services. Good practice guidelines will be published shortly. Users of health services and their carers have drawn attention to the many barriers that can arise through mistaken attitudes and responses, as well as through the problems of physical access. Many people with learning disabilities have difficulties in drawing attention to their health needs, and early indications from several projects to investigate the value of regular health checks suggest that this approach may be beneficial. The publication of *A strategy for people with learning disabilities*[6] in 1995 has been followed nationally by a number of initiatives in health promotion, health education and health screening, and a workshop will draw together some of this work at a conference for service users. Providers of primary care, specialist and health promotion services need to work together to promote good health and to detect health needs in people with learning disabilities. The crucial role of carers must not be overlooked.

(iv)   Mental disability

Mental illness, as noted in the special chapter of last year's Report[7] and on pages 85 and 170, is a significant cause of disability. The 1994 OPCS Survey of Psychiatric Morbidity in Great Britain[8,9,10,11,12,13,14,15] found one in five adults aged 16-64 years reported some sort of neurotic health problem in the week before interview - most commonly mixed anxiety and depressive disorder (77 cases per 1,000), followed by generalised anxiety disorder, depressive episodes, obsessive compulsive disorder, phobia and panic disorder; the overall prevalence of neurotic disorder was 160 per 1,000. The survey also found a strong association between unemployment and psychiatric disorder. Approximately twice as many people with psychiatric disorder were unemployed and economically inactive. Adults with neurotic health problems were four times more likely than the rest of the sample to be permanently unable to work, and of those who were unemployed and seeking work, 70% had been unemployed for a year or more. Compared with the general population, adults with neurosis were twice as likely to be receiving income support and four times more likely to be on invalidity benefit. Nearly one-fifth of adults with a neurotic disorder had difficulty with at least one activity of daily living; this rose to 35% among those with two neurotic disorders.

Advances in the understanding and management of mental illness have helped to create more effective ways to treat and care for such patients, and to minimise their disability. Improved treatment methods, including medication and psychosocial treatments, and changes in treatment settings, with a move from large institutions to a wider variety of local services, have increased flexibility and accessibility of services. The need for greater co-ordination of local services was addressed by the spectrum of care[16] initiative (see page 173). Core components of a comprehensive local service for people with mental health problems to minimise disability include home-based care, day hospitals, crisis accommodation, acute treatment units and psychiatric beds, community mental health centres, social care, social support, special housing, unstaffed group homes, residential care homes, 24-hour nursed residences, specialised services, secure environments, local secure units, medium secure units and special hospitals.

Among children and adolescents, a disability, whether related to physical health, a learning difficulty or a sensory impairment, can act as a risk-factor for a child developing a mental health problem or disorder; likewise, a disability that affects a parent or carer may have a secondary impact on a child. Primary mental health disorders in children and young people can create disability, and may also lead to secondary handicaps such as educational failure. A review[17] of the evidence on the importance of risk-factors indicates that children with chronic medical conditions and associated disability (limitations of usual childhood activities) are at a more than three-fold risk for mental health disorders and considerable risk for social adjustment problems; that the rate of mental health disorder may be increased 4-8-fold among youngsters with cerebral palsy, epilepsy or some other disorder above the brainstem; that the prevalence of mental health disorder in children with hearing impairment is nearly three times that seen in a control group; and that, among three-year-old children, the prevalence of behaviour problems in those with language delay was four times that of the general population, and was a predictor of educational difficulty at eight years-of-age. Disorders more commonly associated with childhood, like attention-deficit hyperactivity disorder, vary in severity and impact; up to one in 200 children in the population may suffer from a severe hyperkinetic disorder, and secondary consequences such as a learning difficulty or conduct disorder frequently occur. Pervasive development disorders - such as autism - and serious mental illness such as schizophrenia, while rare, may cause considerable disability in this age-group.

Among older people, depression and dementia are the most common mental health problems. In England an estimated 550,000 people over the age of 65 years suffer with dementia, and a health authority with a population of 500,000 will include at least 6,000 people aged over 60 years with dementia[18]. Again, a spectrum of care is needed to enable people to remain in a homely setting, often in their own home, for as long as possible, supported by general or specialist community mental health teams, although services should provide a spectrum of care for older people with mental health problems and their carers, and some patients will require inpatient and continuing care services. Demographic factors are a key issue, and the increasing numbers of elderly and very old people (see page 59) is likely to lead to an increase in the number of people with dementia.

References

1. Office of Population Censuses and Surveys. *General Household Survey 1988.* London: HMSO, 1989.
2. Department of Health. *Think dual sensory: good practice guidelines for older people with dual sensory loss.* London: Department of Health, 1996.
3. The Scottish Low Birth Weight Study Group. The Scottish low birth weight study I: survival, growth, neuromotor and sensory impairment. *Arch Dis Childh* 1992; **67:** 675-81.
4. Moss S, Turner S. *The health of people with learning disability.* Manchester: Hester Adrian Research Centre, University of Manchester, 1995.
5. Emerson E, Cairie A, Haiton C. *The clinical psychology of intellectual disabilities: cognitive and behavioural approaches.* Chichester: John Wiley (in press).
6. Department of Health. *The Health of the Nation: a strategy for people with learning disability.* London: Department of Health, 1995.
7. Department of Health. *On the State of the Public Health: the annual report of the Chief Medical Officer of the Department of Health for the year 1995.* London: HMSO, 1996; 13-4, 95-126.
8. Meltzer H, Gill B, Petticrew M, Hinds K. *The prevalence of psychiatric morbidity among adults living in private households.* London: HMSO, 1995 (OPCS Surveys of Psychiatric Morbidity in Great Britain: report 1).
9. Meltzer H, Gill B, Petticrew M, Hinds K. *Physical complaints, service use and treatment of adults with psychiatric disorders.* London: HMSO, 1995 (OPCS Surveys of Psychiatric Morbidity in Great Britain: report 2).
10. Meltzer H, Gill B, Petticrew M, Hinds K. *Economic activity and social functioning of adults with psychiatric disorders.* London: HMSO, 1995 (OPCS Surveys of Psychiatric Morbidity in Great Britain: report 3).
11. Meltzer H, Gill B, Petticrew M, Hinds K. *The prevalence of psychiatric morbidity among adults living in institutions.* London: HMSO, 1996 (OPCS Surveys of Psychiatric Morbidity in Great Britain: report 4).
12. Meltzer H, Gill B, Petticrew M, Hinds K. *Physical complaints, service use and treatment of residents with psychiatric disorders.* London: HMSO, 1996 (OPCS Surveys of Psychiatric Morbidity in Great Britain: report 5).
13. Meltzer H, Gill B, Petticrew M, Hinds K. *The economic activity and social functioning of residents with psychiatric disorders.* London: HMSO, 1996 (OPCS Surveys of Psychiatric Morbidity in Great Britain: report 6).
14. Meltzer H, Gill B, Petticrew M, Hinds K. *Psychiatric morbidity among homeless people.* London: HMSO, 1996 (OPCS Surveys of Psychiatric Morbidity in Great Britain: report 7).

15. Foster K, Meltzer H, Gill B, Petticrew M, Hinds K. *Adults with a psychotic disorder: living in the community.* London: HMSO, 1996 (OPCS Surveys of Psychiatric Morbidity in Great Britain: report 8).

16. Department of Health. *The spectrum of care: local services for people with mental health problems.* London: Department of Health, 1996.

17. Wallace SA, Crown JM, Berger M, Cox AD. *Health care needs assessment: child and adolescent mental health.* In: Stevens A, Raftery J, eds. *Health care needs assessment: the epidemiologically based needs assessment reviews (2nd series).* Oxford: Radcliffe Medical (in press).

18. Department of Health. *A handbook on the mental health of older people.* London: Department of Health (in press).

(e) Re-ablement

Re-ablement involves a wide range of services, any or all of which will have an impact on the life of a disabled person at some time - although for people who have been disabled from birth, the process is not so much one of re-ablement, but of 'ablement', or enabling. Put simply, this process is about removing or minimising the barriers encountered by disabled people. These barriers may be physical or attitudinal - both, if they are not challenged, may prevent disabled people from achieving their potential.

Services for disabled people have the same common objective - to help them to live as fully and as independently as possible in the community by means of[1]:

- participation in the life of local and national communities;

- recognition that discrimination occurs as a result of the barriers disabled people face;

- autonomy, or the freedom of disabled people to make informed choices and to control their own lives;

- partnership between disabled people and service agencies to enable them to work together on an equal basis to plan, implement and evaluate services;

- consultation to ensure services meet the needs and choices of all disabled people; *and*

- information, clearly presented in a way which is accessible to all disabled people.

For a disabled person to have maximum autonomy, choice and participation in the life of the community, information is needed about the opportunities available. More than one agency is often involved, and careful and integrated assessment and planning of services is required. Co-ordination and collaboration between agencies needs to take place at different levels: nationally, where policies are developed; locally, by effective planning of services; and individually, by effective provision of services to a person with a disability.

Education, training and employment services all provide a range of facilities for disabled people, including vocational rehabilitation, and DH is funding an initiative under the aegis of the Inter-Departmental Group on Disability, managed by the Richmond Fellowship, to improve the co-ordination of health, social care, employment, education and training services for disabled people and to encourage consultation between service users and agencies. The steering group for this 'Partnership for rehabilitation' project includes representatives from the Department for Education and Employment (DfEE) and national voluntary organisations. Four regional conferences will be organised in 1997 with a view to the preparation and publication of guidelines on good practice.

Reference

1. Begum N, Fletcher S. *Improving disability services: the way forward for health and social services.* London: King's Fund, 1995 (Living Options Partnership paper no. 3).

(f)   Services for disabled people

Recent years have seen important changes in the style of services, with increasing recognition of the expertise of the disabled person and their carers, and the development of service partnerships.

(i)   NHS services

The NHS provides a wide range of services for disabled people. General practitioner (GP) services provide much of the basic care required and, as well as medicines, can supply many other items, such as continence products. Many GPs work in partnership with other services and most are supported by health care teams which include practice nurses, community nurses and health visitors. Most of the basic care needs of disabled people can be met by the GP practice and community health teams, but GPs can refer disabled patients to other professionals or services if necessary.

In 1992, the Advisory Group on Rehabilitation was set up for a fixed period of three years. Its terms of reference were quite broad, to allow it to advise on the most effective means to promote the development of rehabilitation in England. The work of the Advisory Group will be summarised in *Rehabilitation: a guide*[1], to be published in Spring 1997. The guide outlines the principles of rehabilitation and gives examples of innovative practice. It emphasises the importance of developing 'healthy alliances' to achieve co-ordination and effective collaboration between various agencies.

Community nurses and health visitors

Community nurses have extensive knowledge and expertise in the management and care of disabled people. Health visitors have a particular role in the early identification of childhood disability, providing advice and guidance to parents or guardians on access to other services and voluntary organisations. They are often the key link between education and health, and work closely with GPs and paediatric departments. District nurses provide help to enable disabled people and their carers to manage at home; they have knowledge of the local and national support networks, and provide practical advice and nursing skills to enable people to live an optimum quality of life.

Therapy services

The three main groups of therapy professionals - in physiotherapy, occupational therapy, and speech and language therapy - work in many different settings in the NHS and with a wide range of patients. Occupational therapists are also employed by social services departments, with particular emphasis on assessing people's needs for equipment and home adaptations. All three professions have expanded between 1986 and 1996; for this period, the numbers of qualified therapists (whole-time equivalent) working for the NHS or social services departments in England have increased from 9,150 to 11,010 (up 20%) for physiotherapists; from 4,330 to 7,190 (up 66%) for occupational therapists in the NHS; from 1,050 to 1,580 (up 50%) for occupational therapists in social services departments; and from 2,510 to 3,580 (up 43%) for speech and language therapists.

Physiotherapists

Physiotherapists use a range of techniques to treat, rehabilitate and re-educate people with a wide range of health problems. Disabled people account for a high proportion of the physiotherapy workload, especially those with chronic disabling conditions. Techniques used include manipulation of joints and soft tissues, exercise, electrotherapy and hydrotherapy. Emphasis is placed on enabling people who have lost movement and functional ability, often associated with pain, to resume as active and independent a life as possible. Many of these people will have become disabled through accident, ageing or illness.

In the past, physiotherapists worked mainly in hospitals, but some physiotherapists are now either attached to GP practices or are employed by GP fundholders. Community-based services often involve care for people with long-term conditions such as learning disability, mental illness and physical disability. Many of these services are provided in people's homes, clinics, health centres,

135

special and mainstream schools, nurseries, and so on - often as an integral part of a multiprofessional team.

Hospital services are broad and involve most clinical care groups.

Occupational therapists

The aim of occupational therapy is to prevent disability, to improve function and to achieve an individual's maximum independence in social, domestic and work settings. Therapists also advise disabled people and their carers on the management of disability at home, including provision of equipment and housing adaptations.

Although an increasing number of occupational therapists are now working with GPs and primary health care teams, many work in the hospital sector. Hospital occupational therapists work in rehabilitation departments, psychiatric and geriatric units. One of the prime aims of occupational therapy is to return patients to independent living wherever possible; traditionally, occupational therapists have provided a service in large mental illness and learning disability hospitals, but this role is now more concerned with supporting patients in the community. Many occupational therapists now work in the community in many different settings, including health centres, clinics and special schools.

Speech and language therapists

NHS speech and language therapy services are available across the country and provide assessment, diagnosis, treatment, advice and support across the range of disability. Most speech and language therapists work in the NHS and are often based in the community, working in health, education and local authority settings, including primary health care teams. Priority is usually given to the needs of pre-school children as it is in that period that the best results can be achieved and later social and educational damage minimised. Treatment can involve direct therapy, group work or training parents and other carers to work on programmes designed by professional staff.

Difficulties with speech and communication generally are widespread and, even in their milder forms, can produce disability in an individual's educational, working and social life. The isolation and frustration caused also affects families and carers. Speech and language difficulties can occur at any age, but the most common periods are at the time of normal speech and language development (18 months to two years) and at over 65 years-of-age, when strokes and neurological diseases become more common.

About 15-20% of pre-school children have delayed or disordered speech and language development. Causes range from hearing disability, specific language impairment, generalised learning disability, physical disability or delayed language development due to an impoverished environment. At school entry, 5-15% of children may still have major difficulties and some may require a statement of special educational need.

Many neurological disorders and diseases cause speech and language problems and associated dysphagia; about 50% of patients with multiple sclerosis, 75% with Parkinson's disease and 90% with motor neurone disease will develop difficulty in communicating, particularly during the later stages of their illness. After a stroke, approximately one-third of patients experience difficulty in producing clear speech because of paresis or damage to the central nervous system; traumatic brain injury can produce similar results, depending on the site of the injury.

Each health district will set its own priority for speech and language therapy services but there will normally be help and support for these specific difficulties, as well as for more specialised groups like children with cleft lip and palate, those who stammer and patients who have had head and neck surgery, including laryngectomy. Speech and language therapy services can advise on communication aids, signing systems and other methods of communication where speech is, or becomes, impossible.

Wheelchair services

Wheelchairs are provided by the NHS to anyone who has a clinical need for one due to limited mobility. There are currently 145 wheelchair services in England, most of which are attached to hospital NHS Trusts. Decisions about the type of wheelchair provided are made in the light of specialist therapist assessment of individual need. Any type of wheelchair available in the UK may be supplied depending on local and personal circumstances; people are also able to buy a wheelchair privately if they wish as an alternative to, or in addition to, an NHS chair.

On 23 February 1996, two new wheelchair initiatives were announced: the provision of electrically powered indoor/outdoor wheelchairs (EPIOCs) to severely disabled people who met certain criteria[2], and the introduction of a Wheelchair Voucher Scheme to give wheelchair users more choice[3].

Guidance on the provision of EPIOCs was issued in May 1996[2]. A broad national framework of eligibility was outlined in the guidance, which stated that the severely disabled person should be: unable to propel a manual wheelchair outdoors; able to benefit from the chair through increased mobility leading to improved quality of life; and able to handle the chair safely. Within this broad framework, each health authority then assessed local needs and determined local eligibility criteria. Additional funding for EPIOCs was made available for four years.

Guidance on the Wheelchair Voucher Scheme was issued in December 1996[3]. The aim of the scheme is to give disabled people more choice of wheelchair within the NHS by offering them three options: to accept the wheelchair prescribed, as at present; to contribute to the cost of a more expensive wheelchair of their choice, which would mean that they would then own the wheelchair and be responsible for its maintenance and repair; or to contribute to the cost of a more expensive wheelchair of their choice from a range selected by the local wheelchair service, which would mean that the NHS then owns the wheelchair and is responsible for its maintenance and repair.

The key principles of the scheme are: universal eligibility (anyone assessed as meeting the local eligibility criteria for a wheelchair may apply); assessment and review of needs by the wheelchair service and prescription of a suitable wheelchair in consultation with the user; supply of the wheelchair through agreed suppliers; and continued access to NHS provision of special seating/pressure-relieving cushions if needed.

The voucher (or prescription) is valid for a period which is equivalent to the length of time that the wheelchair user would have had an NHS wheelchair, an average time being about five years. The voucher scheme is being phased in gradually over three years. Additional funding has been made available - £15 million over the first three years of the scheme, becoming recurrent at £8 million annually.

Hearing aid services

NHS hearing aids are available free to anyone who has a hearing loss and could benefit from having a hearing aid fitted. A person with hearing difficulties should first consult their GP who will refer them to a hospital otorhinolaryngology (ENT) department or, in some cases, direct to a hearing aid centre.

Batteries and maintenance of NHS hearing aids are also free. The model supplied is a matter for clinical decision and the range of NHS aids is reviewed regularly. Most NHS aids for adults are behind-the-ear models but an in-the-ear model was introduced in April 1995.

Results of research commissioned into the comparative merits of the traditional method of referral via a hospital ENT consultant and direct referral by the patient's GP to a hearing aid centre indicated that direct referral could, in straightforward cases, provide an equally safe but often quicker service[4]. Hospital managers and GPs may consider the introduction of direct referral where it is likely to improve service and reduce waiting times, as a local decision.

Chiropody, dental and optometry services

Disabled people sometimes have difficulty in gaining access to these services due to physical barriers. The community dental service brings treatment to people whose disability prevents them from visiting a dentist and some dentists will do home visits, as do some opticians.

Opticians play a vital part in the early detection of a number of serious eye conditions which, if not treated, can lead to blindness. Free eye tests are available to people over 40 years-of-age with a family history of glaucoma. People with conditions such as diabetes mellitus especially benefit from regular eye examinations. Opticians can refer patients to ophthalmologists for a full diagnosis and any appropriate treatment.

Disabled people often need help with the care of their feet. As a community health service, chiropody services play a vital role in helping to maintain people's independence by assisting them to maintain their mobility.

(ii)   Social services

Local authority social services departments have a statutory responsibility under welfare legislation to provide, or arrange for the provision of, social care and other personal social services to vulnerable individuals and families in a variety of different situations. They are accountable for the quality of services they provide. There is a wide range of services that may be provided by social services departments after they have assessed the care needs of a disabled person. The individual package of support may include home care or a home-help service to assist with personal and domestic care needs; a meals-on-wheels service to deliver hot meals to homes or day centres and luncheon clubs; and a range of aids and equipment for disabled people to use at home. Social services may also provide day centres, day care, help for carers and respite care, help with independent living and residential care. Social workers and care managers also offer support and help with other issues such as welfare benefits, and work closely with housing departments and housing associations to provide adaptations to disabled people's homes, following professional advice usually given by an occupational therapist.

(iii)   Role of other Government Departments

The Department of Social Security benefit system has a major part to play in the lives of disabled people - not least because, for many disabled people, disability benefits are their main, if not only, source of income. The 1985 OPCS surveys[5,6,7,8,9,10] found that only 36% of disabled men and 31% of disabled women worked; another 11% of men and 4% of women were actively seeking work; about one-third of those sampled in 1985 were classified as permanently unable to work; and a further 25% of women were looking after the family or home. The survey found that disabled adults in work earned less income than their non-disabled colleagues - earning just under three-quarters of the average wage for the general population, partly as a reflection of fewer working hours, but in some instances because of lower hourly rates.

Social Security benefits for disabled people have been rising steadily since the early 1990s. For Great Britain, in 1991/92, a total of £3,700 million were paid by means of Attendance Allowance, Invalid Care Allowance, Severe Disablement Allowance and Mobility Allowance. Five years on (although Mobility Allowance was replaced by Disability Living Allowance and Disability Working Allowance in 1992/93), the total payments of disability benefits in 1996/97 reached a total of £8,400 million.

Between 1992/93 and 1996/97 (for which direct comparisons on the same benefits can be made), expenditure on disability benefits rose by approximately 14% annually in real terms after allowance for inflation, and expenditure on Disability Living Allowance and Invalid Care Allowance grew by about 19% annually for Great Britain as a whole. Over the same period, the number of people receiving disability benefits in Great Britain rose from 2.6 million to 3.7 million, equivalent to a growth of about 9% annually. Growth of benefits is predicted to rise to £11,300 million by 1999/2000.

As well as the contributory disability benefits, Income Support expenditure for long-term sick and disabled people increased in real terms by an average of 19% annually over the same period, during which the number of people who qualified for the disability premium more than doubled from 375,000 to 786,000 for Great Britain as a whole. This increase in Income Support is associated with wider access to the disability premium for those receiving disability benefits.

The DfEE (and its predecessors) has long had a major role in the provision of education for young disabled people, and of employment opportunities. Both these roles will be further enhanced by the Disability Discrimination Act 1995[11]; provisions implemented from 2 December 1996 in the areas of employment, education, property and goods, facilities, services and premises apply to everybody offering goods, facilities and services to ensure equality of opportunity and access for disabled people.

(iv)   Voluntary sector

There are numerous national organisations, large and small, which help to meet the information and support needs of disabled people. Many such organisations serve the needs of people with a particular disability - such as the Multiple Sclerosis Society, the RNIB, MENCAP or the Spinal Injuries Association. Some have networks of local groups, which offer a range of activities and provide some of the services of the national organisation. Local groups often enable disabled people to meet with people who share or understand their particular disability.

One important change regarding the voluntary sector is the growth in recent years of organisations of disabled people, rather than organisations run for disabled people. Organisations of disabled people have played a key role in the campaign for change, often on civil rights issues; some have resource centres to give advice on equipment, services, benefits and grants; and some provide peer counselling by disabled people to disabled people. The British Council of Organisations of Disabled People now represents over 100 such organisations.

Some disability organisations have become providers of care, supported by local authorities. Centres for independent living encourage disabled people to help themselves, and have been at the forefront in the campaign for direct payments to disabled people to enable them to manage their personal care and support by employing their own enablers.

The voluntary sector often has a key role in providing information for disabled people and their carers. Increasingly, the voluntary sector is also addressing the information needs of professionals working with disabled people, and some organisations produce information packs on particular disabilities or issues for health care teams in the community.

(v)   Family and informal carers

Family and informal carers often play a vital role in supporting people with disabilities. When a family member becomes disabled, either through accident, illness or ageing, it can have a profound effect on relationships with partners and other family members. Where personal care is required with toileting and other intimate aspects of personal hygiene, it can be difficult to adapt to needing such help and the inevitable loss of privacy. Sometimes people become closer through these changed circumstances but, unfortunately, a breakdown in partnerships can occur. 'Relate', the charity which provides counselling for relationship problems, can sometimes provide counselling by counsellors who have had training in disability issues, and the organisation SPOD (Sexual Problems of Disabled People) can advise and provide information on a wide variety of subjects related to sex and relationships, and has a confidential telephone counselling line.

The family and carers of disabled people frequently know a great deal about their everyday practical needs. It is estimated that there are currently 6.8 million carers in Great Britain[12]; a surprisingly large number of these are young carers - the Health Services Management Unit at Manchester University has estimated that there are between 15,000 and 40,000 young carers in Great Britain, although the figure may be even higher[13]. Often partners and relatives do not define themselves as carers; caring is a role that is usually thrust upon people due to circumstances beyond their control, and sometimes health and social services alike take for granted that the carer will undertake the role willingly.

Carers are now entitled to ask for a separate assessment of their needs and social workers must take into account the ability of the carer to continue caring[14,15]. Respite care - either at a day centre, by provision of home care while the carer goes out, or residential respite care to enable the carer to have a holiday - can provide practical support. Such breaks are often crucial to ensure that a disabled person is able to continue living at home.

The Carers' National Association, which is run by carers and has over 100 branches in Great Britain, aims to encourage carers to recognise their own needs; to develop appropriate support for carers; to provide information and advice to carers; and to bring the needs of carers to the attention of Government and other policy-makers. There are many smaller carers' organisations and local groups, but frequently carers find themselves unable to benefit from attending meetings because their caring responsibilities prevent them getting there. Thus many carers remain isolated, which can be a particular problem in rural areas.

The expertise and knowledge of the family and carers of a disabled person is often an under-used resource. When a disabled person goes into hospital, there is sometimes an uneasy relationship between the formal and informal carers; the latter may feel that their relative has somehow become 'hospital property' and, although they may welcome the break from daily caring, they may also feel redundant and unimportant. Health and social care professionals need to be sensitive to this possibility and be willing to ask for advice on the care of disabled patients from the patients and carers, as well as to involve them in decision-making and day-to-day aspects of care.

(vi) Partnerships

Working in partnership underpins many of the principles of community care and good practice. Most importantly, partnerships increasingly include disabled people and their families and carers. Joint commissioning has been at the core of local authority community care plans as part of a move towards the provision of a seamless service for all vulnerable groups in society, including disabled people. The benefit of care services will depend to a large extent on the quality of the partnerships involved. In many cases, several agencies will be involved in the provision of care for disabled people, all of whom will have had input to the assessment; most importantly, disabled people want to play a key role in such assessment, and their needs or wishes may not coincide with those of the other agencies involved and the resources available. It is essential to build solid partnerships between the agencies involved and the disabled person to help to ensure that the best possible outcome is achieved.

Responsibilities for continuing care of disabled people and other people with long-term health care needs were discussed in *NHS responsibilities for meeting continuing health care needs*[15]. This guidance confirmed and clarified health service responsibilities after consultation between the NHS and social services departments. Since April 1996, health authorities have published policies and eligibility criteria which make clear their commitment to continuing health care and the basis on which decisions in individual cases are taken. The Disability Discrimination Act[11], the first stages of which came into force in December 1996, has highlighted the importance for the NHS - both as a service provider and as an employer - in responding to the needs and wishes of disabled people.

References

1. NHS Executive. *Rehabilitation: a guide.* Leeds: Department of Health (in press).

2. NHS Executive. *Guidance on the provision of electrically powered indoor/outdoor wheelchairs (EPIOCs).* Wetherby (West Yorkshire): Department of Health, 1996 (Health Service Guidelines: HSG(96)34).

3. NHS Executive. *Guidance on wheelchair voucher scheme.* Wetherby (West Yorkshire): Department of Health, 1996 (Health Service Guidelines: HSG(96)53).

4. Department of Health. *Audiology services: direct referral projects.* Leeds: Department of Health, 1994 (Executive Letter: EL(94)35).

5. Martin J, Meltzer H, Elliot D. *The prevalence of disability among adults.* London: HMSO, 1988 (OPCS Surveys of Disability in Great Britain: report 1).

6. Martin J, White A. *The financial circumstances of disabled adults living in private households.* London: HMSO, 1988 (OPCS Surveys of Disability in Great Britain: report 2).

7. Bone M, Meltzer H. *The prevalence of disability among children.* London: HMSO, 1988 (OPCS Surveys of Disability in Great Britain: report 3).

8. Martin J, White M, Meltzer H. *Disabled adults: services, transport and employment.* London: HMSO, 1989 (OPCS Surveys of Disability in Great Britain: report 4).

9. Smith M, Robus N. *The financial circumstances of families with disabled children living in private households.* London: HMSO, 1989 (OPCS Surveys of Disability in Great Britain: report 5).

10. Meltzer H, Smith M, Robus N. *Disabled children: services, transport and education.* London: HMSO, 1989 (OPCS Surveys of Disability in Great Britain: report 6).

11. *The Disability Discrimination Act.* London: HMSO, 1995.

12. Office for National Statistics. *General Household Survey 1995.* London: Stationery Office (in press).

13. Health Services Management Unit, University of Manchester. *Young carers: an evaluation of three RHA-funded projects.* Manchester: Health Services Management Unit, University of Manchester, 1995.

14. *The Carers (Recognition and Services) Act 1995.* London: HMSO, 1995.

15.	Department of Health. *NHS responsibilities for meeting continuing health care needs.* Wetherby (West Yorkshire): Department of Health, 1995 (Health Service Guidelines: HSG (95)8, Local Authority Circular: LAC(95)5).

## (g)	The way ahead

There are many further opportunities for health and social services to influence the causes and to alleviate the consequences of disability. Examples of work in hand include:

- A programme of workshops to address the needs of disabled children and to draw out messages about good practice and needs for local action based on a recent national inspection of social services, a new analysis of needs, and development work on local registers by the Council for Disabled Children;

- Future initiatives to support self-management to increase independence and autonomy, with a strong research component and co-operation with voluntary organisations (for example the Manic Depression Fellowship, which is publishing a booklet and running a series of workshops; Arthritis Care, which has been funded by NHS Complex and Physical Disabilities Research Programme to evaluate a self-management programme; and a project to identify good practice and to develop standards planned by the Long Term Medical Conditions Alliance, working with its 60 constituent voluntary organisations);

- Assistance for young people with disability to manage the transition to adulthood, as set out in a guidance document *Making connections*[1] - jointly prepared and funded by DH and DfEE, supported by the Prince of Wales' Advisory Group on Disability, SKILL (the National Bureau for Students with Disabilities) and the Disability Unit - which focuses on the transition of disabled young people from school to further education, employment and training, and was distributed to local and health authorities, NHS Trusts, Community Health Councils, and voluntary organisations in March.

- A programme to improve services for disabled people within the NHS, including workshops led by disabled people for health service managers and professionals to enhance their understanding of the challenges which disabled people face in gaining access to health care services (including particular initiatives on hearing impairment and the nutrition of vulnerable people in hospital); *and*

- Further assessment of the role of the NHS in the provision of services for people with learning disability who live in the community, following a workshop held in June 1996, and a series of focus groups involving service users and their carers.

These initiatives will be led by health and social services in partnership with the voluntary sector - but for disabled people to play their full role in society, action will be needed on a broader front: employers, the education sector and the leisure industry all have a major part to play.

Society must recognise the rights of disabled people, as embodied in the Disability Discrimination Act 1995[2]. Disability should not prevent individuals benefiting from being members of society; nor from fulfilling their duties to that society. But for rhetoric to become reality, providers of services must view the world from the range of perspectives of disabled people; work with disabled people; and work across boundaries to alleviate the impact of disability and, where possible, to prevent it[3].

References

1. Department of Health, Department for Education and Employment. *Making connections.* London: Department of Health (in press).
2. *The Disability Discrimination Act 1995.* London: HMSO, 1995.
3. Department of Health. *Public health strategy launched to tackle root causes of ill-health.* London: Department of Health, 1997 (Press release: 97/157).

CHAPTER 5

HEALTH CARE

(a)   Role and function of the National Health Service in England

(i)   Purpose

The purpose of the National Health Service (NHS) is to secure through the resources available the greatest possible improvement in the physical and mental health of the people of England by: promoting health, preventing ill-health, diagnosing and treating disease and injury, and caring for those with long-term illness and disability. In achieving its purpose, the NHS is required to be:

- universal in its reach, available to anyone who wishes to use it;

- of high quality, applying the latest knowledge and the highest professional standards;

- available on the basis of clinical need, and not a patient's ability to pay; *and*

- responsive, by being sensitive to the needs and wishes of patients and carers alike.

In seeking to achieve its purpose, the NHS judges its results under the criteria of:

- *equity:* by improving the health of the population as a whole and reducing variations in health status by targeting resources where needs are greatest;

- *efficiency:* by providing patients with treatment and care which is both clinically effective and a good use of taxpayers' money; *and*

- *responsiveness:* by meeting the needs of individual patients and ensuring that the NHS changes appropriately as those needs change, and as medical technology advances.

(ii)   Policies and strategies

The strategies by which the NHS achieves its purpose have been set out in a number of policy documents.

The Health of the Nation White Paper[1] sets out the approach to improving the overall health of the population, and has formed a central plank of Government policy for the NHS and for NHS planning. It provides a strategic approach to improve the overall health of the population, setting targets for public health gain in five key areas and emphasising disease prevention and health promotion. The NHS continued to make progress towards these objectives, in partnership with other agencies, and integrated the strategy more fully into the general management of the service.

The community care reforms as set out in *Caring for people*[2] aim to allow vulnerable people to live as independently as possible in their own homes or in a homely setting in the community. The emphasis is on the development of more flexible and appropriate care for people. Community care remained a high priority during the year. The Community Care (Direct Payments) Act[3], which was passed and will come into force on 1 April 1997, should allow some people to manage the funds for their care themselves, giving them greater flexibility to deploy those resources to provide the services to suit their own particular needs. Progress was also made to ensure that the NHS was fulfilling its responsibilities to provide continuing health care, including continuing inpatient care, rehabilitation and palliative care, and services in the community.

In November, the Government set out a strategy for health care services in the White Paper *A service with ambitions*[4], which set out the strategic objectives required to achieve a high-quality, integrated health service organised and run around the health needs of individual patients, rather than the convenience of the system or institution:

- *a well-informed public:* who understand about their own health, what symptoms mean, how and when to gain access to services, and who take part in decisions on their own care;

- *a seamless service:* co-ordinated and integrated across the health and social care system around the needs and wishes of individual patients and carers;

- *knowledge-based decision-making:* a service which invests in the future through research and development and which ensures the most effective practice is used throughout the NHS;

- *a highly trained and skilled workforce:* working in teams, promoting health as well as providing treatment and care; *and*

- *a responsive service:* sensitive to different needs and wishes of patients and carers.

A debate on the future of primary care, launched by the Secretary of State for Health in October 1995, and summarised in *Primary care: the future*[5], published in June 1996, set out some principles for the development of primary care which were widely endorsed by those working in primary care and their representatives.

The White Paper *Choice and opportunity*[6], issued in October 1996, set out a number of proposals for legislation to enable evaluation of new approaches to contracting for general practice services, with the aim to improve services, to deal with long-standing problems and to introduce more flexible career structures to meet the needs of a changing workforce. The White Paper also outlined similar proposals for general dental services and for some greater local flexibility in pharmaceutical and optometry services, and proposed changes to the system for appointing single-handed general practitioners (GPs). After consultation, proposals were put before Parliament in the NHS (Primary Care) Bill.

In December, the White Paper *Primary care: delivering the future*[7] set out proposals to improve further the quality and accessibility of primary care services and to offer enhanced development and career opportunities for the professionals who work within them. Proposals were grouped in themes: developing partnerships in care; developing professional knowledge (education and training, research and development, clinical effectiveness and audit); patient and carer involvement and choice; distribution and use of resources; workforce and premises; and better organisation.

The 'Patient's charter'[8] focuses on the delivery of services by setting standards in areas such as waiting times, provision of information, and privacy and dignity issues. The charter is supported by a series of booklets setting out how the charter standards apply to specific services such as maternity, children's and young people's, and mental health services. A new NHS complaints procedure, introduced in April 1996, aims to resolve complaints quickly and simply, and to ensure that information from them is used to improve services. The Health Service Commissioner's powers have been extended to allow investigation of complaints about issues arising from the exercise of clinical judgment and about primary care.

The NHS Executive also set out details of a 'Patient partnership strategy',which aims to support the greater involvement of patients and carers in their own care, and in the development of services. As part of this strategy, a Centre for Quality Health Information will be set up in Spring 1997. Annual performance tables to show comparative performance of NHS Trusts and health authorities against a number of key standards were continued and reviewed.

Six areas, set out in the priorities and planning guidance for 1997/98[9], were identified as priorities for the NHS over the medium term on the basis that they will require particular attention by the Service as a whole:

- *A:* To work towards the development of a primary care-led NHS, in which decisions about the purchasing and provision of health care are taken as close to patients as possible;

- *B:* In partnership with local authorities, GPs and service providers, including the non-statutory sector, to review and maintain progress on the effective purchasing and provision of comprehensive mental health services to enable people with mental illness to receive effective care and treatment in the most appropriate setting in accordance with their needs;

- *C:* To improve the clinical and cost-effectiveness of services throughout the NHS and thereby secure the greatest health gain from the resources available, through supporting research and development (R&D) and formulating decisions on the basis of appropriate evidence about clinical effectiveness;

- *D:* To give greater voice and influence to users of NHS services and their carers in their own care, the development and definition of standards set for NHS services locally and the development of NHS policy both locally and nationally;

- *E:* To ensure, in collaboration with local authorities and other organisations, that integrated services are in place to meet needs for continuing care for elderly, disabled, or vulnerable people and children which allow them, wherever practical, to be supported in the most appropriate available setting; *and*

- *F:* To develop NHS organisations as good employers with particular reference to workforce planning, education and training, employment policy and practice, the development of teamwork, reward systems, staff utilisation and staff welfare.

(iii)   Priority setting

In the White Paper *The National Health Service: a service with ambitions*[4], the Government reaffirmed its approach to priority setting, initially set out in March 1995 in its response to the Health Select Committee on priority setting[10]. Priorities are set at three levels:

- the Secretary of State for Health sets out a framework of national priorities and targets for improvement through annual priorities and planning guidance to the NHS, and through overarching policies such as the Health of the Nation White Paper[1];

- health authorities and GP fundholders assess the needs of the people they serve and decide what treatments and services are required to meet those needs, informed by proper consultation with the public; *and*

- individual clinicians decide the most clinically appropriate treatment and clinical priority for each patient, based on their assessment of that patient's needs.

The values of equity, efficiency and responsiveness should act as a guide to local decision-making. However, these cannot be converted into a universal formula to substitute for informed judgment operating at local level and in full knowledge of the circumstances. No one principle has overriding importance, and they need to be considered together, balancing the interests of individual patients and the community as a whole.

(iv)   Research and development

The research and development strategy

R&D is a core function of the NHS and an integral part of the Department's responsibilities. The R&D strategy comprises two complementary programmes: the Department's policy research programme and the NHS R&D programme. The Department of Health (DH) also promotes strong links with the scientific community, research councils, charities and industry, and has established sound links with the European Union (EU). A national forum of research funders has provided an important means to establish closer working links between research interests in the NHS and elsewhere.

Policy-related research

The policy research programme provides a knowledge base for the development of strategic policy for the health service, for social services and for public health. The programme's remit extends across the whole range of the Department's responsibilities, and is reflected in the broad scope of its research portfolio[11].

This research provides evidence-based findings which can advance Health of the Nation objectives[1]. The coronary heart disease (CHD) and stroke key area is supported by research on nutrition, smoking, hypertension and heavy drinking. For mental illness targets, there are several studies on suicide and a wide range of work to identify cost-effective services for mentally ill people. Studies on breast cancer and cervical screening, on the early detection of melanoma, and on smoking in pregnancy and among adolescents support targets for reducing the incidence of cancer.

The strategic focus extends to other areas where large research programmes are being developed to inform and advance knowledge - including work on primary health care, air pollution and vaccine development. In the light of evidence of a new variant of Creutzfeldt-Jakob disease (nvCJD) emerging during the year[12], the R&D Directorate has led the development of a new strategy for research into the human health aspects of transmissible spongiform encephalopathies (TSEs). This strategy has now been published[13], priority areas highlighted for further research and various research projects are being commissioned (see page 239).

Priority setting draws on advice from the Departmental Research Committee chaired by the Director of Research and Development. Membership is drawn from senior policy and professional colleagues, including the Chief Medical Officer.

Developments in the NHS R&D programme

The NHS R&D strategy has a key role to play in the move to strengthen the scientific basis of health care, and encourages NHS managers and health professionals to convert information needs into answerable research questions, and to track down the best evidence to address the problems that they face in day-to-day practice.

The overall NHS R&D programme comprises a central and eight regional programmes. The programme aims to create a knowledge-based health service in which clinical, managerial and policy decisions are based on sound information from research. The central programme is priority-led, based on widespread consultation and designed to meet the needs of the Service. The resulting programmes of work are managed and commissioned largely through R&D directorates. Research programmes are being funded in various areas, including: mental health, cardiovascular disease/stroke, the interface between primary and secondary care, cancer, asthma, and physical and complex disabilities. The NHS health technology assessment programme[14] is the largest single programme of work within, and a key element of, the central programme. A new national centre, based at the Wessex Institute for Health Research and Development at the University of Southampton, has been established to take forward this work. Results of research programmes are made available world wide through collaboration with the International Network of Agencies for Health Technology.

In the central programme, greater emphasis is now being given to organisational and management issues, and a new programme of work has begun under the direction of an expert group set up to advise on the scope and mechanisms to advance research on service delivery in the light of existing activity and the approach adopted by the health technology assessment programme and other relevant work.

Developments in R&D funding

The R&D funding implications of the NHS reforms were examined by a Task Force chaired by Professor Anthony Culyer[15], Professor of Economics at the University of York. The Task Force's recommendations were largely accepted by Government and are being implemented[16].

Recommendations include new ways to meet the costs which providers of NHS services incur as a result of their involvement in R&D. An initial R&D Levy has been created, bringing together existing central and regional budgets (the R component of SIFTR, the Service Increment for Teaching and Research). The Levy is divided into two parts - one of which provides support to NHS providers for their R&D activity, and the other is used to meet R&D priorities identified by the NHS Executive. NHS Trusts have also completed a declaration of their R&D activity and costs, and a re-basing exercise has removed cross-subsidies between the R&D Levy and other budgets such as patient care. An outline of the new system for R&D support funding for NHS providers of care will be published in early 1997.

References

1.   Department of Health. *The Health of the Nation: a strategy for health in England.* London: HMSO, 1992 (Cm. 1986).

2.   Department of Health. *Caring for people: community care in the next decade and beyond.* London: HMSO, 1989 (Cm. 849).

3.   *The Community Care (Direct Payments) Act 1996.* London: HMSO, 1996.

4.   Department of Health. *The National Health Service: a service with ambitions.* London: HMSO, 1996 (Cm. 3425).

5.   NHS Executive. *Primary care: the future.* Wetherby (West Yorkshire): Department of Health, 1996.

6.   Department of Health, Scottish Office Home and Health Department, Welsh Office. *Choice and opportunity: primary care: the future.* London: Stationery Office, 1996 (Cm. 3390).

7   Department of Health. *Primary care: delivering the future.* London: Stationery Office, 1996 (Cm. 3512).

8.   Department of Health. *The patient's charter.* London: Department of Health, 1991 (revised 1995).

9.   Department of Health. *Priorities and planning guidance for the NHS: 1997/98.* Wetherby (West Yorkshire): Department of Health, 1996.

10.   Department of Health. *Government Response to the First Report from the Health Committee: priority setting in the NHS: purchasing: Session 1994-95.* London: HMSO, 1995 (Cm. 2826).

11.   Department of Health. *Centrally commissioned research programme: commissions in 1994/95.* London: Department of Health, 1995.

12.   Will RG, Ironside JW, Zeidler M, et al. A new variant of Creutzfeldt-Jakob disease in the UK. *Lancet* 1996; **347**: 921-5.

13.   Department of Health. *Strategy for research and development relating to the human health aspects of transmissible spongiform encephalopathies.* London: Department of Health, 1996.

14.   Department of Health. *Health technology assessment: report of the NHS health technology assessment programme, 1996.* Leeds: NHS Executive, 1996.

15. Research and Development Task Force. *Supporting research and development in the NHS*. London: HMSO, 1994. Chair: Professor Anthony Culyer.
16. Department of Health. *Supporting research and development in the NHS: implementation plan*. Wetherby (West Yorkshire): Department of Health, 1995 (Executive Letter: EL(95)46).

(b)   Role of the NHS in maintaining public health

(i)   *Public health and the NHS*

Public Health in England[1], published in July 1994, outlined the public health functions of health authorities. Health authorities are essentially public health organisations that commission health services and work with others to improve the health of the population they serve. The core function of directors of public health (DsPH) and their multidisciplinary teams has been emphasised by making the DPH one of the three statutory executive members of each authority's management board. All health authorities are required to make arrangements to involve professionals in the full range of their work. DsPH are pivotal in ensuring that health professionals contribute to health authority decisions, and have a key role themselves in providing public health advice.

Public health specialists are also working closely with primary care colleagues in the development of the primary care-led NHS, including the provision of evidence-based advice for purchasing decisions. A working group on public health in primary care has been exploring further ways in which public health and primary care professionals can work together for the benefit of patients.

The multidisciplinary base of the public health function in the NHS is strong. A review of progress on public health in England established that a substantial proportion of public health staff in health authorities come from backgrounds other than medicine. There is a need to improve training and development and career opportunities for public health professionals as health authorities evolve the skill-mix they need as public health organisations. The Department is supporting this through a range of initiatives.

(ii)   *Health care needs assessment*

The health care needs assessment series is a long-term programme for the production and dissemination of information to support purchasers of health care in their assessment of local health care needs for a range of conditions. The second series of epidemiologically based health care needs assessments will be published in early 1997[2]. Additional chapters on the black and ethnic minority population, rehabilitation, and the elderly are all in progress. The first series[3] was well received and is now being updated with current information on research

153

and practice. A section in each chapter on primary care issues will be included to make individual chapters more relevant to purchasers of primary care. Work on a third series of health care needs assessments should start in mid-1997.

The health care needs assessment series is part of a wider strategy to promote clinical effectiveness within the NHS and forms part of a range of initiatives commissioned centrally, which include Effective Health Care Bulletins and evidence-based guidelines. Audit of the first series indicates that it was mainly used by health authority public health departments to underpin reviews of services, strategic planning and contract specification. Future publications should now reflect the needs of a wider range of purchasers of health care.

(iii) National Casemix Office and NHS Centre for Coding and Classification

National Casemix Office

The National Casemix Office has been set up to develop, maintain, issue and market patient grouping tools and classification methodologies for use in the NHS. Such groupings allow patient-based data to be aggregated in various ways to assist in analysis. One type of grouping is health care resource groups (HRGs) for use in costing, performance management and monitoring (by NHS Trusts, health authorities and GPs), and for internal resource management. Other types of groupings, for example health benefit groups (HBGs), enable analysis of epidemiological data to assist purchasers to define the needs of their populations and to understand the likely outcome of care purchased. The Office has close working relations with the NHS Centre for Coding and Classification and the Central Health Outcomes Unit, as well as with many local initiatives working to develop packages and profiles of care.

The current programme includes:

- refinement of HRGs for inpatients and day cases;

- pilot projects of HRGs in mental health services and the care of elderly people;

- development of HRGs in outpatient and community services;

- pilot projects and continued development of HBGs to inform purchasing;

- support of the extension of HRG costing in district and GP purchasing in the provision of acute health care;

- review of the definition of 'episode of care' across acute and community services alike;

- provision of casemix-adjusted health service indicators and national HRG statistics; *and*

- support in the implementation of casemix methods in the NHS through training courses, seminars, conferences, and help-desk services.

The National Casemix Office is also collaborating in health needs assessment to include the use of the HRG/HBG framework to identify health needs.

NHS Centre for Coding and Classification

The NHS Centre for Coding and Classification (NHSCCC) continues to maintain and develop the Read Codes - a computerised thesaurus of health care terms and one of the key projects of the information management and technology (IM&T) strategy for the NHS in England (see page 247). The NHSCCC also has responsibility for health care classification and improving the quality of coded clinical data by facilitation of data definitions, standards and training.

The NHSCCC and the Office for National Statistics (ONS) have now established a joint United Kingdom (UK) Collaborating Centre, combining areas of interest, knowledge and expertise. The ONS will continue to have responsibility for mortality data, and the NHSCCC will compile morbidity data within the NHS.

The current programme includes:

- work to help to implement the new Read Codes version 3, with the establishment of pilot sites in primary care to explore issues related to the exchange of clinical records using Read Codes;

- development of a range of mapping tables and specific guidance to enable exchange of clinical messages and migration to systems that use Read Codes version 3;

- development of prototype software to show possible approaches for retrieval and analysis of clinical information from systems that use Read Codes version 3: *and*

- facilitation of the implementation of Read Codes throughout the NHS by the identification of barriers to their use and providing information to users and decision-makers.

(iv)   *National Screening Committee*

In July, DH set up a National Screening Committee to bring together key interests to advise Ministers and the Department on the timeliness and appropriateness for the introduction, review, modification or cessation of national population screening programmes.

Screening is a major health care activity for the NHS, and recent years have seen increased development of novel potential screening technologies. Preliminary results, which are often encouraging, may lead to early pressure and expectation from public and health professionals alike for new screening programmes to be introduced. The Committee will balance all these issues against the capacity and ability of the NHS to provide a high-quality service appropriate to public health needs, rigorous analysis of proposed screening tests and wider consideration of the potential benefits and drawbacks of their introduction.

The Committee will advise Ministers and the NHS Executive on the case for implementing new population screening programmes not presently purchased by the NHS, and for the continuation, modification or withdrawal of existing population screening programmes. Through programme-specific advisory groups and other bodies concerned with national and local population screening, the Committee will monitor and be advised of the progress, problems and research needs of ongoing NHS screening programmes. Where appropriate, it will advise on standards and monitoring arrangements. The Committee is now identifying priorities for its work programme for the next two years.

(v)   *Quality of service and effectiveness of care*

The NHS strategy White Paper, *A service with ambitions*[4] reinforces a commitment to support the NHS in bridging the gap between research findings and routine clinical practice, and to work closely with professional bodies to raise standards of clinical care. Good progress has been made towards providing clinicians with the latest information to support clinical decision-making within the clinical effectiveness framework.

Promoting clinical effectiveness[5], launched in January, described progress with the NHS's clinical effectiveness programme, and was followed up with *Clinical guidelines: using clinical guidelines to improve patient care*[6] and *Clinical Audit in the NHS: a position statement*[7], which focused on progress in particular strands of the clinical effectiveness programme. *Improving the effectiveness of clinical services*[8], issued to the NHS on 18 December, described the portfolio of national effectiveness information resources as a means to support local effectiveness strategies.

Clinical audit is an important tool for changing clinical practice and improving quality of care through constructive, clinician-led developmental review. The Public Account Committee's report, *Clinical audit in England*[9], published in July, supported the progress made, as did the National Audit Office in 1995[10]. The NHS Executive is working to develop the scope of clinical audit by:

- promoting closer working with the medical Royal Colleges and other professional bodies to encourage their leading role in future developments in clinical audit;

- funding a study by the Health Services Management Centre in Birmingham to examine the key data requirements of managing and evaluating the benefits and costs of an effective national programme of clinical audit in the NHS;

- facilitating new leadership and a fresh approach for the National Centre for Clinical Audit (NCCA), which will promote best practice gained from local initiatives and experiences in multiprofessional audit; *and*

- making clinical audit and effectiveness a priority to support continuing professional development.

Professional bodies are mainly responsible to ensure that the latest, appropriate evidence-based guidance is available to and used by their members, but the NHS Executive will continue to provide support in this and other developmental work; it brought four clinical guidelines to the attention of the NHS during 1996. Other publications supported by the NHS Executive as helpful sources of information about clinical effectiveness include the Effective Health Care Bulletins, health care needs assessments and *Effectiveness Matters*.

Local teams are best placed to improve effective local practice at their own pace. Local clinicians, working with health authorities, will develop plans for local action, agree objectives and progress milestones and draw as required on national and local effectiveness resources. Such frameworks for the development of initiatives to enhance effective health care will be sensitive to the needs of local professional staff and local people alike.

(vi)   *Clinical and health outcomes*

Health outcome indicators

An updated version of the set of Population Health Outcome Indicators[11] was published as part of the Public Health Common Data Set 1996 (PHCDS) in December[12]. The Wessex Institute for Health Research and Development was commissioned by the Central Health Outcomes Unit (CHOU) to survey the use of health outcomes assessment and of these indicators by health authorities.

A report on the survey was published in October[13]. Ninety-one representatives of 100 District Health Authorities (DHAs) were interviewed in a telephone survey. Users valued the indicators, wanted national production to continue and made several constructive suggestions to improve them. Details were also obtained on 147 examples of local work, covering over 30 clinical areas, in which population health outcomes assessment had been of most value. Of those, 35% were chosen following publication of national data (with the DHA having an outlier value) or as a result of national initiatives; 45% as a result of local issues; and 20% as a result of national and local issues combined. The Wessex Institute has since been commissioned to prepare, jointly with the DHAs, some 20 case studies of local work for publication during 1997.

The ten working groups set up by the CHOU to develop new outcome indicators continued their work during the year[14]. The Asthma Working Group submitted its report to the Department during 1996, with reviews of published work on outcome measures and effectiveness of health care, along with suggestions for 19 possible outcome indicators that cover a variety of perspectives, including those of patients. Further work is now under way to assess the feasibility of data collection. The other working groups are likely to report during 1997.

Clinical indicators

A first set of 14 clinical indicators, reflecting aspects of clinical care that may raise questions about the quality of care for further investigation, was recommended by a combined Joint Consultants Committee/NHS Executive working group in May 1995. These indicators and their analyses by use of Hospital Episode Statistics data for 1994/95 were developed further during 1996. A consultation document on these indicators will be issued to the NHS during 1997.

Outcomes projects

Alongside its own extensive programme to develop outcome indicators, the CHOU supports a number of projects which aim to develop the methods and information systems necessary to create new indicators. Reports on several projects were made available to DH during 1996 and some have now been published. These reports included: an investigation into variation in hospitalisation rates for 45 selected medical conditions and 32 surgical procedures[15]; the EuroQoL project and development of EQ-5D, an instrument to measure and value general health and well-being; a reliability and validation study of Functional Assessment of Care Environments (FACE), a structured electronic record used to describe physical and mental health, social well-being, the care environment and interventions for people with mental illness and learning disabilities; the development of the Health of the Nation Outcome Scale (HoNOS)[16], a scale for monitoring progress with the mental health key area of the Health of the Nation initiative[17]; outcome measures for ambulatory care[18]; and the Major Trauma Outcomes Study, a national study producing comparative severity-adjusted outcomes data for a selection of hospitals[19].

(vii)   Regional epidemiological services for communicable disease

The surveillance and control of communicable disease is a core function of every health authority. Each authority is required to appoint a consultant in communicable disease control (CCDC), accountable managerially to the DPH, and to ensure that the CCDC has the necessary support for this function - success depends upon an appropriate complement of staff and facilities within the authority itself, and upon effective working relations within the NHS and with local authorities.

CsCDC must be confident that NHS Trusts and primary care organisations have appropriate arrangements in place and that staff will be made available to CsCDC when required to respond to a disease outbreak; many health authorities now make this availability a specific requirement in their contracts with NHS Trusts.

Since 1 April, the NHS Executive has had a contractual arrangement with the Public Health Laboratory Service (PHLS) to provide a regional epidemiologist (RE) and supporting staff. The RE provides advice to the regional director of public health (RDPH) to assist in the performance management of the NHS, to develop regional surveillance and to support CsCDC in the control of individual outbreaks.

References

1.   Department of Health, NHS Executive. *Public health in England: roles and responsibilities of the Department of Health and the NHS.* London: Department of Health, 1994.

2.   Stevens A, Raftery J, eds. *Health care needs assessment: the epidemiologically based needs assessment reviews. (Second series).* Oxford: Radcliffe Medical (in press).

3.   Stevens A, Raftery J, eds. *Health care needs assessment: the epidemiologically based needs assessment reviews (vols I and II).* Oxford: Radcliffe Medical, 1994.

4.   Department of Health. *The National Health Service: a service with ambitions.* London: Stationery Office, 1996 (Cm. 3425).

5.   NHS Executive. *Promoting clinical effectiveness: a framework for action in and through the NHS.* Leeds: NHS Executive, 1996.

6.   Mann T. *Clinical guidelines: using clinical guidelines to improve patient care within the NHS.* London: Department of Health, 1996.

7.   Mann T. *Using clinical audit in the NHS: a position statement.* London: Department of Health, 1996.

8.   NHS Executive. *Improving the effectiveness of clinical services.* Leeds: NHS Executive, 1996. (Executive Letter: EL(96)110).

9.   House of Commons Committee of Public Accounts. *National Health Service Executive clinical audit in England: thirty first report: Session 1995-96.* London: HMSO, 1996 (HC 304).

10. National Audit Office. *Clinical audit in England: report by the Comptroller and Auditor General: Session 1995-96.* London: HMSO, 1995 (HC 27).

11. Department of Health. *Population health outcome indicators for the NHS: 1993: England: a consultation document.* London: Department of Health, 1993.

12. Department of Health. *Public health common data set 1996: incorporating Health of the Nation indicators and population health outcome indicators: data definitions and user guide.* Guildford: National Institute of Epidemiology, University of Surrey, 1996.

13. McColl A, Ferris G, Roderick P, Gabbay J. *How do English DHAs use population health outcome assessments?: telephone survey report of DHAs in England.* Southampton: Wessex Institute for Health Research and Development, University of Southampton, 1996.

14. Department of Health. *On the State of the Public Health: the annual report of the Chief Medical Officer of the Department of Health for the year 1995.* London: HMSO, 1996; 138-9.

15. McPherson K, Downing A, Buirski D. *Systematic variation in surgical procedures and hospital admission rates.* London: Department of Public Health and Policy, London School of Hygiene and Tropical Medicine, 1996.

16. Wing JK, Curtis RH, Beevor AS. *HoNOS: Health of the Nation outcome scales: report on research and development July 1993-December 1995.* London: Royal College of Psychiatrists, 1996.

17. Department of Health. *The Health of the Nation: a strategy for health in England.* London: HMSO, 1992 (Cm. 1986).

18. Hutchinson A. *Outcome measures for ambulatory care: final report of the Department of Health ambulatory care research programme.* Hull: Department of Public Health Medicine, University of Hull, 1996.

19. UK Trauma Audit and Research Network. *Developing effective care for injured patients through outcome analysis and dissemination: a guide for clinicians.* Salford: UK Trauma Network, University of Manchester, 1996.

(c)   Primary health care

(i)   *Organisation of primary care*

During the early part of the year, Ministers mounted a 'listening exercise' to help to develop an agenda for further improvement of primary care services for patients by taking note of service needs as expressed by users, providers and purchasers of such services. The June publication of *Primary care: the future*[1] reflected those views and laid down principles of quality, fairness, accessibility, responsiveness and efficiency to underpin the primary health care service, which should:

- provide continuity of care;

- be properly co-ordinated so that all health care professionals work together to meet patients' needs;

- act as an effective and equitable gatekeeper to secondary care;

- address the health needs of communities as well as individuals; *and*

- offer, in a primary care setting, such services as might feasibly be made available to reflect patients' preferences.

Primary care: the future[1], after further consultation, formed the basis of two White Papers on primary care. *Choice and opportunity*[2] set out the opportunities for possible adaptations in the delivery of primary care to facilitate, where practicable, arrangements to satisfy locally expressed health care needs, and to encourage pilot schemes in the provision of general medical, pharmaceutical and dental services within a primary care setting. The White Paper[2] expressed support for local schemes for enhanced primary care to be further developed by health authorities, and acknowledged the crucial role in service development of those already purchasing or providing such services.

Whilst *Choice and opportunity*[2] mainly addressed the flexibilities needed to develop local primary care services further, the White Paper *Primary care: delivering the future*[3] pointed to increased funding and set out an agenda for action; many items related to quality issues in primary health care services - including commitments to review continuing professional development in general practice, accreditation to the lists for minor surgery, child health surveillance and maternity services, and a focus on resources in inner-city areas. An expressed intention to define primary care indicators at health authority level should help to produce aggregated quality and service markers to assess service developments.

(ii)   *Development of emergency services in the community*

The Chief Medical Officer chaired a review of emergency care other than that provided in hospitals, as announced by the Secretary of State for Health in a statement to the House of Commons and communicated to the NHS by its Chief Executive[4].

The intention of this review, expressed in its terms of reference, was: to develop a clear understanding of what patients require from emergency care services outside hospital; to identify means of meeting those requirements, based on the available evidence; to clarify the roles of different professional staff; and to define appropriate models for the delivery of emergency care (including psychiatric care) to ensure a seamless service across primary and community sectors, as well as social services. In particular, the review considered how best emergency care could be provided to those who develop sudden severe illness in which rapid intervention is necessary to save life or to prevent chronic impairment of health.

The review group comprised a broad range of experts involved in emergency care provision within the NHS as well as from the police, the fire service, voluntary aid societies and patient representative groups. Its broad overview of how people are affected by and manage emergencies, how patients would wish their emergencies to be managed, and how professional resources might be better co-ordinated to facilitate a more integrated emergency care service was supported by a patient focus group study, an expert or Delphi panel exercise and an extensive bibliography.

The review group's conclusions emphasised the need:

- to co-ordinate the provision of emergency care so that a well-planned and well-managed system of appropriate assistance is accessible to patients at any time;

- to ensure that people can recognise emergencies, deal with them and know where to turn to for professional help; *and*

- to investigate the viability of other models of access to emergency care, in particular the evaluation of a freephone helpline for emergencies.

The report of the review, *Developing emergency services in the community*[5], was issued for consultation in November. The conclusions will be reviewed at a final meeting of the working group, taking account of the consultation exercise, and the final report will be presented to the Secretary of State for Health in Summer 1997.

(iii)   *'Out of hours' services*

Agreement was reached with the General Medical Services Committee (GMSC) of the British Medical Association (BMA) in September 1995 on a package of proposals intended to improve the provision of out-of-hours services to patients whilst easing the personal burden on individual GPs and to encourage them, where appropriate, to co-operate even further in the provision of such services. GPs can use deputising services or local co-operatives (where doctors group together in a rota) to provide their out-of-hours services, subject to satisfactory standards and safeguards. Co-operatives appear to have proved particularly popular among practitioners and patients alike, although much current evidence is anecdotal; as deputising services, they facilitate the provision of flexible, responsive emergency general medical services, yet reduce the personal commitment to out-of-hours work of the individual GPs involved. In November 1996, according to the National Association of GP Co-operatives, there were 10,500 GPs working in 130 co-operative schemes in England, with numbers still increasing.

(iv)   *Prescribing*

NHS expenditure on drugs, dressings and appliances prescribed by GPs increased by 8% in 1995/96, reaching £3,500 million; this increase was again less than the previous year (up 9.5% in 1994/95), but it remained higher than the overall increase in NHS expenditure of 4.4%. Generic prescribing reached 60% of prescriptions for the first time; other striking changes were seen in the prescribing of lipid-lowering drugs (up 50% on a cost basis to £93 million), antihypertensive agents (up 17%), antidepressants (up 30%) and antibacterial drugs (down 10%).

Repeat prescribing accounts for 75% of all items prescribed by GPs and for 81% of costs. Indications that the management and clinical care aspects of repeat prescribing may need to be addressed in many practices is therefore of concern[6,7], and the NHS Executive is working with professional groups to take forward improvements in this area.

The National Prescribing Centre (NPC) and the Prescribing Support Unit (PSU) opened in April. The NPC will continue the provision of educational and technical support to health authority prescribing advisors previously provided by the Medical Advisers' Support Centre, the Medicines Resource Centre and the Management Services Information Systems Development Unit, but will also widen the range of services provided to GPs and health authorities. The PSU will continue to support the NHS Executive and health authorities, as did its predecessor the Prescribing Research Unit, and continue to work with external researchers though be less directly involved in research itself. The introduction of novel drugs, some for conditions previously untreatable and others - often more expensive than those they replace - to treat conditions more effectively, and the widening of the indications for existing drugs, point to the need for effective use of NHS resources. The NPC, in consultation with the regional Drug Information Pharmacists Group, is developing a system for tracking drugs in development, and it hopes to publish 8-10 factual bulletins annually to help GPs and health authorities to make sensible preparations for new drug introductions.

The first phase of PRODIGY, a computerised point-of-consultation system to support prescribing decision-making, was completed, and an interim report[8] published in July indicated its potential value to GPs and patients alike, including continuing medical education and patient advice. However, the study revealed various areas where additional features would be valued or improvements were required; these will be incorporated in the second phase of the trial during 1997. A final report of the evaluation is due towards the end of that year. Following widespread consultation with health care professionals, the pharmaceutical industry and patient organisations, it was agreed that a working group that represented all interested parties would be set up to advise on methods to develop advice for decision-support aids of this type.

A large pilot study of nurse prescribing has been successfully implemented in Bolton, and Ministers have agreed to further pilot studies in another seven health authority areas in 1997 to provide further information on training and implementation issues, based on an additional 1,200 nurse prescribers, before the possibility of national implementation in 1998. An evaluation of the nurse prescribing project[9] concluded that current evidence indicates that nurse prescribing was "a professional success", but that more evidence was needed on economic and other indicators.

In *Primary care: delivering the future*[3], the Government announced plans for a review, to start in 1997, which will consider possible new roles for health care professionals in the prescribing, supply and administration of medicines.

References

1.   Dorrell S. *Primary care: the future.* Leeds: NHS Executive, 1996.
2.   Department of Health, Scottish Office, Welsh Office. *Choice and opportunity: primary care: the future.* London: Stationery Office, 1996 (Cm. 3390).
3.   Department of Health. *Primary care: delivering the future.* London: Stationery Office, 1996 (Cm. 3512).
4.   NHS Executive. *Emergency care services.* Leeds: NHS Executive, 1996 (Executive Letter: EL(96)23).
5.   NHS Executive. *Developing emergency services in the community (vols 1 and 2).* London: Department of Health, 1996. Chair: Sir Kenneth Calman.
6.   Harris CM, Dajda R. The scale of repeat prescribing. *Br J Gen Pract* 1996; **46:** 649-53.
7.   Zermansky AG. Who controls repeats? *Br J Gen Pract* 1996; **46:** 643-7.
8.   Sowerby Unit for Informatics, School of Health Sciences, University of Newcastle. *PRODIGY interim report.* London: Department of Health, 1996.
9.   Luker KA, Austin L, Hogg C, et al. *Evaluation of nurse prescribing: final report: executive summary.* Liverpool/York: Universities of Liverpool and York (in press).

(d)   Specialised clinical services

(i)   *Specialised services*

The National Specialist Commissioning Advisory Group (NSCAG) took over the functions of the former Supra-Regional Services Advisory Group from 1 April.

The NSCAG, chaired by Mr Neil McKay, Regional General Manager/Director, Trent Regional Office, has 14 members, representing purchasers of health care, the Joint Consultants Committee (JCC) of the BMA and medical research. The NSCAG has a slightly broader remit than its predecessor that enables it to influence the purchasing of a limited number of highly specialised services which just fail to meet the former Supra-Regional criteria; to pay the service costs during the evaluation of new treatments that are likely, if effective, to meet such criteria; and to commission purchaser guidelines for highly specialised services. An invitation to bid for designated and central purchasing under the revised terms of reference was issued in June; by November, 54 bids had been received and are under consideration.

(ii)   Cancer

The Government's strategy to develop cancer services was set out in *A policy framework for commissioning cancer services*[1], published in April 1995. To support the implementation of its recommendations, further guidance was issued in March 1996 on projected timescales for change - including evidence, where available, on the benefits of specialisation within cancer centres.

Evidence-based guidance for purchasers of health care, *Improving outcomes in breast cancer*[2], published in July, should assist health authorities to identify aspects of care most likely to improve survival rates and quality of life for those with this disease, and covers 11 topics (which include patient-centred care, rapid and accurate diagnostic services, follow-up, palliative care and effective communication), together with summaries of relevant research evidence.

In October, guidance was issued to health authorities on the provision of palliative care to help to ensure that the benefits of advances in pain and symptom control were made available to all with life-threatening diseases.

(iii)   National Confidential Enquiry into Perioperative Deaths

The National Confidential Enquiry into Perioperative Deaths (NCEPOD) has again provided evidence of the high standards of surgical and anaesthetic care in this country[3], with facts and figures brought to life by a selection of well-chosen vignettes that strengthen the educational message and leave no room for complacency. Many of its recommendations are straightforward - like re-emphasis of the importance of clinicians from all disciplines working together; others are backed up by existing evidence and identify areas where further audit or research into areas of practice are needed. Mr Brendan Devlin and Dr John Lunn, two of NCEPOD's founders who have given the initiative invaluable support, announced their retirements from the end of June 1997.

(iv)   Safety and Efficacy Register of New Interventional Procedures

In May, the Safety and Efficacy Register of New Interventional Procedures (SERNIP) was established at the Academy of Medical Royal Colleges to review and register novel invasive procedures. The idea was originally proposed by the Cabinet Office's Advisory Committee on Science and Technology in their report *Medical research and health*[4], which highlighted the lack of formal systems to assess the safety and efficacy of new invasive interventions. The register will initially consider developments in surgery, gynaecology, cardiology and radiology. The SERNIP's advisory committee will meet four times annually and will include nominees from the medical Royal Colleges, the Standing Group on Health Technology, the Medical Research Council (MRC) and DH.

(v)   Osteoporosis

DH and the NHS continued to work to meet the recommendations set out in the report of the Advisory Group on Osteoporosis[5]. In 1996, DH produced education material designed to raise awareness of the condition for patients and professionals alike. The Department worked with the Royal College of Nursing and the National Osteoporosis Society to develop a resource pack for nurses on osteoporosis, which was launched in September[6]. Osteoporosis is also featured in the women's health promotion booklet *Well women: today and tomorrow: health tips for the over 35s*[7], launched in June.

The Committee on Medical Aspects of Food Policy (COMA) set up an expert group to look at the nutritional aspects of bone health. The Clinical Standards Advisory Group also took the report into consideration in working on its own report on community health care for elderly people.

(vi)   Transplantation

During the year, 2,279 organ transplants were performed in England - 171 fewer than in 1995. The number of donors year on year in the United Kingdom (UK) fell from 877 to 831, whilst the number of patients who might benefit by such interventions continued to rise and now stands at around 5,000. The shortage of donor organs reflects increased demand as more patients are identified who might benefit from a transplant, at a time when the main potential source of supply continues to fall because of a continued reduction in fatal road traffic accidents and advances in neurology and neurosurgical techniques. About one-quarter of potential donors are lost because relatives feel unable to consent to organ removal. However, research indicates that where a prior intention to donate organs in the event of death is known to relatives, few will refuse consent. The NHS Organ Donor Register, a permanent, computerised and confidential record of people who wish to donate their organs, which was established in 1994, is now available for local transplant co-ordinators to check at any time; by December 1996, over 3.74 million people had registered.

The Advisory Group on the Ethics of Xenotransplantation, set up by the Secretary of State for Health at the end of 1995[8], consulted organisations with an interest in xenotransplantation (the transplantation of animal organs into humans) and sought views more widely via advertisements placed in the national and specialist press. The Group also hosted a workshop on infection risks that may be associated with xenotransplantation, in association with the Advisory Committee on Dangerous Pathogens. The Advisory Group's report, *Animal tissue into humans*[9], with a Government response[10], will be published early in 1997.

(vii)   National renal review

In May, guidelines[11] were published on renal services following the national renal review[12]. Health authorities were advised to carry out local needs assessments, and to model changes in the numbers of patients who might benefit from renal replacement therapy over the next few years - a figure which is expected to rise considerably; information about how to model such changes was provided.

The guidelines stressed the need to ensure that patients were treated with the most appropriate form of care; many who are unable to receive a transplanted organ will require haemodialysis, and purchasers of health care need to plan for an increase in these facilities. Doctors in specialties other than renal medicine, including GPs, have a major role in the identification of patients at risk of renal disease and their referral for specialist assessment. Effective management of conditions such as hypertension and diabetes mellitus in primary care can do much to reduce the consequences of these conditions, including renal failure, and clinicians should be aware that some ethnic minority populations have a high incidence of these diseases and of related renal failure.

A survey of renal units was repeated in 1996 to update the information provided for the first review, and its findings will be distributed to health authorities in 1997.

(viii)   Adult intensive care

In March, the Department published *Guidelines on admission to and discharge from intensive care and high dependency units*[13], intended to help clinicians to decide which patients should be admitted to intensive-care units (ICUs) and high-dependency units (HDUs). They set out clear and practical definitions of what constitutes intensive and high-dependency care, and included advice on staffing and other resource requirements, the safe transfer of patients and staff training.

A national intensive-care bed register, launched on 1 December[14], brings together information from all adult, neuroscience and paediatric ICUs in England so that any doctor who needs to transfer a patient can now make a single telephone call to find the nearest suitable bed. The information on bed availability held by the register is updated three times daily and the service is available continuously.

Also in December, an extra £4 million were made available to help to alleviate pressures on intensive and high-dependency care facilities, to ensure that an additional 37 ICU beds and 53 HDU beds will be available during Winter 1996-97. A further £5 million from central funds announced for 1997/98 will be supplemented by £15 million from health authorities[15].

(ix)   Emergency care services

Winter 1995-96 saw increased pressures on ambulance services, accident and emergency departments and other acute and community care facilities in NHS Trusts. While such pressures varied across the country, causes appear to include changes in social structure (more people living alone, in particular the elderly and single-parents), increased public expectations, influenza and other similar conditions, respiratory illnesses (particularly pneumonia), and severe weather[16,17,18,19,20,21,22].

In March, following a statement in Parliament by the Secretary of State for Health[23], the Chief Executive of the NHS Executive wrote to health authorities and NHS Trusts to ask them to plan for predictable Winter increases in emergency admissions[24]. The NHS Executive's work programme included:

- the setting up of an Emergency Services Action Team, to work at local, regional and national level on handling winter pressures and to oversee the programme[25];

- a review of emergency services outside hospital by the Chief Medical Officer and consultation on the report *Developing emergency services in the community*[26];

- consultation on a revision of the 'Patient's charter'[27] accident and emergency department immediate assessment standard, linked to the development of a national time-to-treatment standard;

- the introduction of pilot priority systems by NHS ambulance trusts;

- the launch of the national intensive care bed register; *and*

- work with social services on the effects of pressures and incentives related to patients' care needs before, during and after hospitalisation.

(x)   Ambulance performance standards review

The review of the Steering Group on Ambulance Performance Standards was published in July[28]. The Review recommended a change to the present system, under which the same ambulance response is sent to every emergency telephone call regardless of apparent priority. The review indicated that about one-quarter of emergency (999) telephone calls could be classified as immediately life-threatening, where a patient might benefit from life-saving help within minutes; other calls are less urgent. It recommended that ambulance services introduce call prioritisation systems to help to determine the relative urgency of 999 calls. The review estimated that the capacity to reach 90% of life-threatening calls within eight minutes might save the lives of 3,200 people annually from cardiac arrest alone. Call prioritisation systems require the control-room operator to ask a structured series of questions to determine safely the urgency of the call. Such systems are successfully operated in other parts of the world.

References

1.   Department of Health, Welsh Office. *A policy framework for commissioning cancer services: a report by the Expert Advisory Group on Cancer to the Chief Medical Officers of England and Wales: guidance for purchasers and providers of cancer services.* London: Department of Health, 1995.

2.   Department of Health Cancer Guidance Sub-group of the Clinical Outcomes Group. *Guidance for purchasers: improving outcomes in breast cancer (vols 1 and 2).* London: Department of Health, 1996.

3.   National Confidential Enquiry into Perioperative Deaths. *The report of the National Confidential Enquiry into Perioperative Deaths 1993/94.* London: National Confidential Enquiry into Perioperative Deaths, 1996. Chair: Professor John Blandy.

4.   Advisory Committee on Science and Technology. *Medical research and health.* London: HMSO, 1994.

5.   Department of Health. *Advisory Group on Osteoporosis: report.* London: Department of Health, 1994. Chair: Professor David Barlow.

6.   National Osteoporosis Society, Royal College of Nursing. *Osteoporosis resource pack for nurses, midwives and health visitors.* Bath: National Osteoporosis Society, 1996.

7.   Department of Health. *Well women: today and tomorrow: health tips for the over 35s.* In: *Women's health promotion; a resource pack for health care for care purchasers and providers.* London: Department of Health, 1996.

8.   Department of Health. *On the State of the Public Health: the annual report of the Chief Medical Officer of the Department of Health for the year 1995.* London: HMSO, 1996; 144-5.

9.   Department of Health. *Animal tissue into humans: a report by the Advisory Group on the Ethics of Xenotransplantation.* London: Stationery Office (in press).

10. Department of Health. *The Government Response to 'Animal tissue into humans': the report of the Advisory Group on the Ethics of Xenotransplantation.'* London: Department of Health (in press).

11. NHS Executive. *Purchasing renal services.* Wetherby (West Yorkshire): NHS Executive, 1996 (Executive Letter: EL(96)35).

12. Department of Health. *Report of the Health Care Strategy Unit: review of renal services: evidence for the review.* London: Department of Health, 1994.

13. NHS Executive. *Guidelines on admission to and discharge from intensive care and high dependency units.* London: Department of Health, 1996.

14. NHS Executive. *Intensive care bed-state register.* Wetherby (West Yorkshire): NHS Executive, 1996 (Executive Letter: EL(96)76).

15. NHS Executive. *Funding for priority services for 1996/97 and 1997/98.* Wetherby (West Yorkshire): NHS Executive, 1996 (Executive Letter: (EL(96)109).

16. Audit Commission. *By accident or design: improving accident and emergency services in England and Wales.* London: Audit Commission, 1996.

17. Williams B, Nicholl J, Brasier J. *Accident and emergency departments.* In: Stevens A, Raftery J, eds. *Health care needs assessment: the epidemiologically based needs assessments: 2nd series.* Oxford: Radcliffe Medical (in press).

18. Nicholl J, Turner J, Dixon S. *The cost-effectiveness of the regional trauma system in the North West Midlands: medical care research unit.* Sheffield: Sheffield Centre for Health and Related Research, University of Sheffield, 1996.

19. Jones G. *A study of the value of initial patient assessment within the accident and emergency department and the most effective way of achieving this.* London: Department of Health, 1995.

20. Pencheon D, Nicholson D, Hadridge P. *Emergency care handbook.* Milton Keynes: Anglia and Oxford Regional Health Authority, 1995.

21. Department of Health Clinical Standards Advisory Group. *Urgent and emergency admissions to hospital: the report of a CSAG Committee and the Government Response.* London: HMSO, 1995. Chair: Professor Michael Rosen.

22. NHS Executive. *Emergency care services.* Leeds: Department of Health, 1996 (Executive Letter: EL(96)3).

23. House of Commons Parliamentary Debate. Emergency and intensive care: Secretary of State for Health (Mr Stephen Dorrell). *Hansard* 6 March 1996; **273:** col 356-68.

24. NHS Executive. *Emergency care services.* Leeds: Department of Health, 1996 (Executive Letter: EL(96)23).

25. NHS Executive. *Emergency services.* Leeds: Department of Health, 1996 (Executive Letter: EL(96)73).

26. Department of Health. *Developing emergency services in the community (vols 1 and 2).* Leeds: Department of Health, 1996.

27. Department of Health. *The patient's charter.* London: HMSO, 1991.

28. Chapman R. *Review of ambulance performance standards.* London: Department of Health, 1996.

29. NHS Executive. *Patients' charter: progress and new commitments.* Leeds: Department of Health, 1996 (Executive Letter: EL(96)87).

(e)   Mental health

(i)   *Mental health information systems*

During 1996, priority guidance[1] was issued to the NHS requiring health authorities to develop, with their mental health care providers, an information strategy to support clinical care, in particular the Care Programme Approach[2]. DH surveys indicated considerable activity under way in line with this initiative.

Work on the first pilot Minimum Data Set (MDS) for mental health care was completed, and reviewed as part of the efficiency scrutiny of health service information[3]. As well as making recommendations about the nature of and scope for data sets, this review drew attention to the urgent need felt in the NHS for clarity about data sets for mental health and community care, and was underscored by debates at a conference organised by the Royal College of Psychiatrists (RCPsych) in the autumn. Work on the mental health MDS was reviewed in this light, and at the end of the year a new project was established to carry the work forward to a speedy conclusion. Considerable progress was also achieved during the year in the measurement of Health of the Nation mental health targets[4,5] (see page 93).

(ii) Mental health and primary care

Psychological problems are common in primary care settings. Results from the Psychiatric Morbidity Survey[6,7] published in 1995 indicated that, overall, about one in seven adults aged 16 to 64 years had some sort of neurotic health problem in the week before interview. The likelihood of such a score among unemployed people was twice that for those in work, and rates were also higher than average among women, people living alone, those in rented accommodation and city rather than rural dwellers. The most prevalent disorder was mixed anxiety and depression (71 cases per 1,000) followed by generalised anxiety disorder (30 per 1,000), phobia (18 per 1,000) and depression (17 per 1,000). Functional psychosis (mainly schizophrenia and affective disorder) was found to have a prevalence of 4 per 1,000. Despite these figures, and although mental health problems are the second most common reason for consultation with a GP[8], GPs assign a diagnosis for only about half those seen, and only about 5% of these are referred to specialist mental health services. Primary care services thus provide care for most people with mental health problems, and it is clear that support and development for this work must remain a priority.

The Department has funded a range of research, educational and development projects; the 'Defeat depression' campaign, and work on continuing medical education in mental health are examples of collaboration between DH and the Royal College of General Practitioners (RCGP) and the RCPsych. Additionally, during 1996, DH commissioned the Sainsbury Centre for Mental Health to conduct a series of multidisciplinary regional conferences to help the planning of local training for primary care teams in the Care Programme Approach[2]; work has also been taken forward to develop a 'primary mental health care toolkit'.

171

(iii)   *Occupational mental health*

Studies in working populations indicate a high prevalence of minor psychiatric morbidity of 27-37%[7,9]. Minor psychiatric disorder is a major determinant of sickness absence, and is the second most common cause of prolonged absence. Current estimates place the annual cost to industry at over £3,700 million[8]. The Department has been working to increase employers' awareness of the issues and to encourage further action. DH has sponsored conferences, produced booklets for employers and supported the Health and Safety Executive (HSE) to develop training material for business schools. The Health Education Authority (HEA) has also launched *Positive stress at work*[10] to help small employers. A survey by the Confederation of British Industry (CBI) and DH, first undertaken in 1991 and repeated in 1995, indicated that employers' awareness of mental health issues had increased, but few companies had developed policies on mental health in the workplace.

Anecdotal and interim research reports also indicate high levels of psychological symptoms among clinicians and managers in the NHS. DH issued its own policy on mental health in 1994[11], and since then has provided £235,000 annually to support the 'Health at work in the NHS' project, managed by the HEA. Action has been taken to reduce the hours worked by junior hospital doctors and to help GPs set up new out-of-hours services to tackle the issue identified by them as the top cause of stress to doctors. The Department has also provided funding for a senior occupational mental health Fellow to promote the education of occupational health staff about mental health, and two part-time GP Fellows at the RCGP.

To ensure co-ordination of these strategies, DH convened the Mental Health at Work Inter-Agency Group, including representation from the CBI, the Trades Union Congress, the HSE, the Advisory Conciliation and Arbitration Service, the HEA, the Institute of Personnel Management and the Small Business Federation.

(iv)   *Psychological treatment services*

Considerable disability and distress may be caused by mental ill-health, and demand for psychological therapies to complement physical treatments is rising. As many as 30% of GPs employ counselling services directly[12]; such treatments may be the treatment of choice in certain cases, and members of the public may prefer or specifically request them - but few people understand what such treatments involve, how to monitor and evaluate them, or what works for whom. In September, the NHS Executive published a review[13] of policy on psychotherapy services in England. The purpose of the review was to describe the range of psychological therapies used in the treatment of adults and children in primary, secondary and tertiary care, and to collate the evidence on their clinical effectiveness[14], cost-effectiveness, accessibility, appropriateness and acceptability. The review found that psychological treatments can help in many mental health problems - including severe, enduring mental illness - to produce beneficial changes in symptoms and functioning. However, levels of knowledge and provision of such services varied widely, and outcome measurement and audit were not routine. Regional Offices of the Department are arranging a series of workshops which involve commissioners of health care and providers of psychological therapy to improve appropriate provision of these services.

(v)   Child and adolescent mental health services

The mental health of children and young people in England continues to receive increasing attention. During 1996, the Health Select Committee heard evidence on services for children and young people, and several witnesses gave evidence of an increased prevalence of childhood mental health disorders which are aetiologically linked to psychosocial factors[15].

Regional conferences were held to publicise, explain and discuss implementation of policy contained in the *Handbook on child and adolescent mental health*[16]. Children's mental health needs were included in the priorities and planning guidance for the NHS for 1997/98[1] and child and adolescent mental health services (CAMHS) were included in the children's services planning guidance[17]. Health authority purchasing plans for CAMHS are now required to demonstrate agreement with local authorities and GP fundholders. Considerable interest has been generated and a number of innovative joint commissioning projects are being developed.

The review of strategic policy for NHS psychotherapy services in England[13] included a section on child and adolescent services and highlighted the special needs of children in local authority care and children with disabilities. Field trials have also been conducted to develop Health of the Nation outcome scales for children and adolescents; initial reports from the project team from Manchester University and the Royal College of Psychiatrists' Research Unit are encouraging, and these scales are likely to be of practical value to purchasers and providers of care alike.

A report on the feasibility of a survey on the health and development of children and adolescents, with a particular focus on mental health issues, was prepared by the Social Survey Division of the Office for National Statistics (ONS), and work has begun to design and test the methodology to be used.

The Confidential Inquiry into Homicides and Suicides by Mentally Ill People, established in 1992, produced its first report in 1996[18]. Its recommendations included the consideration of: staff training, particularly in risk assessment and the use of legal powers under the Mental Health Act 1983[19]; improved communication between professionals; clarity about care plans; the potential significance of poor compliance with treatment as a risk-factor; and the importance of face-to-face contact between patients and professionals.

Under its Director, Dr William Boyd, the Inquiry established an excellent working relationship with psychiatrists and other mental health workers such that, by the completion of his term, the Inquiry was accepted as a valuable resource to enhance understanding of the relations between mental illness and homicide and suicide. Response rates to the Inquiry have increased as it has progressed, and a firm foundation for future audit established.

The contract for the period 1996-2001 has been awarded to the University of Manchester under a new Director, Professor Louis Appleby. A notification system has been successfully established with district public health departments and NHS Trusts to ensure comprehensive coverage of all suicides that meet the Inquiry's remit. Information about homicides is now to be collected directly from the relevant courts. The next full report is due to be produced in 1998.

(vii)   *Emergency psychiatric services*

Psychiatric emergencies have diverse causes and varied manifestations. Most are managed without the need to refer to specialist mental health services. Although all psychiatric services provide some form of 24-hour emergency response, such services are varied; however, ease of access to and co-ordination of such services are essential for the emergency management of patients at risk.

The Secretary of State for Health asked the Chief Medical Officer to review emergency care (including mental health emergency services) in the community. The emerging conclusions were published for consultation in November[20]. It was argued that when a patient is referred to a mental health service, referrers should be able to speak to a senior clinician to discuss the urgency and the type of response required. Clinicians should have access to a range of assessments, such as: community mental health team emergency assessments; emergency or urgent outpatient appointments; Mental Health Act assessments; court and police station assessments; accident and emergency department assessments; and domiciliary visits.

Although patients may require admission, it was also suggested that there should be a range of alternatives, which might include: support at home; care at a day hospital, day centre or 'drop-in' centre; and residential alternatives such as 'crisis beds' and respite care.

Services should target those at greatest risk. *Building bridges*[21], published in 1995, provides help and advice to clinicians and professional staff who work with and for the protection of people with severe mental illness. However, it is also vital that those who present an immediate suicide risk are responded to. Although local patterns of emergency service provision may still vary, some common principles are now being established, among the most important of which is that all services should be well integrated.

(viii)   *Services for people with severe mental illness*

The Health of the Nation White Paper[4] identified mental illness as one of five key areas and set the target 'to improve significantly the health and social functioning of mentally ill people'.

Since the Mental Health Act 1959[22] there have been considerable advances in our understanding and management of mental illness, which have helped to create more effective ways to assess, treat and care for people with such illness, who may have a wide range of different needs. As well as a vast change in treatment methods there has also been considerable change in treatment settings as large traditional Victorian asylums have been replaced by a wider variety of local services, which now provide more flexible treatment and care to enable people with severe mental illness to adjust and improve more rapidly within the community than after a prolonged stay in institutional care.

February saw the publication of *The spectrum of care: local services for people with mental health problems*[23], which summarised the core components of a comprehensive local service for people with mental health problems and set out the responsibilities of local purchasers to ensure that their plans are co-ordinated with other local service providers; to agree on a flexible approach so that needs receive appropriate care; and to have a clear definition of their responsibilities.

The spectrum of care[23] also emphasised the need for a range of treatments and a range of settings for treatment and social care, including home-based care, day hospitals, crisis accommodation and beds, community mental health centres, housing and social care, residential care, specialised services, secure facilities and special hospitals.

Other developments during the year, which indicate the importance attached to the care and treatment of those with severe mental illness in the community, include publication of a review of 24-hour nursed accommodation[24], undertaken to identify obstacles to the commissioning or use of such accommodation and to make recommendations for action, and which provided detailed advice on the type of services required. The need for this type of accommodation was estimated to be 25 beds per 250,000 population, although there are likely to be considerable variations between districts in levels of need, with increased demand for such services in metropolitan areas.

Despite advances in the care and treatment of people with severe mental illness within the community, the co-ordination of local services needs to be further improved and successful working relations between the different agencies involved may not be easy to achieve. The Green Paper *Developing partnerships in mental health*[25] explores potential changes in the current organisational framework, such as modification to targeted funding mechanisms (eg, the Mental Health Challenge Fund and the Mental Illness Specific Grant), and integration of the Care Programme Approach and care management. Work has also been undertaken in collaboration with the Royal College of Nursing and the RCPsych to review the training needs of the NHS workforce.

(ix)   Services for mentally disordered offenders

Forensic mental health services are only one component of overall mental health services, and mentally disordered offenders form a relatively small group of patients detained under the Mental Health Act 1983[19]. However, the difficult problems they may pose to health, social care and criminal justice agencies have been noted in these Reports since 1991[26,27,28,29,30].

Health authorities have been encouraged to develop a range of services to care for all those with mental illness, and services for mentally disordered offenders have been developed within the NHS. Considerable progress has been made to expand the number of medium-secure places within the health service; from no purpose-built places in 1979, an intensive programme since 1991 - with DH investment of over £47 million with the aim to provide 1,250 purpose-built medium-secure places in the NHS - is now almost complete, so that the Glancy[31] target of 1,000 places nationally has been met. The programme has been supported regionally, and at the end of the year there were 1,509 medium-secure beds for mental illness and learning disabilities plus 1,110 low-secure beds for mental illness; these developments are consistent with the recommendations in the final summary report of the Reed Committee[32].

In April 1996, the High Security Psychiatric Services Commissioning Board (HSPSCB) took responsibility for commissioning high security services[33]. Its terms of reference include the commissioning of high security psychiatric services; the development of longer term secure services for those who no longer require high security (about one-third of high security patients[34,35]); the development of a training and research strategy for forensic staff in high security hospitals and other services; and support for the development of a co-ordinated commissioning strategy for NHS secure services.

Five providers of health have been identified to develop long-term medium-secure services[36], selected from 58 responses to an initial advertisement in 1996. Innovative approaches include the possibility of community forensic mental health teams and a service fully integrated with all local mental health services. North West Region has pioneered a fully integrated range of services which is widely regarded as a model of good practice[37].

The HSPSCB has also established a research and development committee. A major priority for further research is severe antisocial personality disorder, following the recommendations of the 1994 Reed report[38], and a review of published research on treatment outcomes[39]. Pilot schemes with a range of training and education models will underpin the development of an integrated service approach, and DH is also funding the development of other innovative approaches, such as a curriculum for social therapists by Ashworth Hospital, Liverpool and the University of Central Lancashire.

A further objective of the HSPSCB is to develop a commissioning strategy for child and adolescent forensic mental health services to allow this strategy to be considered with that for adults and to achieve congruency of approach - particularly important in preventive activities[40]. Moreover, core skills such as risk assessment are not confined to forensic psychiatry, and are as important for the safe management of many general mental health patients in a variety of settings, including the community, as they are for the management of patients in secure psychiatric settings[41].

(x)   Mental health legislation

Patients detained under the Mental Health Act 1983[19] comprise less than one-tenth of all psychiatric hospital admissions, and services for them need to be developed within, and fully integrated with, mainstream mental health services. However, the needs of such patients are complex, and they may require lengthy periods of inpatient treatment and supervised after-care. During the year, two important advances in the legislation and arrangements for such patients have been a focus for attention.

The Mental Health (Patients in the Community) Act[42] came into effect on 1 April 1996. It introduced new supervised discharge procedures within the Mental

Health Act 1983[19] for some patients who are discharged following detention in hospital. Patients who are subject to supervised discharge "will have been assessed as presenting a substantial risk of serious harm to themselves or other people, or of being seriously exploited, if they do not receive suitable aftercare. They should normally be included on the supervision register..."[43,44]. The NHS Executive will evaluate the use of this new power by research to be commissioned during 1997.

Guidance provided to professionals on their duties under the Mental Health Act 1983[19] was also reviewed. A revised draft Code of Practice was circulated widely for consultation in October, and a final version will be laid before Parliament in 1997. The aim of the intended Code of Practice is to clarify and reinforce messages about the roles and duties of doctors and approved social workers who make assessments under the Act, and the duties and responsibilites of Mental Health Act managers. It will also incorporate a revised chapter on the interface between the Mental Health Act 1983[19] and the Children Act 1989[45]. Publication is subject to Parliamentary approval.

References

1. Department of Health. *NHS priorities and planning guidance: 1997/98.* Wetherby (West Yorkshire): Department of Health, 1996.
2. Department of Health. *Caring for people: the care programme approach for people with a mental illness referred to the specialist psychiatric services.* London: Department of Health, 1990 (Health Circular: HC(90)23).
3. Department of Health. *Seeing the wood, sparing the trees.* Wetherby (West Yorkshire): Department of Health, 1996.
4. Department of Health. *The Health of the Nation: a strategy for health in England.* London: HMSO, 1992 (Cm. 1986).
5. Department of Health. *Mental illness key area handbook, 2nd edn.* London: HMSO, 1994.
6. Meltzer H, Gill B, Petticrew M, Hinds K. *The prevalence of psychiatric morbidity among adults living in private households.* London: HMSO, 1995 (OPCS Surveys of Psychiatric Morbidity in Great Britain: report 1).
7. Department of Health. *On the State of the Public Health: the annual report of the Chief Medical Officer of the Department of Health for the year 1995.* London: HMSO, 1996; 13-4, 95-126.
8. McCormick A, Fleming D, Charlton J. *Morbidity statistics from general practice: fourth national study: 1991-1992.* London: HMSO, 1995 (Series MB5 no. 3).
9. Jenkins R, Warman D. *Promoting mental health policies in the workplace.* London: HMSO, 1993.
10. Health Education Authority. *Positive stress at work.* London: Health Education Authority, 1996.
11. Department of Health. *Mental health policy: a guide for managers.* London: Department of Health, 1994.
12. Sibbald B, Addington-Hall J, Brenneman D, Freeling P. Counsellors in English and Welsh general practices: their nature and distribution. *BMJ* 1993; **306:** 29-33.
13. Parry G, Richardson A. *NHS psychotherapy services in England: review of strategic policy.* London: NHS Executive, 1996.
14. Roth A, Fonagy P. *What works for whom? A critical review of psychotherapy research.* New York: Guilford Press, 1996.

15. Rutter M, Smith D, eds. *Psychosocial disorders in young people*. Chichester: John Wiley, 1995.

16. Department of Health, Social Services Inspectorate, Department for Education. *A handbook on child and adolescent mental health*. London: HMSO, 1995.

17. Department of Health, Department for Education and Employment. *Children's services planning: guidance*. London: Department of Health, Department for Education and Employment, 1996.

18. Steering Committee on the Confidential Inquiry into Homicides and Suicides by Mentally Ill People. *Report of the Confidential Inquiry into Homicides and Suicides by Mentally Ill People*. London: Royal College of Psychiatrists, 1996.

19. *The Mental Health Act 1983*. London: HMSO, 1983.

20. Department of Health. *Developing emergency services in the community (vols 1 and 2)*. London: Department of Health, 1996.

21. Department of Health. *Building bridges: a guide to arrangements for inter-Agency working for the care and protection of severely mentally ill people*. London: Department of Health, 1995.

22. *The Mental Health Act 1959*. London: HMSO, 1959.

23. Department of Health. *The spectrum of care: local services for people with mental health problems*. London: Department of Health, 1996.

24. NHS Executive. *24-hour nursed care for people with severe and enduring mental illness*. Leeds: Department of Health, 1996.

25. Department of Health. *Developing partnerships in mental health*. London: Stationery Office, 1996 (Cm. 3555).

26. Department of Health. *On the State of the Public Health: the annual report of the Chief Medical Officer of the Department of Health for the year 1991*. London: HMSO, 1992; 122-4.

27. Department of Health. *On the State of the Public Health: the annual report of the Chief Medical Officer of the Department of Health for the year 1992*. London: HMSO, 1993; 6, 122-3.

28. Department of Health. *On the State of the Public Health: the annual report of the Chief Medical Officer of the Department of Health for the year 1993*. London: HMSO, 1994; 2, 127-9.

29. Department of Health. *On the State of the Public Health: the annual report of the Chief Medical Officer of the Department of Health for the year 1994*. London: HMSO, 1995; 5-6, 144-5.

30. Department of Health. *On the State of the Public Health: the annual report of the Chief Medical Officer of the Department of Health for the year 1995*. London: HMSO, 1996; 5.

31. Department of Health and Social Security. *Report of a Working Party on NHS psychiatric hospitals*. London: Department of Health and Social Security, 1974.

32. Department of Health, Home Office. *Review of health and social services for mentally disordered offenders and others requiring similar services: final summary report*. London: HMSO, 1992 (Cm. 2088).

33. NHS Executive. *High security psychiatric services: changes in function and organisation*. Leeds: Department of Health, 1995.

34. Maden A, Curle E, Meux C, Burrow S, Gunn J. The treatment and security needs of patients in Special Hospitals. *Criminal Behaviour Mental Health* 1993; **3**: 290-307.

35. Taylor PJ, Butwell M, Dacey R, Kaye C. *Within maximum security hospitals: a survey of need*. London: Special Hospitals Services Authority, 1991.

36. Special Hospitals Services Authority. *Strategies for secure care*. London: Special Hospitals Services Authority, 1991.

37. North Western Regional Health Authority. *Strategy for service provision for mentally disordered offenders*. Manchester: North Western Regional Health Authority, 1995.

38. Department of Health, Home Office. *Report of the Department of Health and Home Office Working Group on Psychopathic Disorder*. London: Department of Health, 1994. Chair: Dr John Reed.

179

39. Dolan B, Coid J. *Psychopathic and antisocial personality disorders: treatment and research issues.* London: Gaskell, 1993.

40. Farrington DP. The development of offending and antisocial behaviour from childhood: key findings from the Cambridge study in delinquent development. *J Child Psychol Psychiatry* 1995; **36:** 929-64.

41. Grounds A. Forensic psychiatry for the millenium. *J Forens Psychiatry* 1996; **7:** 221-7.

42. *The Mental Health (Patients in the Community) Act 1995.* London: HMSO, 1995.

43. Department of Health, Welsh Office. *The Mental Health (Patients in the Community) Act 1995: guidance on supervised discharge (after-care under supervision) and related provisions: supplement to the Code of Practice published August 1993 pursuant to Section 118 of the Mental Health Act 1983.* Wetherby (West Yorkshire): Department of Health, 1996.

44. NHS Executive. *Introduction of supervision registers for mentally ill people from 1 April 1994.* Leeds: NHS Executive, 1994 (Health Service Guidelines: HSG(94)5).

45. *The Children Act 1989.* London: HMSO, 1989.

(f)   Maternity and child health services

(i)   Implementation of 'Changing Childbirth'

Progress continued towards implementation of the recommendations of the Expert Maternity Group's report, *Changing childbirth*[1], focusing on greater continuity of care and choice in maternity services. A further £172,000 were allocated to fund development projects; a total of £1.5 million has been spent on 38 projects since 1994.

During the year, there were several initiatives on education and training which involved the co-operation of professional organisations and consumer groups. DH produced a video for health care professionals about changes in maternity care and, in October, a widespread consumer awareness campaign was launched to enable women to make full use of local maternity services. As part of this campaign, DH and the Changing Childbirth Implementation Team produced a leaflet *How to get the best from maternity services*[2], in association with the National Childbirth Trust. The NHS Executive launched a guidelines booklet[3] for local maternity services liaison committees to help purchasers, providers and users of maternity services to develop services in partnership. In November, a conference on professional education for maternity care was held to provide a framework for the further development of multidisciplinary education and training; a publication of the proceedings is planned for 1997.

(ii)   Confidential Enquiries into Maternal Deaths

The latest report of the Confidential Enquiries into Maternal Deaths in the United Kingdom, for the period 1991-93, was published in June[4,5]. The report - which is the latest of a series which began in England and Wales in 1952, and is the third to cover the UK as a whole - showed that the direct mortality rate from medical conditions specifically caused by pregnancy or childbirth had fallen to 5.5 per 100,000 maternities, compared with 6.1 in the previous triennium[6]. The overall maternal mortality rate, which includes deaths that occur as a consequence of pre-existing disease being aggravated by pregnancy, has also fallen to 9.8 per 100,000 maternities, compared with 10.3 in the previous Report.

The report found:

- that the most common cause of direct death remains thrombosis and thromboembolism, the incidence of which remains static;

- a 50% drop in the number of deaths from ectopic pregnancy and from infection;

- a 30% reduction in deaths associated with high blood pressure;

- a 25% drop in the death rate from antepartum and postpartum haemorrhage; *and*

- a slight increase in conditions (such as coronary thrombosis, aortic aneurysms, and epilepsy) where pregnancy may have hastened, but was not the actual cause of, eventual death.

Whilst the Report is directed mainly to those professionals concerned with obstetric, anaesthetic or midwifery practice, it is also of interest to others likely to care for pregnant women. It contains guidance, produced either by the relevant medical Royal Colleges or authors of the report, covering areas of particular concern such as the diagnosis and management of ectopic pregnancy in primary care and accident and emergency departments, assistance for anaesthetists in obstetric practice, the management of haemorrhage in women who refuse blood transfusion and guidelines for maternal autopsy.

(iii)   Folic acid and prevention of neural tube defects

The Health Education Authority (HEA) continued to promote awareness of the benefits of additional folic acid in the prevention of neural tube defects. The objective is to encourage all women who might become pregnant: to take a daily supplement of 400 micrograms of folic acid; to consume bread and breakfast cereals fortified with folic acid; and to increase consumption of foods naturally rich in folates. The campaign has used advertising and public relations techniques to raise consumer awareness; worked with health professionals to increase their knowledge and ability to provide helpful advice; sought the co-operation of food manufacturers and retailers to promote fortified foods and foods naturally rich in folates; and promoted the development and licensing of supplements. The campaign is being evaluated by assessment of changing levels of public awareness: during the first year of the campaign, unprompted recognition of the benefits of folic acid was shown by 27% of women surveyed, against a baseline of 9%.

The Committee on Medical Aspects of Food and Nutrition Policy (COMA) set up an expert group to review the health aspects of increasing folate/folic acid intake, which is due to report in 1998.

(iv)   Sudden infant death syndrome

In July, the Secretary of State for Health announced publication of the third annual report of the Confidential Enquiry into Stillbirths and Deaths in Infancy (CESDI)[7]. A study on sudden unexplained deaths in infancy was incorporated into this report[7], and a new leaflet issued, *Reduce the risk of cot death*[8]. These publications confirmed associations between sleeping position, various environmental factors and the incidence of sudden infant death syndrome (SIDS, or cot death). The advice that children should continue to be placed on their backs to sleep was repeated and the associations between cot death and babies being exposed to cigarette smoke, and their being subject to overheating, were highlighted. Since the launch in 1991 of the Department's campaign to reduce cot deaths, the number of such deaths in infancy has fallen by about 60% - from 1.4 per 1,000 live births in 1991, to 0.6 per 1,000 in 1995 (for England and Wales, numbers of cot deaths fell from 1,008 in 1991 to 398 in 1995).

(v)   Prophylaxis of vitamin K deficiency bleeding in infants

Additional vitamin K is advised for all newborn babies in order to prevent vitamin K deficiency bleeding. As discussed in earlier reports[9,10,11], the Department awaits the results of commissioned research on this subject before considering whether to issue further guidance on the method of administration.

(vi)   Retinopathy of prematurity

A progress report on a multidisciplinary research project[12], set up to assess and improve the care of infants with retinopathy of prematurity (ROP) in the UK, was received in November. The first phase of the project, a management survey of current screening policies and practices, is complete and the data have been coded and analysed. Preliminary results indicate some well organised and efficient local screening procedures, but others where organisational challenges need to be addressed. The survey has highlighted areas for potential improvement of services, and specific inquiries about the availability of printed information for parents and about record-keeping have prompted new local initiatives. Detailed analysis of the questionnaire survey continues and further reports will follow.

A series of ROP roadshows has been arranged, which cover screening and management of preterm babies; the natural history of the disease; and counselling for parents of babies at risk of, and suffering from, ROP. Attendance by all health care professionals involved in the management of infants with ROP has been most encouraging in the first three roadshows in Taunton, Swansea and Edinburgh, and these educational programmes will continue.

(vii)   Paediatric intensive care

A National Co-ordinating Group was set up in June 1996 to draw up a policy framework for paediatric intensive care, and was asked to report to the chief executive of the NHS Executive by 30 April 1997. The Group's aim has been to build upon the strengths of the paediatric intensive care service, and to produce a clear policy framework for the future. In October, the Group decided to arrange a conference to be held early in 1997 at which to present the wider service with most of the Group's conclusions, to enable and stimulate discussion focused on considerations necessary to realise the longer-term vision of a high quality, integrated paediatric intensive care service, organised to provide for the health needs of individual children. The Group's final report is expected to be available in Summer 1997.

(viii)   Congenital limb reduction defects

The Department's Advisory Group on Congenital Limb Reduction Defects (CLRDs) recommended, in February 1995[13], that a systematic review be undertaken to document what was known about the aetiology of CLRDs. This review was completed in June 1996 and a report, *Congenital limb reduction defects: clues from developmental biology, teratology and epidemiology*[14] was published in October. This report describes the many and varied circumstances associated with a CLRD at birth, and points to advances in scientific knowledge which may shed more light on the condition. It provides a source of reference for doctors and others who investigate the incidence of CLRDs, either individually or in apparent clusters.

The report will be brought to the attention of medical practitioners and copies circulated to all directors of public health. The main findings were to discount the theory of coastal clustering and exposure to sea water as a cause of CLRDs, and to conclude that there is evidence that chorion villus sampling is associated with CLRDs - so that the benefits of this procedure should be weighed carefully against the risk, and parents should be counselled appropriately.

References

1. Department of Health. *Changing childbirth: part 1: report of the Expert Maternity Group.* London: HMSO, 1993. Chair: Baroness Cumberlege.
2. Department of Health, Changing Childbirth Implementation Team, National Childbirth Trust. *How to get the best from maternity services.* Wetherby (West Yorkshire): Department of Health, 1996.
3. NHS Executive. *Guidelines booklet on local maternity services liaison committees.* Wetherby (West Yorkshire): Department of Health, 1996.
4. Department of Health, Welsh Office, Scottish Office Home and Health Department, Department of Health and Social Services Northern Ireland. *Report on Confidential Enquiries into Maternal Deaths in the United Kingdom 1991-1993.* London: HMSO, 1996.
5. Department of Health. *Report of the Confidential Enquiries into Maternal Deaths in the United Kingdom 1991-1993.* London: Department of Health, 1996 (Professional Letter: PL/CMO(96)4, PL/CNO(96)2).
6. Department of Health, Welsh Office, Scottish Office Home and Health Department, Department of Health and Social Services Northern Ireland. *Report on Confidential Enquiries into Maternal Deaths in the United Kingdom 1988-1990.* London: HMSO, 1994.
7. Confidential Enquiry into Stillbirths and Deaths in Infancy. *Report of the Confidential Enquiry into Stillbirths and Deaths in Infancy (CESDI).* London: HMSO, 1996.
8. Department of Health. *Reduce the risk of cot death.* London: Department of Health, 1996.
9. Department of Health. *On the State of the Public Health: the annual report of the Chief Medical Officer of the Department of Health for the year 1993.* London: HMSO, 1994; 132-3.
10. Department of Health. *On the State of the Public Health: the annual report of the Chief Medical Officer of the Department of Health for the year 1994.* London: HMSO, 1995; 148-9.
11. Department of Health. *On the State of the Public Health: the annual report of the Chief Medical Officer of the Department of Health for the year 1995.* London: HMSO, 1996; 148-9.
12. Department of Health. *On the State of the Public Health: the annual report of the Chief Medical Officer of the Department of Health for the year 1994.* London: HMSO, 1995; 149.
13. Department of Health Advisory Group on Congenital Limb Reduction Defects. *Report of the Advisory Group on Congenital Limb Reduction Defects.* London: Department of Health, 1995. Chair: Professor Michael Peckham.
14. Brown N, Lumley J, Tickle C, Keene J. *Congenital limb reduction defects: clues from developmental biology, teratology and epidemiology.* London: Stationery Office, 1996.

(g)   Asthma

One of the keys to achieving a better quality of life for people with asthma is to enable them to manage their own condition as effectively as possible, with help and advice from their GP and others in the primary care team. Asthma sufferers need to know what their individual trigger factors are, and how to avoid them; they also need to know what steps and medicines are needed to control their symptoms, as patient adherence to medication regimens may not always be satisfactory.

DH therefore provided funding in 1996 for a joint project with the National Asthma Campaign to produce a new personal asthma card. The 'Control your asthma' card, which was launched in October by the Chief Medical Officer, is intended to give people the essential information that they need to help them to manage their asthma. Patients can request a card from their GP, who will fill in the relevant parts about their treatment. General practices can order free stocks of the card, and of an accompanying poster for display in surgeries, from the Department[1]; over 400,000 cards had been ordered by the end of the year.

In June, DH helped to fund a British Broadcasting Corporation (BBC) social action radio day of broadcasts on asthma, which included a free booklet and telephone helpline.

The National Asthma Campaign is managing the NHS national research and development programme on asthma management, launched in November 1995. Over 200 outline applications for funding were received by the October 1996 deadline, after which detailed proposals were invited for 44 shortlisted projects.

Reference

1.   Department of Health. Asthma patient card. *CMO's Update* 1996; **12**: 6.

(h)   Complementary medicine

Work progressed further towards the implementation of the Osteopaths Act 1993[1] and the Chiropractors Act 1994[2]. The designate General Osteopathic Council started preparatory work in February 1996, and is to be formally established on 14 January 1997; the statutory register of osteopaths is expected to open early in 1998. The designate General Chiropractic Council is to commence its preparatory work in January 1997 and, subject to progress, should be formally established in the following year. No other complementary therapy group made major advances in 1996 towards similar statutory regulation.

Interest in the provision of complementary therapies within the NHS continued. A two-year pilot scheme of GP fundholder purchasing of osteopathy and chiropractic services was announced in April. The Medical Care Research Unit at the University of Sheffield has been commissioned by DH to evaluate the pilot scheme. This Unit has also started a separate study commissioned by DH on complementary therapy provision in primary care, following on from earlier DH-funded research published in November 1995[3].

References

1.   *The Osteopaths Act 1993*. London: HMSO, 1993.
2.   *The Chiropractors Act 1994*. London: HMSO, 1994.
3.   Thomas K, Fall M, Parry G, Nicholl J. *National survey of access to complementary health care via general practice: final report to Department of Health*. Sheffield: Medical Care Research Unit, University of Sheffield, 1995.

(i)   Prison health care

A long-standing policy that mentally disordered offenders who require specific care and treatment should receive it from health and social services rather than in custodial care was supported by the Reed committee[1], which emphasised the need for very close working with colleagues in the Prison Service to achieve the aims of such a policy.

Court and prison disposals accounted for 7% of formal admissions to NHS hospitals in 1995-96[2]; numbers increased from 1,600 in 1990-91 to 1,940 in 1993-94, but have fallen back in the past two years to 1,740 in 1995-96. In total, 480 prisoners were transferred to hospital under Section 47 (after sentence) of the Mental Health Act 1983[3] or Section 48 (not sentenced) incorporating Section 49 restrictions. For transfers under Sections 47(49), admissions increased from 80 to 170 between 1990-91 and 1993-94, fell back to 125 in 1994-95, and increased to 160 in 1995-96. For transfers under Sections 48(49), admissions increased from 110 in 1990-91 to 320 in 1995-96. However, some differences (partly due to definitions and time periods) exist between DH and Home Office figures, and DH returns may underestimate the true figures.

The three high security hospitals are Rampton, Ashworth and Broadmoor. Most admissions to these hospitals are made under Part III of the Mental Health Act 1983[3], and half of all admissions in 1995-96 were patients transferred from prison and subject to restrictions.

Despite the overall increase in such admissions to NHS and independent sector hospitals and registered mental health nursing homes from prisons, recent surveys indicate unmet need within the prison system[4,5]. Brook et al[4] found a diagnosis of psychosis in 5% of those surveyed in a cross-sectional sample of 750 prisoners, representing 9.4% of the male unconvicted population (including young offenders). Overall, psychiatric disorders were diagnosed in 63% of the study population, including substance misuse (37%), neurotic illness (26%), and personality disorder (11%). Sixty-four were thought to require immediate transfer to an NHS bed. The study did not specify whether individuals would satisfy the criteria for transfer to hospital under the Mental Health Act 1983[3], but Birmingham et al[5] found a 26% prevalence of mental disorder in Her Majesty's Prison (HMP) Durham, with a similar range of disorders. Both studies make the point that, although a number of prisoners required care in hospital settings, many could be appropriately managed within prison health care settings.

A 1992 report by three medical Royal Colleges[6] made recommendations about the training of doctors who work in prison health services, which are being implemented by Nottingham University on behalf of the Health Care Service for Prisoners.

References

1. Department of Health, Home Office. *Review of health and social services for mentally disordered offenders and others requiring similar services: final summary report.* London: HMSO, 1993 (Cm. 2088). Chair: Dr John Reed.
2. Department of Health. *Inpatients formally detained in hospitals under the Mental Health Act 1983 and other legislation: England: 1990-91 to 1995-96.* London: Department of Health (in press).
3. *The Mental Health Act 1983.* London: HMSO, 1983.
4. Brook D, Taylor C, Gunn J, Maden A. Point prevalence of mental disorder in unconvicted male prisoners in England and Wales. *BMJ* 1996; **313:** 1524-7.
5. Birmingham L, Mason D, Grubin D. Prevalence of mental disorder in remand prisoners: consecutive case study. *BMJ* 1996; **313:** 1521-4.
6. Royal College of Physicians, Royal College of General Practitioners, Royal College of Psychiatrists. *Report of the working party of three medical Royal Colleges on the education and training of doctors in the Health Care Service for Prisoners.* London: HM Prison Service, 1992. Chair: Professor Denis Pereira Gray.

CHAPTER 6

COMMUNICABLE DISEASES

(a)   HIV infection and AIDS

Government strategy on HIV infection and AIDS

Targeted health promotion based firmly on epidemiological evidence remains the key to controlling the spread of HIV. Implementation of *HIV and AIDS health promotion: an evolving strategy*[1], which was published in November 1995, continued. This revised and more sharply focused health promotion strategy:

- places greater emphasis on appropriate targeting of high-risk groups (ie, homosexual and bisexual men, people with links to high-prevalence countries, injecting drug users and partners of people from these groups);

- recognises that some national HIV/AIDS campaigns are needed to maintain public awareness;

- acknowledges that community-based and self-help organisations are well placed to develop targeted health promotion work: *and*

- highlights the need for commissioning authorities to use a diversity of approaches and to evaluate outcomes, and for areas of low prevalence to take particular care to avoid complacency.

Epidemiology

AIDS

Surveillance of the epidemic is implemented through the voluntary confidential reporting systems run by the Public Health Laboratory Service (PHLS) AIDS Centre[2,3] and the Government's programme of unlinked anonymous HIV surveys[4].

Details of the AIDS cases reported in England are shown in Table 6.1 and Figure 6.1; 1,743 cases of AIDS were reported in 1996, more than in 1995 and probably reflecting fluctuations in reporting; the cumulative total of AIDS cases reported since 1984 is now 12,644, of whom 8,865 are known to have died.

Figure 6.2 compares the incidence rates of AIDS diagnoses per million population in European Union (EU) Member States for 1995.

Table 6.1: *AIDS cases and known deaths by exposure category and year of report, England, 1982-31 December 1996*

(Numbers subject to revision as further data are received or duplicates identified)

How persons probably acquired the virus	Jan 1995-Dec 1995 Cases		Jan 1996-Dec 1996 Cases		Jan 1982-Dec 1996 Males		Females	
	Males	Females	Males	Females	Cases	Deaths	Cases	Deaths
Sexual intercourse:								
Between men	911	-	1076	-	9057	6597	-	-
Between men and women								
Exposure to 'high risk' partner*	2	22	3	26	37	25	133	90
Exposure abroad†	118	112	180	162	847	474	650	322
Exposure in UK	9	12	6	15	75	51	74	46
Investigation continuing/closed‡	2	2	15	8	22	8	10	2
Injecting drug use (IDU)	47	19	77	29	379	238	160	99
IDU and sexual intercourse								
between men	24	-	33	-	228	155	-	-
Blood								
Blood factor								
(eg, treatment for haemophilia)	80	0	47	0	533	483	5	4
Blood/tissue transfer								
(eg, transfusion)								
Abroad	2	2	7	2	21	10	44	29
UK	1	2	1	1	21	19	24	20
Mother to infant	16	18	15	14	98	52	100	49
Other/undetermined/closed‡	9	2	23	3	111	84	15	8
Total	1221	191	1483	260	11429	8196	1215	669

*Partners exposed to HIV infection through sexual intercourse between men, IDU, blood factor treatment or blood/tissue transfer.

†Individuals from abroad and individuals from the UK who have lived or visited abroad, for whom there is no evidence of 'high risk' partners.

‡Closed = no further information available.

Source: CDSC, PHLS

Figure 6.1: *AIDS cases: total numbers and numbers where infection was probably acquired through sexual intercourse between men and women, England, to 31 December 1996*

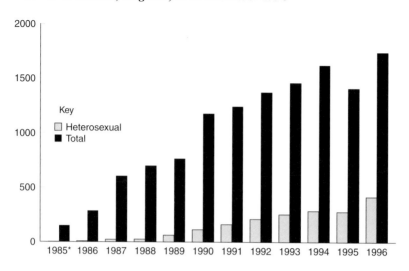

*1985 figure does not include previous years.

Source: CDSC, PHLS

Figure 6.2: *Incidence of AIDS cases diagnosed in Europe in 1995, adjusted for reporting delays: rates per million population*

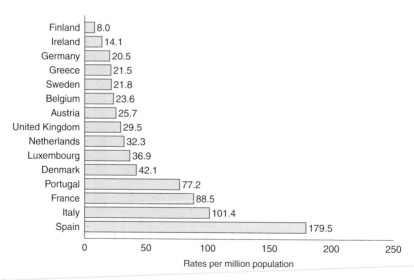

Rates per million population

Source: WHO

HIV infection

Table 6.2 and Figure 6.3 show details of reports of the 2,674 newly diagnosed HIV infections in England, which in 1996 is the highest annual total to date, and bring the cumulative total since 1984 to 25,387. Many factors influence the decision to be tested for HIV, and reported infections underestimate the true number of infections. An increased number of reports in 1996 may reflect an increased demand for testing because of apparent clinical benefits reported with combination antiretroviral therapy.

In response to concerns about inconsistencies in the content of discussions before testing for HIV, and after consultation with the Expert Advisory Group on AIDS, in March the Department of Health (DH) issued guidelines to provide health care workers with a framework for an appropriate discussion with individuals before testing for HIV infection[5].

Unlinked anonymous surveillance

The third report from the Government's Unlinked Anonymous HIV Surveys Steering Group[4] for data to the end of 1995 was published in December. For the first time, in addition to a detailed main report, a summary report presenting key

Figure 6.3: *HIV-antibody-positive people: total numbers and numbers where infection was probably acquired through sexual intercourse between men and women, England, by year of report to 31 December 1996*

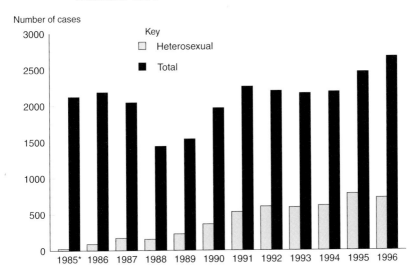

*1985 does not include previous years.

Source: CDSC, PHLS

191

Table 6.2: HIV-1 infected persons by exposure category and date of report, England, to 31 December 1996

(Numbers subject to revision as further data are received or duplicates identified)

How persons probably acquired the virus	Jan 1995 - Dec 1995			Jan 1996-Dec 1996			Nov 1984-Dec 1996		
	Male	Female	NK	Male	Female	NK	Male	Female	NK
Sexual intercourse:									
Between men	1343	-	0	1484	-	0	15773	-	-
Between men and women']									
Exposure to 'high risk' partner*	9	50	0	3	33	0	76	415	0
Exposure abroad†	306	318	0	211	257	4	1891	1880	9
Exposure in the UK	29	40	0	18	20	0	146	227	0
Investigation continuing/closed‡	16	13	0	72	103	2	110	136	2
Injecting drug use (IDU)	115	44	0	90	51	2	1271	595	5
IDU and sexual intercourse between men	26	0	0	41	0	0	410	0	0
Blood									
Blood factor treatment (eg. for haemophilia)	10	0	0	3	0	0	1075	10	0
Blood/tissue transfer (eg. transfusion)									
Abroad/UK	6	6	0	6	13	0	75	86	3
Mother to infant§	25	21	0	10	16	0	173	175	0
Other/undetermined/closed‡	71	15	1	170	52	13	664	135	45
Total	1956	507	1	2108	545	21	21664	3659	64

NK = Not known (sex not stated on report).

*Partner(s) exposed to HIV infection through sexual intercourse between men, with IDUs, or with those infected through blood factor treatment or blood/tissue transfer.

†Individuals from abroad, and individuals from the UK who have lived or visited abroad, for whom there is no evidence of 'high risk' partners.

‡Closed = no further information available.

§By date of report that established infected status of infant.

Source: CDSC, PHLS

192

points in a user-friendly format was produced. These surveys supplement data from voluntary confidential testing and permit a more accurate picture of the epidemic. The surveys are established in a number of genito-urinary medicine (GUM) clinics, centres for injecting drug users (IDUs), London hospitals and antenatal clinics; screening of neonatal dried blood spots also takes place.

Results are summarised in Table 6.3 and show that, whilst prevalence is highest in London, HIV-1 infection is present in high-risk groups in every region surveyed. The prevalence in 1995 among homosexual or bisexual men attending GUM clinics was one in 10 in London and the South East, compared with one in 40 elsewhere.

The prevalence among IDUs was one in 20 for men and one in 30 for women in London and the South-East, and one in 220 for men elsewhere. Prevalence rates among IDUs fell between 1990 and 1995, and there is currently little evidence of substantial HIV transmission in this group. However, about 17% of IDUs report recent sharing of equipment, which indicates a continuing potential for the transmission of blood-borne viruses.

HIV-1 prevalence among women giving birth in London in 1995 was one in 560 (see Figure 6.4). Comparison of data from the surveys with reported births to HIV-1-infected mothers indicate that only 16% of infections have been clinically recognised. Outside London and the South-East, prevalence was one in 10,000 - one-twentieth of that in London.

HIV/AIDS projections

The full report on AIDS projections for England and Wales until 1999 was published in January[6]. At the end of 1999, it is projected that there will be 4,010 people with AIDS alive in the population, and an additional 4,010 people with other forms of severe HIV disease. However, uptake of new combination therapies may influence these forecasts as current evidence indicates that such treatments may increase the incubation period from HIV infection to an AIDS-defining illness.

HIV in blood donations

During 1996, 2.9 million blood donations in the United Kingdom (UK) were tested with anti-HIV-1+2 combined tests. Twenty-four donations (from 14 males and 10 females) were found to be anti-HIV-1-seropositive, or one in 121,454 (0.0008%). The number of new donors tested was 335,714, of whom 10 were seropositive (1 in 33,571, or 0.003%). Again, no donations were found to be anti-HIV-2 seropositive during 1996.

Table 6.3: Prevalence of HIV-1 infection in the unlinked anonymous survey groups, England and Wales, 1995

Survey group	London and South-East England*				England and Wales outside South-East England				Prevalence ratio‡ London vs elsewhere
	Number tested	Number HIV-1 infected	% HIV-1 infected	Prevalence range (%)†	Number tested	Number HIV-1 infected	% HIV-1 infected	Prevalence range (%)†	
Males									
Genito-urinary medicine clinic attenders:									
Homo/bisexual§	4395	434	9.87	3.29, 18.30	1180	29	2.46	0.54, 5.17	4.0
Heterosexual§	12117	95	0.78	0.15, 1.77	14445	14	0.10	0.00, 0.23	7.8
Injecting drug users (IDUs) attending agencies#	571	27	4.73	2.86, 5.55	1557	7	0.45	0.00, 0.61	10.5
Hospital blood counts (sentinel group)	20627	167	0.81	0.16, 2.20	-	-	-	-	-
Females									
Genito-urinary medicine clinic attenders:									
Heterosexual§	17411	90	0.52	0.09, 1.02	12968	16	0.12	0.00, 0.39	4.3
IDUs attending agencies#	186	6	3.23	1.72, 3.91	489	0	-	-	-
Pregnant women at delivery (infant dried blood spots)**	104501	192	0.18	0.00, 0.59	259769	25	0.01	0.00, 0.09	19.1
Pregnant women seeking terminations	8222	64	0.78	0.00, 1.70	-	-	-	-	-
Hospital blood counts (sentinel group)	43534	99	0.23	0.07, 0.38	-	-	-	-	-

* The injecting drug user (IDU) survey includes data from a few agencies in the South-East outside London; all other surveys present data for London.
† The range within a category is the lowest and highest rates recorded in individual genito-urinary medicine clinics (GUM survey), regions (IDU survey), districts (infant dried blood spot survey) or hospitals (termination of pregnancy and antenatal surveys).
‡ The ratio by which the prevalence of infection in London is greater than the prevalence in England and Wales outside South-East England.
§ Excluding known drug users.
# Attending specialist centres for IDUs.
** Prevalence in South-East England outside London was 0.16% (13 of 79,447) in 1995. In Northern and Yorkshire Region data for pregnant women come from the antenatal survey.

Source: Unlinked Anonymous HIV Surveys

Figure 6.4: *Trends in prevalence of HIV-1 infection among women who give birth, by area of residence in Inner London, Outer London, and the rest of England, 1988-95*

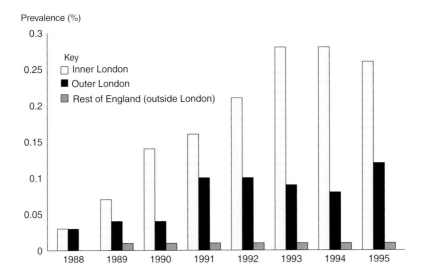

Source: Survey in North Thames and South Thames (West) co-ordinated by Institute of Child Health, London; survey elsewhere co-ordinated by PHLS AIDS Centre (commenced in 1990)

Table 6.4: *HIV in blood donations in the United Kingdom, October 1985 to December 1996*

Year	Donations tested (million)	Donations confirmed HIV-seropositive			
		Male	Female	Total	%
1985	0.6	13	0	13	0.002
1986	2.64	44	9	53	0.002
1987	2.59	18	5	23	0.0009
1988	2.64	18	5	23	0.0009
1989	2.74	25	12	37	0.001
1990	2.82	20*	12	32*	0.001
1991	2.95	23	8	31	0.001
1992	2.90	15	11	26	0.0009
1993	2.92	16	4	20	0.0007
1994	2.91	8	8	16	0.0005
1995	2.90	20	10	30	0.001
1996	2.91	14	10	24	0.0008
Total	*31.52*	*234*	*94*	*328*	*0.001*

*Includes one anti-HIV-2-positive donation.

Source: National Blood Authority and Scottish National Blood Transfusion Service

Table 6.4 shows the number of donations tested in the UK between Autumn 1985 and the end of 1996, together with the number of donations confirmed as HIV seropositive. The male:female ratio of seropositive donations in 1996 was 1.4 to 1, and was 1 to 1.5 for new donors (for those donors where the sex was noted).

Public education and prevention

The Department has contracted out health promotion for the general population and for homosexual and bisexual men, and is considering how best to develop targeted health promotion for those who travel to or have links with countries with a high prevalence of HIV infection.

The integrated AIDS/Drugs Helpline, which was set up on 1 April 1995, continues to play a valuable role in the Government's HIV strategy.

References

1. UK Health Departments. *HIV and AIDS health promotion: an evolving strategy.* London: Department of Health, 1995.
2. Public Health Laboratory Service AIDS Centre. The surveillance of HIV-1 infection and AIDS in England and Wales. *Commun Dis Rep CDR Rev* 1991; **1**: R51-6.
3. Waight PA, Rush AM, Miller E. Surveillance of HIV infection by voluntary testing in England. *Commun Dis Rep CDR Rev* 1992; **2**: R85-90.
4. Department of Health. *Unlinked anonymous HIV prevalence monitoring programme: England and Wales: data to the end of 1995: summary report from the Unlinked Anonymous Surveys Steering Group.* Wetherby (West Yorkshire): Department of Health, 1996.
5. Department of Health. *Guidelines for pre-test discussion on HIV testing.* Wetherby (West Yorkshire): Department of Health, 1996.
6. Public Health Laboratory Service. The incidence and prevalence of AIDS and prevalence of other severe HIV disease in England and Wales for 1995 to 1999: projections using data to the end of 1994: report of an Expert Group convened by the Director of the Public Health Laboratory Service on behalf of the Chief Medical Officers. *Commun Dis Rep CDR Rev* 1996; **6**: R1-24.

(b)   Other sexually transmitted diseases

All figures for sexually transmitted diseases (STDs) are derived from the KC60 reporting form for consultations in National Health Service (NHS) GUM clinics; cases diagnosed and managed elsewhere are not included. The KC60 form was redesigned for 1995, so direct comparisons with previously published total aggregate figures cannot be made. The total number of new cases seen in GUM clinics in England in 1995 was 404,638 (see Table 6.5). Of these, approximately 23% were for wart virus infection, 18% for non-specific genital infection, 10% for *Chlamydia*, 7% for herpes simplex virus and 3% for gonorrhoea.

Table 6.5: *Sexually transmitted diseases, and other infections that may be sexually transmitted, reported by NHS genito-urinary medicine clinics, England, in year ending 31 December 1995*

Condition	Males	Females	Persons
Total number of new cases seen	176423	228215	404638
All syphilis	912	505	1417
Infectious syphilis	*187*	*96*	*283*
All gonorrhoea	7649	4710	12359
Uncomplicated gonorrhoea	*6619*	*3343*	*9962*
Gonococcal ophthalmia neonatorum	*5*	*4*	*9*
Epidemiological treatment of suspected gonorrhoea	*979*	*1200*	*2179*
Gonococcal complications	*46*	*163*	*209*
All *Chlamydia*	17922	21367	39289
Uncomplicated Chlamydia infection	*12672*	*16431*	*29103*
Complicated Chlamydia infection	*260*	*876*	*1136*
Chlamydial ophthalmia neonatorum	*23*	*14*	*37*
Epidemiological treatment of suspected Chlamydia	*4967*	*4046*	*9013*
All Herpes simplex	11550	15515	27065
Anogenital Herpes simplex - first attack	*5902*	*9141*	*15043*
Anogenital Herpes simplex - recurrence	*5648*	*6374*	*12022*
All Wart virus infection	52460	40857	93317
Anogenital warts - first attack	*26213*	*25047*	*51260*
Anogenital warts - recurrence	*20278*	*11281*	*31559*
Anogenital warts - re-registered cases	*5969*	*4529*	*10498*
Chancroid/LGV/Donovanosis	60	31	91
Uncomplicated non-gonococcal/non-specific urethritis in males	44539	-	44539
Epidemiological treatment of NSGI	4353	15964	20317
Complicated non-gonococcal/non-specific infection	1930	7206	9136
Trichomoniasis	249	5237	5486
Anaerobic/bacterial vaginosis, male infection & other vaginosis/vaginitis/balanitis	13161	45600	58761
Anogenital candidiasis	8690	60742	69432
Scabies/pediculosis pubis	4245	1233	5478
Antigen-positive viral hepatitis B	523	174	697
Other viral hepatitis	1124	515	1639
Other	7056	8559	15615

LGV = lymphogranuloma venereum; NSGI = non-specific genital infection.

Source: Form KC60

In 1995, total reports of gonorrhoea rose by 5% compared with 1994 to 12,359, which is equivalent to a rate of 39 per 100,000 population (see Figure 6.5). The Health of the Nation target[1] to reduce the incidence of gonorrhoea among men and women aged 15-64 years by at least 20% by 1995 was achieved in 1992, when the rate fell to 45 cases per 100,000 population. Whilst an increase over a single year needs to be interpreted with caution, it is a reminder of the continuing need for messages about safer sex.

The total number of reports of uncomplicated chlamydial infection rose by 7% to 39,289 (an increase of 2% in men and 8% in women). Uncomplicated non-specific genital infections fell by 2% from 65,974 in 1994 to 64,856 in 1995. There was a small increase in reports of all syphilis (2%), but a small decrease in reports of infectious syphilis (283 cases in 1995 compared with 304 in 1994).

First attacks of herpes simplex virus (HSV) infection fell by 2% to 15,043, the first annual fall since 1989. First attacks of HSV declined in males by 6% but first attacks rose slightly (by less than 1%) in females and accounted for 61% of reports in 1995. Recurrent attacks rose by some 5% overall, and accounted for 44% of all reports of HSV infection during 1995. Total reports of viral warts rose by 8% and recurrent attacks accounted for 45% of all reports of wart virus infection during 1995.

Figure 6.5: *All gonorrhoea: number of new cases seen at NHS genito-urinary medicine clinics, England, 1980-95*

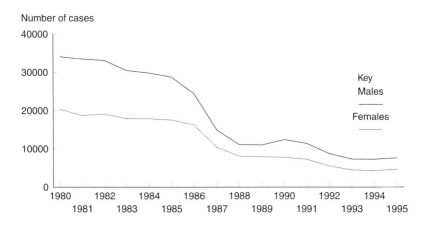

Source: Forms SBH60 and KC60

198

Other aspects of GUM clinic workload are reported in the *Statistical Bulletin*[2]: for example, 84,000 other conditions requiring treatment were identified and 125,000 individuals received pre-test discussion for HIV testing, of whom 84% underwent an HIV test.

A high proportion of reports of STDs come from patients in younger age-groups (see Table 6.6).

References

1.   Department of Health. *The Health of the Nation: a strategy for health in England.* London: HMSO, 1992 (Cm. 1986).
2.   Department of Health. *Sexually transmitted diseases: England 1995: new cases seen at NHS genito-urinary medicine clinics.* London: Department of Health, 1996 (Statistical Bulletin: 1996/14).

(c)   Immunisation

Progress continues to be reported in immunisation coverage, with increases in all antigens except measles, mumps and rubella (MMR) vaccine, which has remained static at 91%. By a child's second birthday, coverage for diphtheria, tetanus (DT) and polio vaccines is 96%; for vaccine against *Haemophilus influenzae* type b (Hib) it is 95%; and is 94% for pertussis. Notifications and laboratory reports for target diseases remain at extremely low levels. There has been no upsurge of pertussis in line with previous four-yearly epidemics, and since the measles, rubella immunisation campaign of November 1994, control of measles has been striking. Despite nearly 10,000 notifications of measles, evidence from the national salivary antibody surveillance scheme shows that only 1% of more than 6,000 samples from suspected cases were confirmed; around one-third of these cases were probably imported[1]. A routine second dose of MMR vaccine at the time of the pre-school DT and polio boosters was introduced for all children in October 1996.

In 1988, the World Health Assembly announced the goal of global eradication of poliomyelitis by the year 2000. The Americas have already been certified by an international commission to have eliminated transmission of wild virus poliomyelitis. The process of certification of countries in the World Health Organization (WHO) European Region has now started and the United Kingdom (UK) will be among the first group of countries being considered for certification.

Reference

1.   Gay N, Ramsay M, Cohen B et al. The epidemiology of measles in England and Wales since the 1994 vaccination campaign. *Commun Dis Rep CDR Rev* (in press).

Table 6.6: New cases of selected conditions reported by NHS genito-urinary medicine clinics by age (in years), England, 1995

Condition	Sex	All ages	Under 16	16-19	20-24	25-34	35-44	45 and over	Estimated median age
Infectious syphilis*	M	107	1	2	13	38	26	27	34
	F	30	0	2	8	13	3	4	28
Post-pubertal uncomplicated gonorrhoea	M	6619	37	663	1681	3150	821	267	27
	F	3343	128	994	1109	899	171	42	22
Post-pubertal uncomplicated Chlamydia	M	12672	42	1126	4200	5703	1256	345	26
	F	16431	378	4711	6253	4230	699	160	22
Herpes simplex - first attack	M	5902	12	266	1348	2731	1017	528	29
	F	9141	121	1580	2827	3167	992	454	25
Wart virus infection - first attack	M	26213	86	1714	8928	11064	2967	1454	27
	F	25047	450	6427	9160	6470	1705	835	23

*Primary and secondary syphilis only.

Source: Form KC60

(d)   Viral hepatitis

Data on viral hepatitis given below are obtained through the voluntary confidential reporting by laboratories of confirmed cases to the PHLS Communicable Disease Surveillance Centre (CDSC).

Hepatitis A

The incidence of hepatitis A infections fluctuates, the most recent peak being in 1990 when 7,248 cases were reported to the CDSC for England. Reports have decreased in each of the six successive years, with 1,024 reports being received in 1996 (see Figure 6.6). Most cases of hepatitis A infection seen in England are acquired in the UK and while most are sporadic, outbreaks do occur. However, a history of travel abroad in the six weeks before the onset of illness was recorded in 157 (15%) of cases reported to the CDSC in 1996.

Hepatitis B

Reports of acute hepatitis B in England peaked in 1984 with 1,889 reports, and subsequently fell (see Figure 6.7). The CDSC received reports of 532 cases in 1996. Information about exposure risk was available in 366 (69%) cases; of these, 44% were likely to have acquired infection as a result of injecting drug use, 24% as a result of sexual intercourse between men and women, and 16% as a result of sexual intercourse between men. In the last four years there has been a fall in reports related to sex between men, but a rise in reports among IDUs. Much acute hepatitis B is subclinical, not diagnosed and hence not reported.

Hepatitis C

Hepatitis C infection infrequently produces an acute symptomatic illness with jaundice, and hence very few incident cases are diagnosed. Some 80% of those infected become carriers of the virus. Evidence of infection is detected by testing for antibodies to the virus, although such tests do not distinguish between previous resolved infection and established chronic infection. Laboratory reports of the presence of antibodies to hepatitis C received by the CDSC for England increased from 27 in 1991 to 1,911 in 1996. This rise is consistent with the increasing frequency of testing during that period. During the year, the Department commissioned work to look at the feasibility of using the unlinked anonymous serosurvey samples to determine and monitor prevalence of hepatitis C as well as HIV infection. In addition, £1 million were made available for research projects to study the prevalence, modes of transmission and natural history of hepatitis C.

Figure 6.6 : *Reports of hepatitis A to CDSC, England, 1980-96*

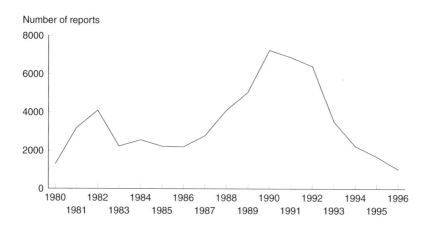

Source: PHLS, CDSC

Figure 6.7: *Reports of hepatitis B to CDSC (all reports and reports in injecting drug users), England, 1980-96*

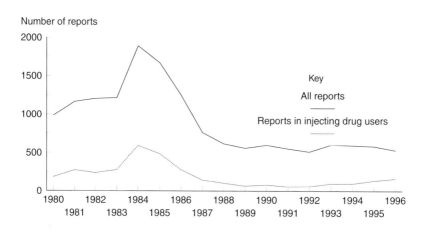

Source: PHLS, CDSC

Hepatitis E

Hepatitis E is spread by the faecal-oral route, and large outbreaks have occurred in some endemic areas in association with faecally contaminated drinking water. The virus is not endemic in the UK. In 1996, the CDSC received reports of 48 cases for England; in the 47 for which information was available, all were associated with a history of recent travel abroad to endemic areas, mainly the Indian sub-Continent. No cases of secondary spread within the UK were reported. In outbreaks in endemic areas, hepatitis E has been associated with high mortality rates among infected pregnant women, and there is currently no vaccine against hepatitis E.

(e)   Influenza

Influenza followed its usual pattern of seasonal winter increases associated with considerable morbidity, and evolving changes in the circulating viruses. Clinical illness continued to be monitored by the Royal College of General Practitioners' Research Unit in Birmingham from data supplied by sentinel practices across the country. Virological surveillance by the PHLS incorporates analysis of routine samples and a structured surveillance scheme in general practice.

The winter 1995-96 influenza season, which had peaked in the first week of December 1995, ended early in the new year with general practitioner (GP) consultation rates for new episodes of influenza-like illness back to baseline levels (less than 50/100,000 population per week) by the end of January 1996. Clinical influenza increased again towards the end of December 1996; a sharp increase in total deaths and in deaths from respiratory causes was attributed to a combination of influenza, other respiratory viruses, including respiratory syncytial virus, and a spell of extremely cold weather.

At the beginning of the year, $A(H_3N_2)$ viruses predominated, but had been largely replaced by $A(H_1N_1)$ isolates towards the end of the 1995-96 season. All were covered by the vaccine. Elsewhere in the world, a significant antigenic drift in H_3N_2 viruses led the World Health Organization (WHO) to recommend a change in this component of the vaccine for 1996-97 to an A/Wuhan/359/95-like strain. The change proved correct - most of the viruses isolated in the UK later in the year were $A(H_3N_2)$ subtypes related to the vaccine strain.

The UK continues a selective influenza immunisation policy aimed to immunise people of any age with conditions which predispose them to serious illness from influenza - especially those with chronic heart, respiratory or renal disease, diabetes mellitus or immunosuppression due to disease or treatment. Doctors were reminded of this policy in May[1] and again in September[2]. Two information leaflets for patients - *'Flu vaccination*[3] and *What should I do about 'flu?*[4] were

produced, and a press conference, run jointly with the Association for Influenza
Monitoring and Surveillance, launched Influenza Awareness Week in October.
In Autumn 1996, 6.2 million doses of influenza vaccine were distributed - the
highest number ever.

References

1.   Department of Health. Influenza immunisation. *CMO's Update* 1996; **10**: 7.
2.   Department of Health. *Influenza immunisation.* London: Department of Health, 1996
     (Professional Letter: PL/CMO(96)7).
3.   Department of Health. *'Flu vaccination.* Wetherby (West Yorkshire): Department of Health,
     1996.
4.   Department of Health. *What should I do about 'flu?* Wetherby (West Yorkshire): Department
     of Health, 1996.

(f)   Meningitis

During 1996, the previously reported increase in cases of meningococcal
infection continued - exceeding the total for 1995, itself the highest for 50 years.

Table 6.7 shows the numbers of cases of meningococcal disease (meningitis and
septicaemia) reported to the Office for National Statistics (ONS) and to the
Meningococcal Reference Unit (MRU) between 1989 and 1996. The change to a
higher proportion of cases reported as septicaemia continues. The total
provisional number of deaths in 1996 was 234, higher than in 1989, the last peak
year. The overall case-fatality rate is stable, but the rate for meningococcal
septicaemia continues to fall - which may reflect a change in reporting practice,
with more cases being reported as septicaemic[1].

In October, DH information on meningococcal infection, in advance of the start
of the 'meningococcal season', was supplemented by a Health Education

Table 6.7: *Notifications of meningitis to the Office for National Statistics
(ONS) and the Meningococcal Reference Unit, England and Wales,
1989-96*

Year	Notifications to ONS			MRU reports
	Meningitis	Septicaemia	Total	
1989	1133	229	1362	1354
1990	1138	277	1415	1500
1991	1117	273	1390	1405
1992	1067	277	1344	1301
1993	1053	398	1451	1298
1994	938	430	1368	1129
1995	1142	705	1847	1468
1996	1177	1136	2313	1496

Source: ONS and MRU

Authority (HEA) leaflet for students of college age, warning of the early signs and symptoms of meningococcal infection. Demand for the leaflet was high and independent market research indicates that the leaflet was well received.

Reference

1. Ramsay M, Kaczmarski E, Rush M, Mallard R, Farrington P, White J. Changing patterns of case ascertainment and trends in meningococcal disease in England and Wales. *Commun Dis Rep CDR Rev* (in press).

(g)   Tuberculosis

Notifications of, and deaths from, tuberculosis continued at levels similar to those of the last three years. 5,654 cases of tuberculosis were notified in England and Wales during 1996, compared with 5,608 in 1995 and 5,591 in 1994; 420 deaths were attributed to tuberculosis.

The first two reports on the prevention and control of tuberculosis in the UK from the Inter-Departmental Working Group on Tuberculosis (IDWGTB) were issued in July. The first, on recommendations for the prevention and control of tuberculosis at local level[1], outlines the aims of national policy:

- to halt and reverse the recent rise in incidence of tuberculosis in the UK;

- to reduce avoidable mortality associated with this disease;

- to minimise morbidity and the transmission of infection by early diagnosis and effective treatment; *and*

- to prevent the emergence of drug-resistant tuberculosis.

This report identifies co-ordination of the many measures required to achieve these aims as a key element in a successful local policy. The second report, *Tuberculosis and homeless people*[2], concentrates on the particular problems associated with the control of tuberculosis in this population group.

Drug resistance in isolates of mycobacteria submitted to the PHLS Mycobacterial Reference Laboratories continues to be monitored through the UK Mycobacterial Resistance Network. Although overall levels remain very low, they have increased, and a second outbreak of multidrug-resistant tuberculosis, mainly involving HIV-infected patients, occurred in a London hospital. The expert working group of the IDWGTB, established at the end of 1995 to prepare more detailed guidance on the prevention of transmission of HIV-related and drug-resistant tuberculosis, completed a draft report for consultation.

The Joint Committee on Vaccination and Immunisation (JCVI) reviewed the current epidemiology of tuberculosis in the UK and recommended that BCG immunisation of school-age children should continue to be part of national policy[3]. Selective BCG immunisation of neonates at higher risk of exposure to tuberculosis also continues; the JCVI noted that monitoring of this part of the programme needed to be improved.

References

1. Inter-Departmental Working Group on Tuberculosis. *The prevention and control of tuberculosis at local level.* London: Department of Health, Welsh Office, 1996.
2. Inter-Departmental Working Group on Tuberculosis. *Tuberculosis and homeless people.* London: Department of Health, Welsh Office, 1996.
3. Department of Health. *Tuberculosis: two reports of the Inter-Departmental Working Group on Tuberculosis.* Leeds: Department of Health, 1996 (Executive Letter: EL(96)51).

(h)   Hospital-acquired infection

The number of patients affected by methicillin-resistant *Staphylococcus aureus* (MRSA) increased in 1996. During the year, the PHLS recorded 2,107 incidents involving three or more people in the same hospital who were colonised or infected with the same strain within a month, compared with 1,616 in 1995. Most of these incidents involved the epidemic (EMRSA) strains 15 and 16. The proportion of bloodstream infections with *Staph. aureus* reported to be due to MRSA also rose, to 13%. Revision of the clinical guidelines on the control of MRSA, which were published in 1990[1] and are endorsed by DH[2], was taken forward during the year, and a new version is expected to be issued in 1997.

In May, the Department issued a package of guidance on MRSA in the community[3], which included leaflets for managers of nursing and residential homes and health service and local authority staff responsible for their registration, and emphasised that people colonised or infected with MRSA can safely be cared for in community settings. This guidance addressed the concerns of health and social care staff in the community that the spread of MRSA in hospitals might pose a risk to their patients, which in some places has led to inappropriate delay in hospital discharge of people colonised by MRSA. The package also included guidance on general infection control measures in nursing and residential homes.

Laboratory reports of *Clostridium difficile*-associated diarrhoea rose steadily from about 3,000 in 1992 to over 11,000 in 1996[4]. Improved ascertainment accounts for some, but probably not all, of this increase. The great majority of cases were hospital inpatients, and three-quarters were aged over 65 years. The risk is much higher in patients who have received broad-spectrum antibiotics in the preceding month. DH/PHLS guidance stresses that avoidance of inappropriate antibiotic usage and efforts to control the spread of infection are the most important preventive measures[5].

In late 1995, the Department funded the PHLS to establish a Nosocomial Infection National Surveillance Scheme (NINSS). By the end of 1996, pilot studies of the first two modules of the scheme - for bloodstream and surgical wound infections - were under way. This scheme will become fully operational in 1997, and will provide participating hospitals with comparative data on infection rates from other (anonymised) hospitals to assist them to target preventive efforts and to investigate rates which seem disproportionately high.

The topic of communicable disease and infection control, in hospitals and in the community alike, was included as a new baseline requirement in the NHS planning and priorities guidance, issued in June[6].

References

1. Hospital Infection Society, British Society for Antimicrobial Chemotherapy. Revised guidelines for the control of epidemic methicillin-resistant *Staphylococcus aureus:* report of a combined working party of the Hospital Infection Society and the British Society for Antimicrobial Chemotherapy. *J Hosp Infect* 1990; **16:** 351-77.
2. Department of Health. *Improving the effectiveness of the NHS.* London: Department of Health, 1994 (Executive Letter: EL(94)74).
3. Department of Health. *Methicillin-resistant Staphylococcus aureus in community settings.* London: Department of Health, 1996 (Professional Letter: PL/CMO(96)3, PL/CNO(96)1, CI(96)12).
4. Public Health Laboratory Service. Clostridium difficile. *CDR Weekly Commun Dis Rep* 1997; **7:** 34.
5. Department of Health. *The prevention and management of Clostridium difficile infection.* London: Department of Health, 1994 (Professional Letter: PL/CO(94)4).
6. NHS Executive. *NHS priorities and planning guidance: 1997/98.* Leeds: Department of Health, 1996 (Executive Letter: EL(96)45).

(i)   Emerging and re-emerging infectious diseases

Established diseases such as malaria, tuberculosis, cholera and, now, HIV/AIDS, continue to represent the main causes of morbidity from communicable disease world wide, and showed no signs of abating in 1996.

Nonetheless, concern continued to focus on international preparedness to detect and to respond to challenges posed by new and re-emergent infectious diseases. The EU further discussed a proposal to create a European network for the surveillance and response to communicable diseases; a Task Force was established to create an early warning surveillance and response system for communicable diseases between the EU and the United States of America (USA). Three working groups were established to look at surveillance, research and training, and capacity building, and will work closely with the WHO. The WHO began work to revise the International Health Regulations.

Incidents of note during 1996 included two outbreaks of Ebola haemorrhagic fever in Gabon in February and in October (the latter included a physician in South Africa who had been working in the infected area), and an outbreak of Lassa fever, mainly affecting adolescent females, in an endemic area of Sierra Leone. Several African countries in and adjacent to the recognised 'meningitis belt' reported large outbreaks of meningococcal infection, and malaria increased in southern Africa following heavy rains. After many years without polio transmission, an outbreak of paralytic poliomyelitis occurred in Albania. An outbreak of typhoid fever occurred in Tajikistan. An outbreak of *Escherichia coli* O157 (VTEC) infection occurred among schoolchildren in Japan and outbreaks of this infection also occurred in the UK. In the UK, cases of a new variant of Creutzfeldt-Jakob disease (nvCJD) with a distinct pathology were a cause of concern (see page 239)[1]. However, the diphtheria epidemic in the Russian Federation showed signs of having reached a plateau.

Reference

1.   Will RG, Ironside JW, Zeidler M et al. A new variant of Creutzfeldt-Jakob disease in the UK. Lancet 1996; **347:** 921-5.

(j)   Travel-related disease

Malaria

Cases of imported malaria reported to the PHLS Malaria Reference Laboratory from the UK increased by just over 20% from the 1995 figure to 2,500 cases; there were 11 deaths. The greatest increases were in vivax malaria from Asia and falciparum malaria among travellers to southern Africa, where higher than expected malaria transmission rates followed heavy rains.

Mefloquine, the recommended antimalarial drug of first choice for travellers to most of sub-Saharan Africa[1], was the subject of media publicity. The controversy surrounded the adverse reactions attributed to mefloquine, which include depression, headache, anxiety and panic reactions, and occasionally more severe neuropsychiatric reactions, in relation to its undoubted efficacy as an antimalarial against most chloroquine-resistant falciparum malaria. The Medicines Control Agency (MCA) and the Committee on Safety of Medicines (CSM) have carefully monitored the safety of mefloquine since it was authorised in 1989. In the light of accumulating experience, the product information for

'Lariam' has been amended on five occasions to provide more extensive information for doctors and patients on its use and safety. Information on the safety of mefloquine was also published in May[2] and July[3]. The PHLS Malaria Reference Laboratory convened a meeting of experts to review the guidelines for malaria prophylaxis for travellers from the UK; their report is expected in 1997.

Other travel-related infections

One hundred and fifty seven cases of hepatitis A (15% of reported cases) were reported as travel-related, as were 47 of the 48 reported cases of hepatitis E. There were 175 notified cases of typhoid fever and 32 notifications of cholera.

Ninety-six of the 200 reported cases of legionnaires' disease in England and Wales were possibly or probably acquired abroad. Following a review of the response to recent outbreaks of legionnaires' disease associated with accommodation abroad, the travel industry introduced a check-list for good management of water systems for use by resort staff.

References

1. Bradley DJ, Warhust DC. Malaria prophylaxis: guidelines for travellers from Britain. *BMJ* 1995; **310:** 709-14.
2. Department of Health. Mefloquine for malaria prophylaxis. *CMO's Update* 1996; **10:** 5.
3. Committee on Safety of Medicines. Malaria (Lariam) prophylaxis and neuropsychiatric reactions. *Curr Probl Pharmacovigilance* 1996; **22:** 6

(k)   Microbiological risk assessment

Microbiological risk assessment (MRA) underpins the Department's work on infectious disease hazards. The Advisory Committee on Dangerous Pathogens' (ACDP's) detailed consideration of the issue, in *Microbiological risk assessment: an interim report*[1] recognised that a structured approach to the assessment of risk would aid the decision-making process and provide a clear record of how and why decisions were made. The report makes recommendations to encourage the development and application of microbiological risk assessment and highlights many practical applications - for example, in assessing the risks from foodborne pathogens. As part of the Department's continuing work in this area, the ACDP hosted a seminar on microbiological risk assessment to stimulate scientific debate and help to identify future priorities.

Reference

1. Advisory Committee on Dangerous Pathogens. *Microbiological risk assessment: an interim report.* London: HMSO, 1996.

CHAPTER 7

ENVIRONMENTAL HEALTH AND FOOD SAFETY

(a)   Chemical and physical agents in the environment

(i)   Small Area Health Statistics Unit

The Small Area Health Statistics Unit (SAHSU) is funded by Government to investigate claims of unusual clusters of disease or ill-health in the vicinity of point sources of pollution from chemicals and/or radiation, such as industrial installations[1,2]. The SAHSU was originally based at the London School of Hygiene and Tropical Medicine but, in April 1996, it transferred to the Imperial College School of Medicine at St Mary's Hospital.

During 1996, the SAHSU published a study of cancer incidence near municipal solid waste incinerators, field work for which was completed in 1995[3]; the results were reassuring, although a small, probably artifactual, raised incidence of liver cancer is being investigated further[4]. A study of cancer incidence and mortality around the Pan Britannia Industries pesticide manufacturing site at Waltham Abbey, Hertfordshire, found only limited and inconsistent evidence for a local excess of cancer near the site. Publication of the results of this study, and of studies of leukaemia incidence near high-power radio transmitters and of angiosarcoma of the liver near vinyl chloride sites, is anticipated in 1997.

(ii)   Air pollution

A sub-group of the Committee on the Medical Effects of Air Pollutants (COMEAP) has been established to estimate more precisely the effects of air pollutants on health in the United Kingdom (UK). During the past seven years, the COMEAP and its predecessor, the Advisory Group on the Medical Aspects of Air Pollution Episodes (MAAPE), have extensively investigated the possible effects of air pollution on health. However, it remains difficult precisely to estimate the number of people who may be affected annually, and extrapolation of data on air pollution and health from studies done in other countries may not accurately reflect environmental exposure to air pollution in the UK.

External environmental atmospheric measurements might not be fully representative of the challenges faced; indoor exposure to air pollution may be more important in terms of effects on health than outdoor exposure. The Department of Health (DH) has increased the amount of attention given to potential effects of indoor air pollution and the COMEAP is examining the generation of nitrogen dioxide by gas cookers, and other issues, in collaboration with the Department of the Environment (DoE).

The provision of public information on the effects of air pollutants on health remains a priority: during the year, the COMEAP considered the current Air Quality Banding System and, in collaboration with the DoE, proposed some revisions. Particles require special attention: as reported in *Non-biological particles and health*[5], there is no clear threshold of effect, and no completely safe level of exposure can be defined.

The Expert Panel on Air Quality Standards has continued to recommend standards for air pollutants. In November, the Panel recommended a standard of 150 parts per 1,000 million (ppb) for nitrogen dioxide, measured as an hourly average concentration, and that further research was required and should be reviewed to set a longer-term standard[6].

Findings of a public consultation on the UK National Air Quality Strategy, undertaken by the DoE, will be published in Spring 1997 (see page 24).

(iii)   *Radiation*

During 1996, work continued on the revision of guidance to health authorities and National Health Service (NHS) Trusts on the arrangements needed to deal with the consequences of accidents involving radioactivity. In October, this guidance was issued as a chapter in the revision of the handbook *Emergency planning in the NHS: health services arrangements for dealing with major incidents*[7,8]. Contributions to the revision were provided by the National Radiological Protection Board, and by a Departmental expert working group.

The revised guidance sets out the planning background and the responsibilities of Government Departments and health authorities in the event of a radiological emergency, and possible counter-measures that can be taken. It includes updated guidance on distribution and pre-distribution of stable iodine tablets in the event of a nuclear accident, and on arrangements to deal with radiation casualties and to arrange radiation monitoring for members of the public.

The revised chapter forms part of the first phase of the revision of the *Emergency Planning Handbook*[8]. Further work will be carried out on the content and layout of the chapter during the second phase of the *Handbook's* revision. DH arrangements are tested on a regular basis in emergency exercises led by other Government Departments.

(iv)   *Environment and health*

DH continued to advise other Government Departments on health implications of chemicals in the environment in support of policy development and regulatory activity by those Departments. The Medical Research Council (MRC) Institute for Environment and Health has carried out a number of projects on public health aspects of chemicals in the environment for DH and the DoE.

A major action agreed in the World Health Organization's (WHO's) environmental health action plan for Europe (EHAPE) was that each country would prepare its own national environmental health action plan (NEHAP). The UK NEHAP was published in July[9] following public consultation, which had led to an extensive revision of the original draft document, including the addition of a chapter on noise. The final document sets out a range of over 150 actions, across the spectrum of environmental health, to remedy identified problems or to secure further improvements; these establish the means to achieve the objectives of the EHAPE and of WHO's 'Health for All' targets.

The European Environment and Health Committee (EEHC), chaired by the Chief Medical Officer, met twice during 1996. The UK Government agreed to host the third Ministerial Conference on Environment and Health in London in June 1999. The EEHC, as well as discussing wider or transboundary issues of environment and health, acts as the steering committee for the London conference. During the year, Member States were canvassed on topics for the London conference to support the theme of implementation of environmental health action plans, as a first step in planning the programme of the conference.

(v)   *Surveillance of diseases possibly due to non-infectious environmental hazards*

The monitoring of non-infectious diseases is not as extensive as that for communicable diseases. During the year, DH, in consultation with the NHS, developed its arrangements for a consistent local response to chemical emergencies, and for the local surveillance and reporting of health effects of chemicals in the environment. After a preliminary study and consultation[10], it was concluded that local arrangements should be strengthened through support from specialist provider units, and that a new national co-ordinating focus for this work should be commissioned. In December, the Department appointed the Welsh Combined Centres for Public Health to provide the national Focus for work on response to chemical incidents and surveillance of health effects of chemicals in the environment. The Focus will take on and develop a central and co-ordinating role on the response to chemical incidents, and will also support the NHS in the national surveillance of health effects of ambient levels of chemicals in the environment, promote suitable training in these areas, and promote consistency of response and approach.

References

1. Department of Health. *On the State of the Public Health: the annual report of the Chief Medical Officer of the Department of Health for the year 1991.* London: HMSO, 1992; 152.
2. Department of Health. *On the State of the Public Health: the annual report of the Chief Medical Officer of the Department of Health for the year 1994.* London: HMSO, 1995; 192.
3. Department of Health. *On the State of the Public Health: the annual report of the Chief Medical Officer of the Department of Health for the year 1995.* London: HMSO, 1996; 184.
4. Elliott P, Shaddick G, Kleinschmidt I, et al. Cancer incidence near municipal solid waste incinerators in Great Britain. *Br J Cancer* 1996; **73:** 702-10.
5. Committee on the Medical Effects of Air Pollutants. *Non-biological particles and health.* London, HMSO, 1995. Chair: Professor Stephen Holgate.
6. Department of the Environment Expert Panel on Air Quality Standards. *Nitrogen dioxide.* London: HMSO, 1996. Chair: Professor Anthony Seaton.
7. NHS Executive. *Emergency planning in the NHS: health services arrangements for dealing with major incidents.* Wetherby (West Yorkshire): Department of Health, 1996 (Executive Letter: EL(96)79).
8. NHS Management Executive. *Emergency planning in the NHS: health services arrangements for dealing with major incidents.* London: Department of Health, 1990.
9. Department of the Environment, Department of Health. *United Kingdom national environmental health action plan.* London: HMSO, 1996.
10. Department of Health. *On the State of the Public Health: the annual report of the Chief Medical Officer of the Department of Health for the year 1995.* London: HMSO, 1996; 186-7.

(b)   Food safety

(i)   Foodborne and waterborne diseases

Foodborne diseases

Provisional figures from the Office for National Statistics (ONS) show that there were 83,233 reported cases of food poisoning in England and Wales in 1996 (formally notified and ascertained by other means) (see Table 7.1). Although this figure represents a small rise of about 1.5% on the 1995 figure of 82,041, for the second year in a row the figures have not shown the striking upward trend seen in 1992-94.

The number of laboratory reports of human faecal *Salmonella* isolations has remained fairly constant over the past six years, with around 30,000 recorded annually. The number of *Salmonella enteritidis* isolates increased in 1996 by 14% compared with 1995, of which *Salmonella enteritidis* phage type 4 (PT4) increased by 6%. Laboratory reports of *Salmonella typhimurium* fell by 17%, although *Salmonella typhimurium* definitive type 104 (DT104) showed a rise of 2%. The number of cases of infection due to *Listeria monocytogenes* remained low, and a further slight fall was seen in the incidence of *Campylobacter*

Table 7.1: *Food poisoning: reports to the Office for National Statistics, England and Wales, 1982-96*

Year	Total*
1982	14253
1983	17735
1984	20702
1985	19242
1986	23948
1987	29331
1988	39713
1989	52557
1990	52145
1991	52543
1992	63347
1993	68587
1994	81833
1995	82041
1996	83233**

* Statutorily notified to ONS and ascertained by other means.
**Provisional.

Source: ONS

infection. The number of faecal isolations of verocytotoxin-producing *Escherichia coli* (VTEC) O157 fell by 16% compared with 1995, although the 1995 figure (792) was much higher than in earlier years.

Campylobacter enteritis

Campylobacter remains the most commonly isolated bacterium associated with acute gastro-enteritis in human beings. There was a 3.5% fall in the number of laboratory-confirmed faecal isolates reported to the Communicable Disease Surveillance Centre (CDSC) - 42,345 in 1996 compared with 43,902 in 1995.

Salmonellosis

In 1996, the number of isolates of *Salmonella* from human beings in England and Wales recorded on the Public Health Laboratory Service (PHLS) Salmonella Data Set was provisionally 29,111, compared with 29,314 in 1995 (see Table 7.2).

Salmonella enteritidis PT4 continues to be the commonest phage type to cause human salmonellosis in England and Wales: in 1996, provisionally, there were 13,184 cases reported, compared with 12,482 in 1995. The second most prevalent *Salmonella* to cause human infection is *Salmonella typhimurium* DT104: in 1996, provisionally, there were 3,821 reported cases compared with 3,746 in 1995. About 95% of *Salmonella typhimurium* DT104 are resistant to a number of antibiotics. The Advisory Committee on the Microbiological Safety of Food (ACMSF) has set up a working group to consider antibiotic-resistant micro-organisms in relation to food safety (see page 206).

Table 7.2: *Salmonella in human beings, England and Wales, January to December (inclusive), 1995 and 1996*

Serotype	1995		1996*	
	Total cases	Imported cases	Total cases	Imported cases
S. enteritidis				
Phage type 4	12482	950	13184	754
Other phage types	3562	670	5112	743
S. typhimurium				
Definitive type 104	3746	128	3821	117
Other definitive types	2997	298	1752	240
Other serotypes	6341	1378	5015	1161
Others untyped	186	35	227	33
Total	*29314*	*3459*	*29111*	*3048*

*1996 data provisional.

Source: PHLS Salmonella Data Set

Verocytotoxin-producing Escherichia coli (VTEC)

During 1996, there were provisionally 660 laboratory reports of faecal isolates of VTEC O157 in England and Wales, compared with 792 in 1995 - a fall of nearly 17%. This figure still represents a considerable increase on the 1994 figure (411), the rise being partly explained by rapid implementation of the ACMSF's recommendation that all diarrhoeal stool specimens should be examined for VTEC O157[1].

Listeria

Cases of human listeriosis in England and Wales continue to be reported at a low level: during 1996, there were 116 reported cases, compared with 91 in 1995.

Advisory Committee on the Microbiological Safety of Food (ACMSF)

The ACMSF published its report on poultry meat in January[2]. The report made recommendations aimed to reduce pathogen carriage rates throughout the poultry meat supply chain. The Committee's working groups on foodborne viral infections and on microbial antibiotic resistance in foodborne pathogens hope to report by Spring 1998.

Developments in food surveillance

The ACMSF has the responsibility to advise the Government on its microbiological food surveillance programme, and the Microbiological Food

Surveillance Group (MFSG) co-ordinates relevant work undertaken by DH, other Government Departments, the PHLS and the local authorities' co-ordinating body on food and trading standards. The MFSG, which includes representatives from industry and research institutions, held two meetings in 1996. The Group's food microbiological surveillance strategy and future work programme were endorsed by the ACMSF in May.

An Epidemiology of Foodborne Infections Group has been established in parallel with the MFSG. The objective of this new Group is to collate and assess available information on animal and human infections, and to advise on the need for action where necessary.

The ACMSF VTEC report[1], published in 1995, made several research and surveillance recommendations and, following an open competition, DH funded 13 proposals in a programme of work in this area. A two-day meeting with the ACMSF was held in November to review DH-funded work in relation to research and surveillance recommendations in an interim report on *Campylobacter*[3]. The Department has developed a microbiological food safety surveillance and research strategy, to be published in 1997.

The Department is also funding a major study of Infectious Intestinal Disease (IID) in England. Microbiological work was completed in Spring 1996; analysis of epidemiological and microbiological data will continue into 1997, with the final report expected to be published by the end of that year.

A small focus group on food microbiology has been established to improve the communication between and to co-ordinate the activities of DH, the Ministry of Agriculture, Fisheries and Food (MAFF) and the PHLS. This group held its first meeting in September.

Waterborne diseases

Five outbreaks of cryptosporidiosis were reported: three were associated with drinking water, one strongly and the other two probably associated. No other outbreaks of waterborne disease were reported.

Five outbreaks of gastro-enteritis associated with molluscan shellfish were reported, all associated with oysters. An aetiological agent was identified in two outbreaks: astrovirus was found in one, and small round structured viruses (SRSVs) in the other.

Following the drought of 1995, advice on issues to be addressed to protect public health during cuts to water supplies was sent to all water companies and directors of public health from the Chief Medical Officer.

(ii) Food hazard management

The Food Incident Team investigated 144 food incidents reported through UK and European Union (EU) networks. Food Hazard Warnings were issued on 19 occasions, where a wider or more serious risk to public health was identified.

There were two major food hazard incidents during 1996. One was an attempted extortion in which DH and the Police, in a co-ordinated operation, prevented the threatened contamination with micro-organisms of several food products.

The other incident concerned a UK cheese producer, some of whose farm cheese production was contaminated with *Salmonella gold-coast*. Careful investigation of the source and extent of contamination was required to assist the dairy company with product withdrawal and the subsequent production and release of independently analysed cheese to ensure the protection of public health.

(iii) Biotechnology and novel foods

Although a small number of genetically modified (GM) foods have been on sale in the UK for some time, during the year the imminent importation of GM soya and maize into the UK led to widespread public health debate on the safety of such foods.

The safety of a wide range of novel foods, including GM foods, is assessed by the Advisory Committee on Novel Foods and Processes (ACNFP), an independent expert committee that advises Government Ministers. In recent years, the ACNFP has evaluated an increasing number of GM foods, a trend that continued in 1996. The Committee evaluated a range of processed food products derived from GM crops such as oilseed rape, maize and cottonseed which had been genetically modified to confer resistance to certain herbicides or insect pests. The ACNFP also recommended food safety clearance for riboflavin (vitamin B_2) derived from a GM bacterium, *Bacillus subtilis*.

The ACNFP also evaluated a number of non-GM novel foods - including guarana, an extract from the South American shrub *Paullinia cupana* which is used in a range of drinks and as an infusate, and green tea extract for use in table-top sweeteners.

(iv) Toxicological food safety

Chemical contaminants and infant feeding

The presence of potentially harmful chemicals in the human diet is always a matter of public health concern, which may be heightened further if there are raised concentrations of such chemicals in the diet of infants. During the year, the Committee on Toxicity of Chemicals in Food, Consumer Products and the Environment (COT) reviewed the toxicity of certain compounds which are oestrogenic and found in human diets. Two classes of compounds were specifically examined - the phthalic acid diesters (phthalates) and phytoestrogens; chemicals of both classes have been detected in infant milk formulas[4,5,6].

Phthalates, members of a group of organic chemicals with various industrial uses, are common environmental contaminants. An in-vivo rodent study had indicated that pre-natal and postnatal exposure to one particular compound might affect testicular development[7]. During its review, the COT noted the problems of using the results of a study in rodents to assess risks to human beings, but considered that phthalates in milk formulas were unlikely to pose a risk to the health of infants. The COT endorsed the action taken to trace the sources of phthalates identified in infant formulas.

Phytoestrogens are chemicals, present in plants, of two main structural classes - isoflavones and coumestans - which can affect fertility in experimental animals. Consumption of isoflavones associated with soy proteins will occur in populations where soya products are regularly eaten. Although they may have some beneficial effects, soy isoflavones have been shown to affect the menstrual cycle. Because of the possibility that they might adversely affect the sexual development of infants, the COT endorsed DH advice that breast milk and cows' milk formulas are the preferred sources of nutrition for infants. However, if parents have been advised by a health professional to use soy-based formulas they should continue to do so[6,8].

Naturally-occurring toxicants

Plants can produce a wide variety of toxic compounds. As well as on phytoestrogens, the COT provided advice on other natural toxicants which had been considered in a report prepared by the MAFF Working Party on Naturally Occurring Toxicants in Food[8]. The compounds reviewed included glycoalkaloids of potatoes, furocoumarins of parsnips or celery and natural hydrazine derivatives found in mushrooms.

Traditional and herbal remedies

The final results of a project to investigate adverse health effects arising from the use of traditional remedies or dietary supplements became available during the year[9], and were announced in October[10]. The project was carried out on behalf of DH and the MAFF by the Medical Toxicology Unit of Guy's and St Thomas' Hospital Trust, London. The project involved the investigation of inquiries which were made to the Unit about cases that appeared to involve either herbal preparations or food supplements.

During the five years in which the project ran, the majority of cases were associated with the use of herbal preparations rather than with dietary supplements. It was rarely feasible to assign more than a 'possible' causal relation to the association of any preparation and any symptoms (including one case where the use of Chinese herbal medicines was associated with liver problems). Cases in which a causal relation was 'probable' included allergic reactions to bee products, flushing from a herbal stimulant and hair darkening from a rejuvenating product.

Allergy and food intolerance

The possibility of a person having an allergy to a constituent of food is well recognised. In extreme cases, individuals may suffer a fatal anaphylactic reaction on exposure to the food item to which they are sensitive. Mechanisms not involving allergy and the immune system may result in less specific symptoms associated with food intolerance. In a new departure, during 1996 the COT decided to form working groups to study the topics of peanut allergy and of food intolerance in general; these two groups will include COT members and outside experts, and will report back to the COT.

(v)   Pesticides

The new European Union (EU) system for authorisation of plant protection products, established by Directive 91/414/EEC[11], requires that all existing active ingredients used in pesticides and approved under national legislation be reviewed on an EU-wide basis. The evaluation stage of this process began in 1992. The first eight evaluations, including four produced by the UK, were discussed by a series of EU working groups in the latter part of 1996; monographs on some 75 other active ingredients are in various stages of preparation.

The Advisory Committee on Pesticides (ACP) was asked to review the standards applied when approving pesticides for non-commercial use. It was agreed that a slightly more flexible approach was required than for commercial usages, with greater emphasis on risk assessment and risk management for pesticide products used in the home or garden. Full details of the ACP's recommendations will be published in 1997, and there will be public consultation before any proposed revisions to the approvals rules are made.

A second edition of the booklet, *Pesticide poisoning: notes for the guidance of general practitioners*[12], was published by the Department and distributed to general practices and some other clinicians in April. It gives a concise summary of the clinical effects of pesticides, guidance on first aid, sources of further advice and arrangements for reporting pesticide incidents.

A survey of organochlorine residues in human milk samples by Working Party on Pesticide Residues was started in 1996. The first survey of this type was conducted in 1963, and human milk samples have since been monitored at approximately five-yearly intervals. Many organochlorines are no longer permitted for use in the UK and previous surveys have shown downward trends in the concentrations of these compounds in human fat and milk. This latest survey will measure current levels of these compounds in human milk samples taken throughout the UK.

(vi)   Veterinary products

Organophosphate sheep dips

On 21 March, the Veterinary Products Committee (VPC) undertook its latest review of organophosphate (OP) sheep dips. The safety of OP sheep dips was further discussed by the VPC's Medical and Scientific Panel in December, in the context of recently published research. DH continued to contribute to the funding of epidemiological research into the health of those who dip sheep, carried out by the Institute of Occupational Medicine.

On 29 October, the Chief Medical Officer wrote to the Presidents of the Royal Colleges of Physicians and Psychiatrists to express support for the establishment by the medical Royal Colleges of a Working Group to draw up guidance on the management of people who attribute ill-health to exposure to OP sheep dip. It is anticipated that the Working Group will first convene in 1997, and will meet representatives of those affected.

Other veterinary products

The Department provided advice to the MAFF Food Science Division, the Veterinary Medicines Directorate and the European Medicines Evaluation Agency on human safety aspects of veterinary medicines and materials in animal feedstuffs. DH also provided advice on human safety considerations for European authorisations of drugs and the setting of acceptable daily intakes (ADIs) and maximum residue limits (MRLs) for pharmacologically active ingredients by the Committee on Veterinary Medicinal Products, under EU legislation, and provided advice on human safety aspects of European approvals of micro-organisms and enzymes used in animal feedstuffs.

The Appraisal Panel for Human Suspected Adverse Reactions to Veterinary Medicines and the Advisory Group on Veterinary Residues continued to advise the VPC on human adverse reactions to veterinary products and the monitoring of residues of veterinary drugs in foods, respectively.

References

1. Advisory Committee on the Microbiological Safety of Food. *Report on verocytotoxin-producing Escherichia coli.* London: HMSO, 1995.
2. Advisory Committee on the Microbiological Safety of Food. *Report on poultry meat.* London: HMSO, 1996.
3. Advisory Committee on the Microbiological Safety of Food. *Interim report on Campylobacter.* London: HMSO, 1993.
4. Ministry of Agriculture, Fisheries and Food. *Phthalates in food.* London: Ministry of Agriculture, Fisheries and Food, 1996 (Food Surveillance Information Sheet no. 82).
5. Ministry of Agriculture, Fisheries and Food. *Phthalates in infant formulae.* London: Ministry of Agriculture, Fisheries and Food, 1996 (Food Surveillance Information Sheet no. 83).
6. Ministry of Agriculture, Fisheries and Food, Department of Health. *Natural toxicants: phytoestrogens in soya based infant formulae.* In: *FAC meeting.* London: Ministry of Agriculture, Fisheries and Food, 1996; 1-2 (Food Safety Information Bulletin no. 75).
7. Sharpe RM, Fisher JS, Millar MM, Jobling S, Sumpter JP. Gestational and lactational exposure of rats to xenoestrogens results in reduced testicular size and sperm production. *Environ Health Perspect* 1995; **103**: 1136-43.
8. Ministry of Agriculture, Fisheries and Food. *Inherent natural toxicants in food: the 51st report of the Steering Group on Chemical Aspects of Food Surveillance.* London: Stationery Office, 1996 (MAFF Food Surveillance Paper no. 51).
9. Shaw D, Kolev S, Leon C, Bell G, Colbridge M, Murray V. *Toxicological problems resulting from exposure to traditional medicines and food supplements.* London: Guy's and St Thomas' Hospital Trust, 1996 (Project no. N2656, 1991-96).
10. Ministry of Agriculture, Fisheries and Food. *Traditional remedies and dietary supplements.* London: Ministry of Agriculture, Fisheries and Food, 1996 (Food Surveillance Information Sheet no. 94).
11. Council of the European Communities. Council directive of 15 July 1991 concerning the placing of plant protection products on the market (91/414/EEC). *Off J Eur Commun* 1991 L230/1: 1-32.
12. Proudfoot A. *Pesticide poisoning: notes for the guidance of medical practitioners (2nd edn).* London: HMSO, 1996.

CHAPTER 8

MEDICAL EDUCATION, TRAINING AND STAFFING

(a)   Junior doctors' hours

The 'New Deal'[1] is an initiative to create better training opportunities for junior doctors, and improved patient care. The final 'New Deal' target date was December 1996. By September, 97% of junior posts had achieved the target for contracted hours. Progress has been slower in meeting the 56-hour ceiling on actual working hours. Overall, 78.4% of junior posts now comply with this target. Although 21,000 junior doctors are working no more than 56 hours a week, other posts - notably house officer and senior house officer (SHO) grades in acute specialties - need further action to reduce long hours and work intensity.

The 'New Deal' is supported by a central budget to create extra doctors and promote local projects; 1,300 extra consultant and staff grade posts have been funded centrally and targeted where they would best help to reduce junior doctors' hours. The cost in 1996/97 alone is £180 million, including new allocations of £15 million. National Health Service (NHS) Trusts have funded another 1,300 doctors from local resources.

As well as this increased funding, 'New Deal' activity has helped to stimulate organisational change - including new working patterns, better team-working and cross-cover, effective skill-mix initiatives across all grades (notably the increase in nurse practitioners), more daytime surgery and other service improvements.

A new system for increasing out-of-hours payments where work intensity remained too high, introduced in April, has helped to identify problems and to encourage action to improve working practices. The Department of Health (DH) continues to work closely with junior doctors themselves to ensure that actual hours of work are monitored accurately, and regional task forces routinely involve junior doctors in the validation of these figures.

Reference

1.   Department of Health. *Hours of work of doctors in training: the new deal.* London: Department of Health, 1991 (Executive Letter: EL(91)82).

(b) Advisory Group on Medical and Dental Education, Training and Staffing, the Specialist Workforce Advisory Group and the Medical Workforce Standing Advisory Committee

The Advisory Group on Medical Education, Training and Staffing (AGMETS), chaired by the Chief Medical Officer, comprises NHS managers, academic and research interests, and representatives of the medical profession. It continued to meet on a regular basis during the year to advise the Department about the development, implementation and monitoring of medical and dental staffing and education policies.

Medium-term planning of the number of higher specialist trainees is the function of the Specialist Workforce Advisory Group (SWAG). The Group's recommendations for a considerable increase of 1,500 higher specialist trainees, particularly in specialties facing recruitment difficulties, were approved by Ministers and announced on 8 March[1] for implementation in 1996/97. At least 300 new specialist registrar (SpR) posts are expected to be created. The remainder of the increase will be achieved by means of converting posts currently occupied by SHOs and visiting registrars into SpR posts. An extra £5.7 million were provided during 1996/97, with available resources being particularly targeted at: accident and emergency medicine, anaesthetics, diagnostic radiology, forensic psychiatry, general surgery, medical oncology, obstetrics and gynaecology, old age psychiatry, paediatrics, palliative medicine, psychiatry (mental illness), radiotherapy (clinical oncology) and urology.

Longer term planning of the medical workforce is undertaken by the Medical Workforce Standing Advisory Committee (MWSAC); its second report[2], published in 1995, recommended an increase of 500 in the annual intake of medical students, to reach 4,970 by the year 2000. Good progress has been made towards the implementation of this recommendation. The Committee has begun to prepare for its third report, due to be published in late 1997: the key issues being assessed include future demand for doctors, the increasing proportion of women doctors in the medical workforce, skill-mix, grade-mix, changes in delivery of care between the primary and secondary sectors, hours of work, retirement patterns, use of overseas doctors and wastage from United Kingdom (UK) medical training.

References

1. NHS Executive. *Specialist Workforce Advisory Group recommendations: higher specialist training numbers 1996/97.* Leeds: Department of Health, 1996 (Executive Letter: EL(96)18).
2. Department of Health Medical Workforce Standing Advisory Committee. *Planning the medical workforce: Medical Workforce Standing Advisory Committee: second report.* London: Department of Health, 1995.

(c)   Postgraduate and specialist medical education

Specialist medical training

Implementation of the reforms of higher specialist medical training in response to the recommendations of the Working Group on Specialist Medical Training (the Calman Report)[1] is being co-ordinated by a Steering Group chaired by Professor John Temple, postgraduate medical dean for the West Midlands. Considerable progress was made to implement these reforms during the year, including the largely administrative process of moving trainees into the new SpR grade. Full implementation will require educational changes to ensure that higher specialist trainees, in addition to acquiring effective clinical skills, are also able to respond to service changes and to develop a wider range of competencies, including team-working and communication skills. The pace at which such changes can be made will have to take account of the capacity of the NHS to absorb the impact of any changes within available resources. Progress in implementing the reforms has been aided by the medical Royal Colleges and Faculties, universities and postgraduate deans, and by consultants, trainees, supervisors, tutors and advisors.

The establishment of the Specialist Training Authority of the medical Royal Colleges (STA) as the competent authority for specialist medical training in the UK was a key component of the European Specialist Medical Qualifications Order 1995[2], which came into force on 12 January 1996. The STA is legally responsible for ensuring that postgraduate medical training in the UK complies with the training requirements stipulated in the European Union's (EU's) Medical Directive, which includes the award of a Certificate of Completion of Specialist Training (CCST) to doctors who have successfully completed a specialist medical training programme. The Order also designates the General Medical Council (GMC) as the UK's competent authority responsible for the mutual recognition arrangements stipulated in the EU Directive, and requires the GMC to maintain and publish the Specialist Register. From 1 January 1997, a doctor must be on the Specialist Register before taking up a substantive or honorary NHS consultant appointment.

Following the successful introduction of the SpR grade in two vanguard specialties (general surgery and diagnostic radiology) in December 1995, a rolling programme to introduce the new grade in all other specialties began on 1 April 1996 - the grade commissioning date. The final group of 14 specialties will begin transition to the new grade on 1 January 1997; when completed, over 12,000 higher specialist trainees in 52 different specialties will have entered the new structured training programmes.

After an extensive consultation exercise with the NHS and discussions with other interested parties, a revised edition of *A guide to specialist registrar training*[3] (the 'orange guide') was issued in March. The revised guide is designed as an operating manual covering all aspects of the SpR grade from entry through to the arrangements for leaving the grade. In addition, an *Academic and research medicine supplement*[4] to the guide was published in November, providing additional information on the opportunities and flexibilities that exist under the new training arrangements to enable doctors to gain experience of research and academic medicine.

General practice vocational training

Work has continued during 1996 towards the regulatory introduction of summative assessment - a four stage assessment of the general practice element of vocational training. The four elements, all of which must be passed, have been designed by the profession and consist of: a test of general professional knowledge through a multiple-choice questionnaire; written submission of practical work; assessment of consultation skills by video; and a structured trainer's report.

Summative assessment was introduced in September as a professionally led initiative, but with the full support of the Government and on the understanding that the necessary amendments to Regulations would be brought forward during 1997.

Management of postgraduate medical and dental education

A number of changes were made to the management and funding arrangements for postgraduate medical and dental education (PGMDE) to take account of the abolition of Regional Health Authorities on 1 April. PGMDE is managed on a regional basis by postgraduate deans, with responsibility for training for general practice devolved to directors of postgraduate general practice education (DPGPEs). From April, postgraduate deans have been employed on interdependent university and civil service contracts with appointments made jointly by universities and Regional Offices. DPGPEs are normally also part of Regional Offices, with contracts similar to those of postgraduate deans.

Junior doctors' contracts

From 1 April, junior doctors' contracts of employment have been held by NHS Trusts and public health trainees' contracts held by health authorities, with postgraduate deans tasked to ensure that junior doctors' educational needs are met. The necessary legal powers were taken to ensure that junior doctors on training rotations could be employed by NHS Trusts whilst maintaining their continuity of service for employment purposes.

Funding arrangements

From 1 April 1996, funding for PGMDE has been raised by a levy on purchasers known as the Medical and Dental Education Levy (MADEL). These funds totalled over £530 million in 1996/97 and were administered regionally by postgraduate deans on behalf of the NHS Executive. These regional budgets support 50% of the basic salaries of full-time doctors in training and 100% of the basic salaries of part-time and public health trainees, as well as the costs of study leave, the training infrastructure, local training for managers and regional PGMDE management.

The MADEL central budgets provided support for postgraduate dentistry, educational activities of medical Royal Colleges, the Standing Committee on Postgraduate Medical and Dental Education (SCOPMDE) and various initiatives to enhance medical education.

Monitoring arrangements were developed to ensure that all MADEL budgets were properly managed.

References

1. Department of Health. *Hospital doctors: training for the future: the report of the Working Group on Specialist Medical Training.* London: Department of Health, 1993. Chair: Dr Kenneth Calman.
2. *The European Specialist Medical Qualifications Order 1995.* London: HMSO, 1995 (Statutory Instrument: SI 1995 no. 3208).
3. Department of Health, Welsh Office, Scottish Office Home and Health Department, Department of Health and Social Services Northern Ireland. *A guide to specialist registrar training.* London: Department of Health, 1996.
4. UK Health Departments. *Academic and research medicine: supplement to a guide to specialist registrar training (March 1996).* London: Department of Health, 1996.

(d)   Equal opportunities for doctors

Improved arrangements for flexible training have been introduced with the launch of the new SpR grade. These new arrangements will increase flexible training opportunities, be more responsive to local and specialty needs, and should ensure that part-time trainees are treated on the same basis as full-time trainees in terms of entry requirements and training standards.

(e)   Retention of doctors

Cohort studies by the United Kingdom (UK) Medical Careers Research Group at Oxford University[1] have examined retention and career patterns of doctors after qualification. A survey of 1983 qualifiers ten years after qualification showed:

- that around 85% were still working in medical practice in the UK (this retention rate is slightly higher than those who qualified in the mid-1970s); *and*

- that of those who were not practising medicine in the UK, the majority were abroad, and most of those were in medical practice.

An initial survey of 1993 qualifiers examined career intentions and indicated a fall in interest in entering general practice; a further survey of this cohort some three years into their careers is now under way.

Reference

1.   Lambert TW, Goldacre MJ, Parkhouse J, Edwards C. Career destinations in 1994 of United Kingdom medical graduates of 1983: results of a questionnaire survey. *BMJ* 1996; **312**: 893-7.

(f)   Undergraduate medical and dental education

Close co-operation between the NHS and universities is essential for the successful management of medical and dental education and research. The Steering Group on Undergraduate Medical and Dental Education and Research (SGUMDER) advises the Secretaries of State for Health and for Education and Employment on the arrangements for and service implications of undergraduate medical and dental education and research. Its membership includes senior representatives from the NHS and universities.

The Group published its fourth report in March[1], which includes a revision of the 'ten key principles' that underpin the close co-operation which exists between universities and the NHS for the successful management of medical and dental education and research. The report also made a number of recommendations for effective NHS/university liaison, and good progress had been made to implement many of these by the end of the year.

Reference

1.   Department of Health Steering Group on Undergraduate Medical and Dental Education and Research. *Undergraduate medical and dental education and research: fourth report of the Steering Group.* Wetherby (West Yorkshire): Department of Health, 1996.

(g)   Maintaining medical excellence

Continued implementation of the report *Maintaining medical excellence*[1] will help to ensure that the quality of medical practice is maintained at a high level. In May, a meeting was held with the main parties responsible for implementation of the recommendations of the report. A key recommendation concerned the introduction of systems for mentoring. The SCOPMDE was asked to draw together existing work on various different approaches to mentoring, both within and outside the medical profession. A working group, chaired by Dr Trevor Bayley, set up a workshop on the subject and its report should be published in mid-1997. The GMC has also considered the need to supervise trainee doctors and to identify early signs of potential problems arising in the provision of care to patients, and proposes to publish guidance early in 1997.

Any guidance on conduct and disciplinary procedures will need to reflect changes in the NHS and in professional practice. Work has focused in particular on the recommendation that professional responsibility to monitor the standard of colleagues' performance needed to be reinforced, and concluded that, in part, this would best be achieved in a culture and a climate of opinion within the NHS which is sympathetic to the challenges faced by clinicians, but which also took into account the needs and expectations of patients and the public at large. Chief executives and medical directors of NHS Trusts have been informed of the views of professional and NHS management organisations as to how best colleagues should be encouraged to take appropriate action themselves before patients suffer or other actions might be needed[2]. In particular, it has been stressed that the job descriptions of all medical directors of NHS Trusts should include their responsibility to put into place and make known their Trust's procedures for doctors to report any concerns about the conduct, performance or health of medical colleagues. In addition, the GMC has reminded practising doctors of their professional responsibilities by issuing the annual retention certificate accompanied by the 14 principles as set out in their publication *Duties of a doctor*[3].

References

1.   Department of Health. *Maintaining medical excellence: review of guidance on doctors' performance: final report.* Leeds: Department of Health, 1995.
2.   Department of Health. *Maintaining medical excellence.* London: Department of Health, 1996 (Miscellaneous Circular: MISC(96)67).
3.   General Medical Council. *Duties of a doctor: guidance from the General Medical Council.* London: General Medical Council, 1995.

CHAPTER 9

OTHER TOPICS OF INTEREST IN 1996

(a)   Medicines Control Agency

(i)   *Role and performance*

The Medicines Control Agency (MCA) is an Executive Agency which reports through its Chief Executive, Dr Keith Jones, to the Secretary of State for Health. Its primary objective is to safeguard public health by ensuring that all medicines available in the United Kingdom (UK) meet appropriate standards of safety, quality and efficacy. Safety aspects encompass potential or actual harmful effects; quality relates to all aspects of drug development and manufacture; and efficacy is a measure of the beneficial effect of the medicine on patients.

Public health is protected through a system of licensing and the monitoring of medicines after they have been licensed. The MCA has an inspectorate that monitors the standards of pharmaceutical manufacturers and wholesalers. The Agency also supports the work of the British Pharmacopoeia Commission in setting quality standards for drug substances. The MCA has responsibilities for medicines control policy within the Department of Health (DH), plays a full role in the European Union (EU) and represents UK interests in respect of pharmaceutical regulatory matters in other international settings.

The Agency is financed by fees charged to the pharmaceutical industry and, in 1996, reduced these fees by 2% overall such that its fees were set at a lower level than in 1993. During the year, the MCA met virtually all of its key licensing and safety targets. It became the leading reference Member State in the mutual recognition procedure, and is one of the leading Member States in the centralised procedure of the new EU marketing authorisation (licensing) system. The Agency was highly commended in the annual 'Chartermark' awards announced in December. The MCA's annual report for 1995/96 was among the top ten Government Agency reports in the annual competition run by Price Waterhouse, and was judged to be the best at identifying its audience and focusing clearly on it throughout.

(ii)   *Legal reclassification of medicinal products*

The Prescription Only Medicine (POM) Order[1] was amended twice in 1996[2,3]. Two substances were reclassified to allow over-the-counter sale from pharmacies: azelastine hydrochloride for the treatment of seasonal allergic rhinitis, and nizatidine for the prevention of symptoms of food-related heartburn. The existing exemptions from POM classification for famotidine, mebeverine hydrochloride, mebendazole and pseudoephedrine hydrochloride were widened. Famotidine may now be supplied for the prevention of the symptoms of heartburn and indigestion, including sleep disturbance, when associated with consumption of food or drink. Mebeverine hydrochloride may be supplied at a higher dose for the symptomatic relief of irritable bowel syndrome. Mebendazole may be supplied in a larger family pack, and pseudoephedrine hydrocholoride in controlled-release formulations may be supplied at a higher maximum dose. Six topical products were also reclassified for pharmacy sale (P): three that contain aciclovir for cold sores, two that contain hydrocortisone, and one that contains hydrocortisone with clotrimazole.

Amyl nitrite, previously available for pharmacy sale, was reclassified as a POM for safety reasons following concerns about abuse; an exemption was made to allow pharmacists to continue to supply amyl nitrite without prescription to agriculture workers who use CYMAG gas to poison moles, who may need amyl nitrite as an antidote to cyanide poisoning.

(iii)   Drug safety issues

Oral contraceptives and breast cancer

The MCA reviewed new evidence from a meta-analysis of studies on a possible association between oral contraceptives and a small increase in the risk of breast cancer, published in June[4]. The practical impact of the increased risk of diagnosis of breast cancer is greatest for older users of oral contraceptives (OCs), but after cessation of use the extra risk reduces. Breast cancer diagnosed among users of OCs appeared to be less likely to have spread than in non-users. Initial advice was provided to health professionals through the Chief Medical Officer's Epinet system, accompanied by an information sheet for patients[5]. A working party of the MCA and the Committee on Safety of Medicines (CSM) examined the issue in detail. It recommended that changes should be made to product information for doctors and patients, and these are being implemented.

Hormone replacement therapy and venous thromboembolism

There has been considerable debate as to whether use of hormone replacement therapy (HRT) might influence the risk of deep vein thrombosis and/or pulmonary embolism (together described as venous thromboembolism [VTE]). In October, several studies were published which showed a consistent increase in risk of VTE in association with use of HRT. Although the absolute excess risk was small, the MCA and the CSM provided preliminary advice to health professionals in an article in *Current Problems in Pharmacovigilance*[6], together with an information leaflet for patients, shortly after the publication of the new studies. Appropriate warnings are being added to product information for doctors and patients alike.

(iv) *Pharmaceutical developments in the European Union*

The new EU marketing authorisation (licensing) system began operation in January 1995. The European Commission has since embarked on a legislative programme that includes a proposed Directive on good clinical practice and clinical trials, a 'Codification Directive' to combine all existing pharmaceutical Directives for human medicines into a single Directive, and a Regulation on 'orphan medicines' (for treating rare diseases). There was also a proposal for a Directive to govern the control of materials used in the manufacture of medicinal products, but development of this proposal was postponed to 1997.

During the year, considerable progress was made to meet various concerns raised by individual Member States, including the UK. It is expected that the Directive on good clinical practice and clinical trials will improve the transparency of national procedures, which will allow continuation of the UK's successful Clinical Trials Certificate and Exemption schemes. The 'Codification Directive', which is now unlikely to make significant amendments to the original text of individual Directives, should be published towards the end of 1997.

Negotiations also continued on the European Commission proposal for a Council Regulation on fees payable to the European Medicines Evaluation Agency (EMEA). A proposal for a definitive Fees Regulation will be submitted to the Council in early 1997; a new Regulation should be in place by 1 January 1998.

References

1. *The Medicines (Products Other Than Veterinary Drugs) (Prescription Only) Order 1983.* London: HMSO, 1983 (Statutory Instrument: SI 1983 no. 1212).
2. *The Medicines (Products Other Than Veterinary Drugs) (Prescription Only) Amendment Order 1996.* London: HMSO, 1996 (Statutory Instrument: SI 1996 no. 1514).
3. *The Medicines (Products Other Than Veterinary Drugs) (Prescription Only) Amendment Order (Number 2).* London: Stationery Office, 1996 (Statutory Instrument: SI 1996 no. 3193).
4. Collaborative Group on Hormonal Factors in Breast Cancer. Breast cancer and hormonal contraceptives: reanalysis of individual data on 53,297 women with breast cancer and 100,239 women without breast cancer from 54 epidemiological studies. *Lancet* 1996; **347:** 1713-27.
5. Department of Health. *Oral contraceptives and breast cancer.* London: Department of Health, 1996 (Cascade Electronic Message: CEM/CMO(96)7).
6. Committee on Safety of Medicines. Information on the risk of blood clots for women taking hormone replacement therapy (HRT). *Curr Probl Pharmacovigilance* 1996; **22:** 9-10.

(b)   Medical Devices Agency

Role

The Medical Devices Agency (MDA) is an Executive Agency of the Department which reports through its Chief Executive, Mr Alan Kent, to the Secretary of State for Health. The role of the Agency is to advise Ministers and to take all reasonable steps to safeguard public health by ensuring that all medical devices meet appropriate standards of safety, quality and performance, and comply with relevant European and UK legislation.

Developments in the European Union

The UK has played an active part in the initiatives and negotiations to bring about a single European Market in medical devices. In its implementation of European Directives, the Agency has introduced two sets of regulations to control the sale and supply of medical devices on the UK market:

- The Active Implantable Medical Devices Regulations[1] came into force on 1 January 1995. From that date, all active implants had to comply with the relevant Regulations although, as permitted by the Regulations, the Secretary of State for Health has allowed a few active implantable devices without such a marking to be used on humanitarian grounds.

- The Medical Devices Regulations 1994[2] took effect on 1 January 1995, with a transition period until 13 June 1998.

Negotiation of a third Directive covering in-vitro diagnostic medical devices began early in 1996, and is expected to be finalised during 1998.

The MDA acts as the UK's Competent Authority to implement the provisions of, and to monitor compliance with, the European Medical Devices Directives, and to take any necessary enforcement actions. The work of the Agency as a regulatory authority continued to increase during the year. The eight independent certification organisations, or Notified Bodies, which assess manufacturers' compliance against the essential requirements of the Regulations, were regularly audited throughout 1996 to assess their continued competence to carry out their functions satisfactorily. Additionally, 58 applications were received for products that required clinical investigation assessments before being placed on the market. A panel of external expert assessors set up to assist the Competent Authority in the assessment of clinical investigation submissions has continued to provide valuable advice.

Fees charged by the Agency for Notified Body designation and clinical investigation assessment were unchanged from the 1995 level.

Adverse incident reporting centre/vigilance system

During 1996, the Agency received over 4,200 adverse incident reports, of which 36 involved fatalities[3]. The number of adverse incidents of CE-marked devices reported by manufacturers in line with their obligations under the Medical Devices Regulations increased from 49 in 1995 to 128 in 1996. As a result, the MDA sent out 14 reports to other European Competent Authorities to alert them of measures taken or contemplated to prevent recurrence. The MDA also received 16 reports from other Competent Authorities, and this number is expected to increase as other Member States begin to implement their vigilance systems.

As a result of adverse incident investigations, 12 Hazard Notices, 37 Safety Notices and six Pacemaker Technical Notes were issued.

Evaluation programme

During the year, over 160 reports (including surveys of various products on the market) were published on pathology test kits and instrumentation, diagnostic imaging equipment (including those for breast screening), other diagnostic and monitoring devices, equipment used in surgery and in intensive care, and equipment for people with disabilities. One new venture was the publication of a quarterly Diagnostic Imaging Review, which gives news and views on the latest technology and developments in imaging, and emphasises safety aspects for patients and users alike.

Other publications

Device Bulletins, which were first issued in 1995, provide guidance and information on important medical device issues. They summarise experience gained from adverse incident investigations and review published information, together with information from users, the Agency's evaluation centres and manufacturers. The Bulletins highlight recurrent problems which can be solved by good training and practice rather than by modification and withdrawal of the device. Recent topics have included latex sensitisation[4]; decontamination of endoscopes[5]; the purchase, operation and maintenance of benchtop steam sterilisers[6]; wheelchair and vehicle passenger lifts[7]; and guidance on the safe use of lasers in medical and dental practice[8,9].

References

1. *The Active Implantable Medical Devices Regulations 1992*. London: HMSO, 1992 (Statutory Instrument: SI 1992 no. 3146).
2. *The Medical Devices Regulations 1994*. London: HMSO, 1994 (Statutory Instrument: SI 1994 no. 3017).

3.   Medical Devices Agency. *Adverse incident reports 1996*. London: Medical Devices Agency (in press).

4.   Medical Devices Agency. *Latex sensitisation in the health care setting (use of latex gloves)*. London: Medical Devices Agency, 1996 (Device Bulletin: MDA DB 9601).

5.   Medical Devices Agency. *Decontamination of endoscopes*. London: Medical Devices Agency, 1996 (Device Bulletin: MDA DB 9607).

6.   Medical Devices Agency. *The purchase, operation and maintenance of benchtop steam sterilisers*. London: Medical Devices Agency, 1996 (Device Bulletin: MDA DB 9605).

7.   Medical Devices Agency. *Wheelchair and vehicle passenger lifts: safe working practices*. London: Medical Devices Agency, 1996 (Device Bulletin: MDA DB 9606).

8.   Medical Devices Agency. *Guidance on the safe use of lasers in medical and dental practice*. London: Medical Devices Agency, 1996 (Device Bulletin: MDA DB 9602).

9.   Department of Health. Safe use of lasers. *CMO's Update* 1996, **10**: 2.

(c)   National Blood Authority

The National Blood Authority (NBA) is a Special Health Authority set up in April 1993 to manage the National Blood Service (NBS) in England. The NBS comprises the Bio-Products Laboratory, the International Blood Group Reference Laboratory and the Blood Centres (which until April 1994 were managed by the then Regional Health Authorities), and celebrated its 50th anniversary in 1996.

In November 1995, Ministers announced that they had accepted proposals put forward by the NBA to reorganise the blood service on an integrated national basis to improve the safety, reliability and efficiency of the service, and to meet the changing needs of the National Health Service (NHS)[1,2]. The plans included improved administration arrangements, with the creation of three administrative zones and the introduction of a national computer system; the consolidation of bulk donation processing and testing activities from 15 to 10 centres; and an increase in the number of NBS blood banks.

The zonal reorganisation was completed in 1996 and introduction of the new computer system remained on schedule. The rationalisation of processing and testing work, which is scheduled for completion in March 1998, was accelerated in December 1996 with the closure (a year ahead of schedule) of those activities at the Cambridge centre.

During 1996, steps were taken to monitor the performance of the NBS in terms of the service provided to hospitals and donors alike. An independent NBS user group, chaired by Professor Edward Gordon-Smith, Professor of Haematology at St George's Hospital, London, was set up to monitor the service provided to hospitals. The national group held its first meeting in October; its first annual report is expected to be submitted to the Secretary of State for Health in Summer 1997. Local user committees, reporting to the national group, were also established in each of the NBS zones.

The NBA has been exploring various ways to improve the service received by donors and to increase the number of regular donors to meet the rising hospital demand for blood and blood products. Measures have included extension of the hours when blood is collected, arrangement of donor sessions at times more suited to donors' needs, and pilot schemes to investigate the use of appointments in some areas. A joint review by the NBA and DH of the interim 'Blood donors' charter'[3], as announced when the Charter was first introduced in November 1995, was also started in late 1996.

References

1.   Department of Health. *On the State of the Public Health: the annual report of the Chief Medical Officer of the Department of Health for the year 1995.* London: HMSO, 1996; 208.

2.   Department of Health. *Plans for the future of the National Blood Service.* London: Department of Health, 1995.

3.   Department of Health. *The patients' charter: blood donors: interim charter.* London: Department of Health, 1995.

(d)   National Biological Standards Board

The National Biological Standards Board (NBSB), a non-Departmental public body set up in 1976, has a statutory duty[1,2] to assure the quality of biological substances used in medicine. The Board fulfils this function through its management of the National Institute for Biological Standards and Control (NIBSC). The NIBSC is a multidisciplinary scientific organisation which tests the quality, reliability and safety of biological medicines such as vaccines, products derived from human blood and those produced by biotechnology; develops the biological standards necessary for such testing; and carries out associated research.

The Board and the Institute work within the Government's overall public health programme to:

- respond to and advise on public health problems involving biological agents;

- address new developments in science and medicine; *and*

- take a leading role in developing the scientific basis for the control and standardisation of biological agents in Europe.

The NIBSC examines almost 2,000 batches of biological medicines annually, in addition to testing over 3,000 plasma pools for virological safety. The Institute is designated an Official Medicines Control Laboratory within the EU, and is one of only two laboratories to have achieved independent quality accreditation for testing biological agents. This accreditation is to the internationally recognised quality standard EN45001.

The Institute is a World Health Organization (WHO) International Laboratory for Biological Standards and prepares and distributes the bulk of the world's international standards and reference materials. These activities are certified to the quality standard ISO9001.

During the year, the NBSB commissioned an external international review of the standardisation and control of biological medicines, chaired by Sir Leslie Turnberg, to set out a vision for the future of this rapidly changing area of medicine.

References

1.   *The Biological Standards Act 1975.* London: HMSO, 1975.
2.   *The National Biological Standards Board (Functions) Order 1976.* London: HMSO, 1975 (Statutory Instrument: SI 1976 no. 917).

(e)   National Radiological Protection Board

The National Radiological Protection Board (NRPB) is a non-Departmental Public Body which reports to the Secretary of State for Health. The functions given to the Board[1,2] are:

- by means of research and otherwise, to advance the acquisition of knowledge about the protection of mankind from radiation hazards (for both ionising and non-ionising radiation); *and*

- to provide information and advice to persons (including Government departments).

The NRPB contributes to the Health of the Nation[3] strategy by a combination of formal advice, the publication of scientific reports and the provision of advice directly to health professionals and others involved with radiation work, as well as to the general public. Its main contributions during the year were concerned with important radionuclides in food and environmental materials[4], radon-affected areas in England and Wales[5] and risks from deterministic effects of ionising radiation[6]. A pocket-sized version of the NRPB statement[7] on the hazards of ultraviolet radiation was sent to general medical practitioners and public health and occupational physicians in the UK by the medical Royal Colleges.

The NRPB Advisory Group on Ionising Radiation is studying the heterogeneity of response to radiation, the risks of second cancers following radiotherapy, and the assessment of reference doses for clinical radiology; a detailed study of the most recently published data from atomic bomb survivors is also under way. The

NRPB Advisory Group on Non-ionising Radiation is studying the health effects of power lines and mobile telephones to provide advice to all with an interest in these issues.

The WHO has invited the NRPB to become a Collaborating Centre for ionising and non-ionising radiations and has identified specific areas of work. The NRPB will become part of the WHO Radiation Emergency Medical Preparedness Assistance Network, and establish WHO training courses for public health professionals on actions to be taken in a radiation accident or incident.

The *At-a-Glance* leaflets published by the NRPB remain very popular and cover topics such as medical radiation, radon and non-ionising radiation.   A new leaflet on radio waves has been produced to explain the nature and effect of radiation from such devices as mobile telephones.

The NRPB assumed the administrative support for the Administration of Radioactive Substances Advisory Committee (ARSAC) and the Committee on the Medical Aspects of Radiation in the Environment (COMARE) during 1996, and staff were seconded to the Department further to strengthen links between the two organisations for protection against ionising and non-ionising radiations.

References

1. *The Radiological Protection Act 1970.* London: HMSO, 1970.
2. *Extensions of Functions Order 1974.* London: HMSO, 1974.
3. Department of Health. *The Health of the Nation: a strategy for health in England.* London: HMSO, 1992 (Cm. 1986).
4. National Radiological Protection Board. *Generalised derived limits for radioisotopes of strontium, ruthenium, iodine, caesium, plutonium, americium and curium.* Oxford: National Radiological Protection Board, 1996 (Doc. NRPB 7, no. 1).
5. National Radiological Protection Board. *Radon affected areas: England and Wales.* Oxford: National Radiological Protection Board, 1996 (Doc. NRPB 7, no. 2).
6. National Radiological Protection Board. *Risk from deterministic effects of ionising radiation.* Oxford: National Radiological Protection Board, 1996 (Doc. NRPB 7, no. 3).
7. National Radiological Protection Board. *Board statement on effects of ultraviolet radiation on human health.* Oxford: National Radiological Protection Board, 1995 (Doc. NRPB 6, no. 2).

(f)   United Kingdom Transplant Support Service Authority

The UK Transplant Support Service Authority (UKTSSA) was established as a Special Health Authority on 1 April 1991 to provide a 24-hour support service to all transplant units in the UK and the Republic of Ireland, taking over the work of the UK Transplant Service. Its main functions include the matching and allocation of organs for transplantation on an equitable basis and in accordance with agreed methodologies; the provision of support and quality assurance to local tissue-typing laboratories; the maintenance and analysis of the national database of transplant information; and the production of audit reports on the status of transplantation and organ donation and use.

The UKTSSA also provides a forum at which transplant and organ donation issues can be discussed and is responsible for the maintenance of the NHS organ donor register, which was established in 1994. By December 1996, over 3.74 million people had registered their willingness to donate their organs in the event of sudden death. In November, an audit of cardiothoracic transplant activity and outcome[1] was published in a series of audit reports based on data submitted to the National Transplant Database.

Reference

1.   United Kingdom Transplant Support Service Authority. *Cardiothoracic organ transplant audit 1985-1995.* Bristol: UK Transplant Support Service Authority, 1996.

(g)   Public Health Laboratory Service Board

The Public Health Laboratory Service (PHLS), established under the National Health Service Act 1946[1], celebrated its 50th anniversary on 6 November. The PHLS Board was formally constituted as a non-Departmental public body in 1960 to exercise functions which are embodied in statute in the National Health Service Act 1977[2], as amended by the Public Health Laboratory Service Act 1979[3], and is accountable to the Secretary of State for Health and the Secretary of State for Wales.

The PHLS exists to protect the population of England and Wales from infection by maintaining a national capability for the detection, diagnosis, surveillance, prevention and control of infections and communicable diseases.

During 1996, the PHLS implemented major organisational changes, enhanced its support of public health professionals and successfully helped to protect public health through prompt identification of potential hazards and advice on control. The year included:

- the restructuring of the network of public health laboratories into nine regional groups to enhance management and effectiveness of services;

- the establishment of regional epidemiology units to provide support to health professionals with statutory and field responsibilities for communicable disease control;

- a major review of research and development to identify project priorities;

- the detection of a small number of false-negative HIV results associated with a particular test kit, which led to a national programme of rapid re-testing and follow-up of patients;

- the investigation of clusters of meningococcal infection, for which the PHLS provided expert advice and operational support - enhanced by the development of novel techniques and additional investment in automated equipment; *and*

- the detection and investigation of an outbreak of *Salmonella gold-coast* associated with cheddar cheese.

During the national week of science, engineering and technology in March, the PHLS held open days, exhibitions in shopping centres and other venues, including schools, and collaborated with universities to provide lectures to students. A description of the work of the PHLS, to celebrate its golden jubilee, was printed and widely distributed with private sector funding, and a special exhibition about the history and work of the PHLS to mark its 50th anniversary was opened at the Science Museum in London.

References

1. *The National Health Service Act 1946*. London: HMSO, 1946.
2. *The National Health Service Act 1977*. London: HMSO, 1977.
3. *The Public Health Laboratory Service Act 1979*. London: HMSO, 1979.

(h)   Microbiological Research Authority

The Microbiological Research Authority is a Special Health Authority which directs the work of the Centre for Applied Microbiology and Research (CAMR) at Porton Down, Salisbury. The CAMR's special resources include containment facilities for the handling of the most dangerous pathogens and biological toxins. The CAMR Research Steering Group provides a systematic assessment of the research work commissioned and funded by DH, and its membership comprises representatives from the PHLS, DH and independent external assessors. Projects are grouped into the areas of pathogenesis, diagnostics, biotherapeutics, vaccines, environmental microbiology and cell culture. These are assessed individually - for example, in terms of their scientific quality, relevance to policy, achievement towards targets and value for money. Included in the current public health research programme are projects related to HIV, *Campylobacter*, *Salmonella* and vaccine development, such as vaccines against meningococci and pneumococci.

(i)   National Creutzfeldt-Jakob Disease Surveillance Unit

The National Creutzfeldt-Jakob Disease (CJD) Surveillance Unit, established in 1990 and funded by DH and the Scottish Office, monitors the incidence of CJD and investigates its epidemiology, paying particular attention to occupation, eating habits and medical history. In March 1996, the Unit identified a previously unrecognised form of CJD[1] in 10 patients aged under 42 years. Now known as new variant CJD (nvCJD), this disease presents with unusual clinical features and shows a distinctive appearance in brain tissues; all cases so far identified are in patients aged under 50 years. The independent expert Spongiform Encephalopathy Advisory Committee (SEAC) concluded that the most likely explanation was that these cases were linked to exposure to bovine spongiform encephalopathy (BSE) before the introduction of the specified bovine offals ban in 1989.

During 1995, there were three deaths attributed to nvCJD; in 1996, 10 patients have so far been identified as having died from nvCJD, and at the end of the year there were two cases of nvCJD in patients who were still alive (confirmed by brain biopsy) - a total of 15 confirmed cases of nvCJD to the end of December 1996. Altogether, there were 57 deaths in definite or probable cases of CJD and Gerstmann-Sträussler-Scheinker syndrome (GSS) during 1996. All figures remain provisional until 1996 data are finalised (see Table 9.1).

The identification of nvCJD, and public awareness and concern about BSE and nvCJD and their possible public health implications, stimulated much further work during the year. The Department has worked closely with colleagues in the Ministry of Agriculture, Fisheries and Food (MAFF) to ensure that all issues related to transmissible spongiform encephalopathies (TSEs) with potential public health implications are considered by the SEAC, and that the Committee's recommendations for the measures required to protect public health - including strengthening of existing controls to prevent potentially infective material from entering the human food chain - were put in place as quickly as possible, in some instances going further than the SEAC advice. In March, following the announcement to Parliament about nvCJD[2], the Government implemented a ban on the use for any purpose of meat from bovine animals aged over 30 months, and in September a ban was introduced on the consumption of sheep and goat heads.

The Department has also informed professionals and the public alike about subsequent developments. Activities have included a scientific press briefing, regular publication of statistics on the incidence of CJD via monthly press releases, communications from the Chief Medical Officer to all doctors[3,4,5] and preparation of an information pack to be issued to all directors of public health, environmental health officers and consultants in communicable disease control[6]. In addition, a grant of some £150,000 over three years was awarded to the Alzheimer's Disease Society to help to set up a network to provide information, advice and support to the families of patients with CJD.

Knowledge about nvCJD remains sparse, and a link between nvCJD and BSE has not been definitely established, although evidence has emerged during the

Table 9.1: Deaths due to definite and probable cases of Creutzfeldt-Jakob disease (CJD) and Gerstmann-Sträussler-Scheinker syndrome (GSS), and referrals to the UK CJD Surveillance Unit, United Kingdom, 1985-96

Year	Referrals	Creutzfeldt-Jakob disease				GSS	Total	Sporadic incidence/ million population*
		Sporadic	nvCJD	Iatrogenic	Familial			
1985	-	26	-	1	1	0	28	0.45
1986	-	26	-	0	0	0	26	0.45
1987	-	23	-	0	0	1	24	0.40
1988	-	21	-	1	1	0	23	0.36
1989	-	28	-	2	2	0	32	0.48
1990	53	27	-	5	0	0	32	0.47
1991	75	32	-	1	3	0	36	0.55
1992	96	44	-	2	4	1	51	0.76
1993	78	38	-	4	3	2	46	0.66
1994	116	52	-	1	3	3	59	0.90
1995	86	34	3	4	2	3	46	0.64
1996†	129	38	10	4	2	3	57	0.83

nvCJD = new variant CJD (included from 1995).

*Based on UK population of 57.78 million (1991 Census Update).

†Provisional figures.

Note: These figures may differ from those published previously because the Unit is still identifying cases from previous years.

Source: UK CJD Surveillance Unit

course of the year to support such a possibility. A new strategy for research and development into the human health aspects of TSEs has been developed to target research at priority health questions, and to ensure that the research efforts are properly co-ordinated across Government Departments; this strategy[7] was published on 11 November, and will be kept under continuous review.

References

1. Will RG, Ironside JW, Zeidler M et al. A new variant of Creutzfeldt-Jakob disease in the UK. *Lancet* 1996; **347**: 921-5.
2. *Hansard* 20 March 1996; vol 275; col 375.
3. Department of Health. *New variant of Creutzfeldt-Jakob disease (CJD)*. London: Department of Health, 1996 (Professional Letter: PL/CMO(96)5).
4. Department of Health. New variant of Creutzfeldt-Jakob disease. *CMO's Update* 1996; **11**: 4.
5. Department of Health. New variant of Creutzfeldt-Jakob disease. *CMO's Update* 1996; **12**: 4.
6. Department of Health. *Creutzfeldt-Jakob disease (CJD) and bovine spongiform encephalopathy (BSE) information pack.* London: Department of Health (in press).
7. Department of Health. *Strategy for research and development relating to the human health aspects of transmissible spongiform encephalopathies.* London: Department of Health, 1996.

(j)   Bioethics

(i)   Research ethics committees

In 1991, each district health authority was required to establish a Local Research Ethics Committee (LREC). In 1996, the Department consulted widely on a proposal to streamline the process of ethical approval for health-related multi-centre research, which recommended that a Multi-centre Research Ethics Committee (MREC) should be established in every English health region. An MREC would advise nationally, not just within its host region, on the science and general ethics of multi-centre research protocols it considered. LRECs would not be able to request amendments to these protocols, but would continue to advise on local acceptability. The response to the consultation was encouraging, and plans were drawn up to implement MRECs in 1997.

A number of LREC members and other colleagues with experience of NHS research helped the Department to develop a briefing pack for research ethics committee members[1], which was sent for preliminary evaluation to six LRECs in December. The final guidance will complement the Standards Framework[2] issued to LREC members in 1995, and help to clarify the objectives of LRECs and to promote good and consistent practice.

(ii)   Bioethics in Europe

The Council of Europe's Convention on Human Rights and Biomedicine was adopted in November 1996 after more than five years' work, and will be opened for signature in April 1997. The Convention[3], which comprises 38 Articles, emphasises the importance of consent, privacy, and the avoidance of unjustified discrimination. Whilst recognising the importance of scientific research, the Convention provides strict safeguards for the protection of research subjects. Detailed provisions address standards which must be met before patients who are not able to give informed consent can be involved in research or the donation of regenerative tissue for transplantation. Four protocols - on research, organ transplantation, genetics, and the protection of the embryo and fetus - are planned under the Convention.

(iii)   *Human genetics and the Human Genetics Advisory Commission*

Last year's Report[4] recorded the work of the House of Commons Select Committee on Science and Technology inquiry into human genetics[5]. A Government response was issued in January 1996[6], followed by a follow-up report[7] and a second Government response[8] in April and June 1996, respectively.

The key outcome has been the establishment of the Human Genetics Advisory Commission (HGAC), with a remit to review progress in human genetics and to report to health and industry ministers on issues expected to have wider social, ethical or economic consequences - for example insurance, employment and patents. The appointment of Sir Colin Campbell, Vice Chancellor of the University of Nottingham, to chair the Commission was announced, along with the membership, in December. The HGAC will meet for the first time in Spring 1997.

(iv)   *Advisory Committee on Genetic Testing*

The Advisory Committee on Genetic Testing (ACGT), chaired by the Reverend Dr John Polkinghorne, was established during 1996 to advise Health Ministers on developments in genetic tests and testing services. The ACGT began work in July, and its first priority has been consideration of the marketing of human genetic testing services offered direct to the public. A draft code of practice on such services was prepared and a consultation paper on the draft issued in November[9]. In the light of comments received, and subject to the approval of the ACGT and Ministers, guidance and a code of practice will be issued in 1997.

The ACGT identified the use of predictive tests for late-onset disorders as its next area of work, and has established a sub-group to take forward work on this topic.

(v)   *Gene Therapy Advisory Committee*

The Gene Therapy Advisory Committee (GTAC) continues to review protocols for gene therapy research. Baroness Lloyd's term of office as chair of the GTAC came to an end in 1996; her contribution to the high standing of the UK system to oversee gene therapy has been considerable. Professor Norman Nevin will take on the chair from 1 January 1997.

The GTAC met three times during 1996 and was content, in principle, for five protocols for gene therapy research in human beings to proceed; two revised proposals were approved and a further five protocols are still under consideration.

The major developments during the year were the increased industrial sponsorship of research trials in the UK, reversing the picture since 1993 (previously most trials have been supported through Medical Research Council [MRC] and cancer research charity funding), and the resubmission of protocols, with changes to patient eligibility criteria, with a view to including either less ill or more easily accessible patient groups.

A total of 17 gene therapy trials have been approved in the UK since 1993 and, by the end of 1996, 13 had started. Most of these trials are in the area of cancer research.

In addition, the GTAC has identified several other areas of work, including the wider dissemination of information on gene therapy to the public, and will hold an open workshop in March 1997.

(vi)   Assisted conception

The Human Fertilisation and Embryology Authority (HFEA) was established by the Human Fertilisation and Embryology Act 1990[10,11]. It is responsible for the regulation of certain techniques for the treatment of infertility, including in-vitro fertilisation, and research on embryos. A review of the Authority was conducted during 1996, which concluded that there was a continuing need for both the executive and advisory functions of the HFEA, and that no other existing body could carry these out more cost-effectively.

The statutory maximum storage period for frozen human embryos was extended by regulations from five to ten years in certain circumstances.

The Royal College of Obstetricians and Gynaecologists has been sponsored by the Department to review its 1992 clinical guidelines for the management of infertility treatment.

A review of the consent requirements in the 1990 Act[10], to be carried out by Professor Sheila McLean, Professor of Law and Ethics in Medicine at the University of Glasgow, was announced on 5 December.

(vii) Protection and use of patient information

Guidance on the protection and use of patient information was issued to the NHS in March[12]; it explains the principles to be applied when handling such information and the legal duty of everyone working in the NHS to protect patient confidentiality. The guidance recognises that, to function effectively, the NHS may need to use patient information (anonymised whenever possible) for reasons other than direct patient care, but requires patients to be informed, in general terms, what those uses may be. Every NHS body was required to adopt clear policies and procedures on the use and protection of patient information and to review (and where necessary, amend) their security arrangements against the guidance requirements by November 1996.

A working group, chaired by Dame Fiona Caldicott, was set up to review the uses of patient information outside direct patient care and research.

Jointly chaired by the Chief Medical Officer and Dr Alexander Macara, Chairman of Council of the British Medical Association (BMA), a working group looked at issues surrounding the privacy of patient information and the phased introduction of networked information technology systems throughout the NHS. A joint statement, *Working together to secure the privacy of personal health information in the NHS*[13], was issued in October.

References

1. Department of Health. *Briefing pack for research ethics committee members.* London, Department of Health (in press).
2. Department of Health. *Standards for Local Research Ethics Committees: a framework for ethical review.* London: Department of Health, 1994.
3. Council of Europe. *Convention for the protection of human rights and dignity of the human being with regard to the application of biology and medicine: convention on human rights and biomedicine.* Strasbourg: Council of Europe, 1996 (ETS 164).
4. Department of Health. *On the State of the Public Health: the annual report of the Chief Medical Officer of the Department of Health for the year 1995.* London: HMSO, 1996; 215.
5. House of Commons Science and Technology Committee. *Human genetics: the science and its consequences: third report from the Science and Technology Committee: Session 1994-95.* London: HMSO, 1995 (HC41; Vol I-IV).
6. Department of Trade and Industry. *Human genetics: the science and its consequences: Government response to the third report of the Science and Technology Select Committee: Session 1994-95.* London: HMSO, 1996 (Cm. 3061).
7. House of Commons Science and Technology Committee. *Human genetics: the Government's response: Session 1995-96.* London: HMSO, 1996 (HC 231; vol I-II).
8. Department of Trade and Industry, Office of Science and Technology. *Human genetics: Government response to the third report of the Science and Technology Select Committee: Session 1995-96.* London: HMSO, 1996 (Cm. 3306).
9. Advisory Committee on Genetic Testing. *Draft Code of Practice for genetic testing offered commercially direct to the public.* London: UK Health Departments, 1996.
10. *The Human Fertilisation and Embryology Act 1990.* London: HMSO, 1990.

11. *The Human Fertilisation and Embryology Act 1990 (commencement no. 2 and Transitional Provision) Order 1991*. London: HMSO, 1991 (Statutory Instrument: SI 1991 no. 480 c.10).
12. Department of Health. *The protection and use of patient information*. Wetherby (West Yorkshire): Department of Health, 1996.
13. Department of Health. *Working together to secure the privacy of personal health information in the NHS*. London: Department of Health (in press) (Miscellaneous Circular: MISC(97)1).

(k) Complaints

The new NHS complaints procedure, outlined in last year's Report[1], was introduced on 1 April. Final guidance on implementing the new procedure was issued to the NHS in March[2]; training material for local resolution had already been issued in January[3], and training events for conveners and lay chairpersons of panels involved in independent review aspects of the procedure took place in the Spring and Autumn. A public information leaflet[4] and a poster were also produced and sent to all NHS bodies, citizens' advice bureaux and main public libraries.

The Health Service Commissioners (Amendment) Act 1996[5] also came into force on 1 April. It extended the remit of the Health Service Commissioner to include complaints about matters arising from the exercise of clinical judgment and about family health services, such that the Commissioner can now investigate complaints about all aspects of NHS care.

Early indications are that the new system is working successfully, particularly in regard to local resolution. Concerns have emerged about independent review, but mainly on operational issues rather than matters of principle. Work on an extensive evaluation of the implementation of the new procedure will start early in 1998.

References

1. Department of Health. *On the State of the Public Health: the annual report of the Chief Medical Officer of the Department of Health for the year 1995*. London: HMSO, 1996; 216-7.
2. NHS Executive. *Complaints: listening...acting...improving: guidance on implementing the NHS complaints procedure*. Wetherby (West Yorkshire): Department of Health, 1996 (Executive Letter: EL(96)19).
3. Department of Health. *Acting on complaints national training initiative - local resolution: a training resource pack*. Wetherby (West Yorkshire): Department of Health, 1996.
4. NHS Executive. *Complaints: listening...acting...improving*. Leeds: Department of Health, 1996.
5. *The Health Service Commissioners (Amendment) Act 1996*. London: HMSO, 1996.

(l)   Research and development

Collaboration with other research funders

The Department's research and development (R&D) strategy promotes strong links with the science base and with other major research funders. A national forum of research funders has provided an important means to establish closer working links between research interests in the NHS and elsewhere, including the Research Councils, the Association of Medical Research Charities, industry and universities. It meets twice a year to exchange and share information on activities and priorities to improve understanding and co-ordination (see page 150).

Collaboration between the UK Health Departments and the Medical Research Council (MRC) is formalised in a Concordat. Concordats have also been established with the Engineering and Physical Sciences, the Biotechnology and Biological Sciences, and the Natural Environment Research Councils; a new Concordat with the Economic and Social Research Council is being finalised.

European research

The Department, with the MRC, has helped to shape the EU's Biomedicine and Health Research Programme (BIOMED) to ensure consistency with national programmes and to create opportunities for UK scientists and researchers. The Department has other research interests in the EU's Fourth Framework Programme for Research and Technological Development (FP4) such as the health care and disabled and elderly people sectors of the telematics programme, and the radiation protection programme in EURATOM. DH is participating with other Government Departments in the consultation process to establish UK views on priorities for the Fifth Framework Programme (FP5)

(m)   Use of information technology in clinical care

The NHS information management and technology (IM&T) strategy is directed towards the use of information technology (IT) as an aid to the delivery of effective and efficient health care. It has a number of key programmes - such as NHS-wide networking and NHS number replacement - on which work continued during the year; taken together, these programmes will provide the necessary infrastructure to support health care in the future. During 1996, a number of important developments were seen.

There are real advantages to clinicians if appropriate information can be made available at the point of care. Prescribing benefits have been seen during work on the electronic patient record project at the Wirral NHS Trust and, at Burton NHS Trust, laptop computers allow clinicians direct access to all computerised notes at the bedside in some wards.

Practical experience of integrating information by use of clinical workstations has been gained during a project run at the Horizon, Bethlem and Maudsley, and Winchester NHS Trusts. This integrated clinical workstation project, with the electronic patient record project, addressed many of the complex cultural and technical issues that underlie the use of information technology to support clinical care. A simulator of a clinical workstation was developed and demonstrated.

The IM&T training programme for clinicians has continued to develop IM&T as an integral part of clinical training programmes, in pre-registration and post-registration training alike. A second successful workshop with UK medical schools was held in December. The database of training resources (now known as the Gateway to Health Informatics in Teaching [GHIFT]) has been completed. Various other initiatives to support the training and development of IM&T knowledge and skills for practising clinicians have been put in hand.

The 'Patients not paper' efficiency scrutiny[1] highlighted the need to reduce paperwork flowing into and out of general practices and stressed that best use of IM&T was needed to achieve this. Work continued to ensure that all general practitioners (GPs) will be linked via the NHS-wide network to health authorities and providers of health care. This linkage will support the development of a primary-care led NHS.

GP records have potentially the richest source of morbidity and health data in the NHS. Work continued to address the necessary recording standards and confidentiality policies that are needed before such data can be shared and used to support achievement of health strategy targets[2] and locality purchasing. The options for transferring electronic GP records between practices have also been examined.

Security and confidentiality of personal health information is a major ethical concern, which also has an important technical dimension. Jointly chaired by the Chief Medical Officer and the Chairman of Council of the BMA, Dr Alexander Macara, a working group began in January to resolve a number of issues that surround the privacy of personal health information and the phased introduction of networking of IT systems throughout the NHS. Two further working groups were established: one, chaired by Dame Fiona Caldicott, past president of the Royal College of Psychiatrists, will examine the use of personal health information outside the setting of immediate clinical care and research; another, chaired by Professor Alastair Bellingham, President of the Royal College of Pathologists, will advise on the security of large databases, in particular the NHS-wide Clearing Service.

Work progressed on health care resource groupings for use in costing, performance management and monitoring (by NHS Trusts, health authorities and GPs), and internal resource management (see page 154). The use of health benefit groupings for analysis of epidemiological data to assist purchasers of health care to define their needs continued.

The Read Code project (see page 154) maintained and developed an agreed computerised health care thesaurus of clinical terms after work which involved over 55 specialty working groups and over 2,000 clinicians. Introduction of the new NHS number continued. By the end of January, everyone in England and Wales had been allocated their new NHS number by the NHS Central Register, and by the end of the year all health authorities, bar one, had completed the roll-out to GPs. The transmission of electronic messages that use nationally agreed standards continued in a number of key areas - such as referral and discharge summaries, and radiology and pathology test requests and results.

As the national IM&T infrastructure develops, so the potential benefits from the use of information technology to support the provision of health care to individual patients can be more fully realised.

References

1.   NHS Executive. *Patients not paper: report of the efficiency scrutiny into bureaucracy in general practice.* Wetherby (West Yorkshire): Department of Health, 1995.
2.   Department of Health. *The Health of the Nation: a strategy for health in England.* London: HMSO, 1992 (Cm. 1986).

(n)   Dental health

(i)   *Dental health of the nation*

Dental epidemiological research as part of the National Diet and Nutritional Survey programme (see page 77) included an analysis of the dental health of elderly people to assess the impact of nutritional status and age upon oral and dental disease; the results should be published during 1997.

Results from surveys conducted for health authorities in 1995/96 show a mean of 41% of 5-year-old children in England had some experience of dental caries. Wide regional variations in dental health still remain; 33% of 5-year-olds in the

West Midlands had experienced dental caries, rising to 54% of that age-group in the North West. The mean number of teeth with known decay experience in this age-group was 1.6, as found in 1983. It appears that the decline in dental caries in deciduous teeth may now have halted in many areas, and among those 5-year-olds who do have dental caries, more teeth appear to be affected. These findings emphasise a continuing need for preventive dental health measures - such as water fluoridation and oral health education.

The mean number of filled deciduous teeth in 5-year-old children in England fell from 0.3 in 1993 to 0.21 in 1996.

(ii)   General dental services

On 30 September, there were 15,280 principals, 560 assistants and 496 vocational trainees in general dental practice, a total of 16,336 dentists providing dental care in NHS general dental services in England. A total of 26,761,820 registered NHS dental patients were recorded in England on 30 June, comprising 19,734,906 continuing care (adult) and 7,026,914 capitation (child) registrations.

On 12 June, the Government announced agreement with the profession on a package of reforms designed to improve patient services, and to provide stability and security for dentists as well as a firm foundation for future work. The reforms involved three main components. From 1 September, dentists were paid for individual child treatments in addition to the capitation payments already received, to ensure continued improvements in child dental health by relating payments more closely to oral disease in the children treated. The registration period for children and adults alike was harmonised to provide continuing dental care for 15 months following each course of treatment, which should streamline administrative procedures and focus payments on those patients who require and receive active interventions. From 1 December, a more rigorous scheme for prior approval of treatments was introduced: all treatment necessary to secure and maintain oral health is, and will remain, available, and criteria based on clinical effectiveness will be developed to ensure the best use of existing resources. A joint Working Party between the UK Health Departments and the dental profession will develop these proposals further.

The Minister for Health, Mr Gerald Malone MP, also announced that, in view of the profession's agreement on these proposals, the Government would agree a total waiver of overpayments that had arisen under the former remuneration system, and the General Dental Services Committee of the British Dental Association (BDA) announced the end of the dental dispute that it declared in 1992.

For the longer term, the Government confirmed its intention to pilot and evaluate systems of local commissioning between health authorities and dental practices by including legislative powers in *Primary care: delivering the future* published on 20 November[1].

Selected health authorities were also allocated a total of £800,000 for 1996/97 from a newly created Access Fund to enable them to make payments to dentists to improve the availability of general dental services where there was evidence of unmet demand.

(iii)   Community dental services

Clinical community dental staff continued to experience increased complexity of the work that they carry out and a shift away from the routine treatment of children to the dental care of those with special needs. The community dental service expressed concern that the Government policy of strengthening its 'safety net' function was becoming increasingly difficult to meet, and that the responsibility of the service to provide dental care to those individuals unable to obtain care through the general dental services - the 'safety net' function - might compete with services for people with special needs, whose oral health requirements will not be met elsewhere. The UK Health Departments considered that resource decisions were for individual health authorities to decide, based on local priorities rather than by central direction.

On the basis of joint evidence submitted by the UK Departments of Health and the BDA, the Review Body on Doctors' and Dentists' Remuneration recommended that an additional increment should be added to the senior dental officer (SDO) scale, thus restoring the link between the SDO and associate specialist grades[2]. One consequence of this additional award was that the top point of the SDO scale was higher than the top point of the Assistant District Dental Officer (ADDO) scale, whereas the differential had previously been in favour of the latter. The BDA invited the Review Body to reinstate the differential in favour of the ADDO grade in their next review.

(iv)   Hospital dental services

The number of hospital dentists in England rose by 5.8% from 1,289 to 1,364 between September 1994 and September 1995. In September 1995, there were 445 consultants in post, an increase of 2.5% over the previous year. The number of senior registrars fell by 2.0% from 101 to 99. The number of registrars rose by 2.0% from 150 to 153, and the number of senior house officers rose by 14.2% from 324 to 370. (Figures given refer to whole-time equivalent posts.)

The basis for reporting outpatient activity in dental hospitals is being revised. It is therefore not possible to report on outpatient activity in dental specialties for the period September 1994 to September 1995.

(v)   Continuing education and training for dentists

There were 445 trainees in 45 regionally based vocational training schemes in England on 1 September 1995 (44 schemes in the general dental services and one in the community dental services). The Committee for Continuing Education and Training identified the following priority areas for the training of general dental practitioners in 1995/96: providing training in informatics skills; supporting the oral health strategy; 'hands-on' courses; sedation techniques; pain control and the management of anxious patients; the management of elderly or disabled patients and those with special needs; courses to reinforce distance learning programmes; the training of trainers, advisers and examiners; research techniques relevant to general dental practice; training practice staff; and courses to promote peer review and clinical audit in general dental practice. These courses are arranged by postgraduate dental deans or directors of dental education and funded by DH under the provisions of Section 63 of the Health Services and Dental Public Health Act 1968[3].

During the year, DH continued to fund the development, production and distribution of distance learning material for general dental practitioners, including further computer-assisted learning (CAL) programmes. Some 18 different CAL programmes for general dental practitioners have been distributed or are in development, and may be obtained free of charge from dental postgraduate deans or via the 'Dentanet' information network.

(vi)   Dental research

Diet and oral health

A feasibility study to test oral health survey procedures as part of the National Diet and Nutrition Survey programme of those aged 4 to 18 years was conducted successfully by a team from the Office for National Statistics and the Universities of Birmingham and Newcastle-upon-Tyne.

NHS research and development programme

Development of the NHS national research programme in primary dental care, managed by the North West region of the NHS Executive, continued; three workshops on the commissioning of development work were attended by 121 individuals from general dental practice, dental public health, academic and research dentists, community dentistry, patient groups and NHS management.

References

1. Department of Health. *Primary care: delivering the future.* London: Stationery Office, 1996 (Cm. 3512).
2. Review Body on Doctors' and Dentists' Remuneration. *25th Report 1996.* London: Stationery Office, 1996 (Cm. 3090).
3. *The Health Services and Public Health Act 1968.* London: HMSO, 1968.

CHAPTER 10

INTERNATIONAL HEALTH

(a)   England, Europe and health

Many of the health challenges encountered in England and the United Kingdom (UK) as a whole are also found in the rest of Europe; diseases have no respect for national boundaries. The pace of technological advance, ageing populations and rising expectations are leading to growing demands on health care services throughout Europe and beyond. The challenges of drug dependence and other lifestyle-related health problems are common to many countries.

The opportunity to work together on common problems within the European Community (EC), and in international bodies such as the World Health Organization (WHO) and the Council of Europe, brings great benefits. The UK has much expertise to offer, but can also benefit greatly from the knowledge of others, the insight provided by international comparisons, and the greater resources that international co-operation can bring into play.

(i)   The European Union

The Health Council

The Council of Ministers is a key decision-making body of the European Union (EU), in which all Member States are represented. Councils of Ministers with particular responsibilities, such as health, meet regularly to deal with relevant EC business.

In 1996, the Health Council held general meetings on 14 May and 12 November. It adopted conclusions on transmissible spongiform encephalopathies (TSEs) designed to enhance understanding of the pathogenesis and transmissibility of Creutzfeldt-Jakob disease (CJD) and to extend related epidemiological surveillance. The Council also noted action being taken to develop a global early-warning system and response network for communicable diseases, within the context of the EU-United States action plan agreed in December 1995.

Negotiations on the European Commission's proposal for Community action on the prevention of drug dependence were concluded. Discussions on a separate proposal for a Community programme of action on health monitoring were continuing at the year's end; a decision on this programme is expected to be adopted in the first half of 1997.

The Council adopted Resolutions on a strategy for promoting blood safety and self-sufficiency of supplies in the EC; on reduction of cigarette smoking in the EC; and on the integration of health protection requirements into other Community policies.

The European Commission's proposal to establish a Community-wide network for the epidemiological surveillance and control of communicable diseases continued to be discussed; agreement on a common position is expected at the Health Council meeting in June 1997.

High Level Committee on Health

During the year, the European Commission convened two meetings of its informal Advisory Committee on Health. It gave the Commission opinions on the scope of future Community activities in the field of public health and on the links to be made between public health policy and research.

Meetings of European Chief Medical Officers

The Chief Medical Officers of the Member States meet informally twice a year to exchange professional views on Community health policy, and on relevant WHO and Council of Europe programmes. Their meetings, which are attended by representatives of the WHO and the Council of Europe, provide an ideal opportunity to promote closer collaboration between the EC, the WHO and the Council of Europe.

Other European Community programmes

The European Commission held meetings of experts from the Member States during the year and, in the light of their advice, is expected to bring forward further proposals during 1997 for programmes of action on pollution-related illnesses, accidents and injuries, and rare diseases.

Free movement of people

Health professionals

The number of health professionals from other Member States of the European Economic Area (EEA) working in the UK is small and most come for short periods of time to gain experience. In 1996, 2,067 doctors with recognised qualifications from other Member States obtained full registration with the

General Medical Council; 360 dentists with the General Dental Council; 35 pharmacists with the Royal Pharmaceutical Society of Great Britain; 1,035 nurses and 52 midwives with the UK Central Council of Nursing, Midwifery and Health Visiting; and 275 individuals with the Council for the Professions Supplementary to Medicine (comprising 1 chiropodist, 12 dietitians, 74 occupational therapists, 1 orthoptist, 180 physiotherapists, and 7 radiographers).

Patients

EC Social Security Regulation 1408/71 continued to operate satisfactorily, co-ordinating health care cover for people moving between EEA Member States. The main categories covered were temporary visitors, detached workers and pensioners transferring their residence to another Member State. In addition, during 1996, 864 applications by UK patients for referral to other Member States specifically for treatment of pre-existing conditions were approved by the Department of Health (DH); 419 citizens of other Member States were treated in the UK on the same basis.

(ii)   Council of Europe

During 1996, the Council's European Health Committee took forward work on blood products, organ transplantation, health care in prisons, the use of medical examinations in the field of employment and insurance, and the legal protection of persons with mental disorders who are placed as involuntary patients.

The Council adopted a convention on human rights and biomedicine that will be opened for signature by Member States in 1997. A recommendation on measures to ensure the traceability of blood and blood products was also adopted.

In November, a Ministerial meeting approved a Charter on equity and patients' rights within health care systems.

(iii)   Relations with Central and Eastern Europe

In 1996, the Czech Republic and Slovenia applied to join an enlarged European Union. These applications will be assessed with those of the other eight countries who have already applied.

Plans of co-operation were renewed with Slovakia and the Russian Federation, by which support is given to short-term exchanges of health professionals.

(b)   The Commonwealth

A Commonwealth Health Ministers' Meeting was held on 19 May, immediately before the World Health Assembly. The Chief Medical Officer led the British delegation to the meeting, which agreed that high priority should be attached to continued work on women and health, building on progress following the 11th triennial meeting held in Cape Town, South Africa, in December 1995[1].

For the future, it was agreed that the Commonwealth Secretariat should emphasise its role as an advocate, broker and catalyst, and that it should undertake only limited project work when resources were available. It was further agreed that the Secretariat's health activities should include annual objectives, targets, budgets and programme expenditure.

Reference

1.   Department of Health. *On the State of the Public Health: the annual report of the Chief Medical Officer of the Department of Health for the year 1995.* London: HMSO, 1996; 227-8.

(c)   World Health Organization

(i)   *European Regional Committee*

The 46th session of the European Regional Committee was held in Copenhagen in September; the Chief Medical Officer led the UK delegation. The Committee agreed a programme budget for the 1998-99 biennium, which set the same headline figure as the previous biennium. The Chief Medical Officer, as chair of the Environment and Health Committee, reported on the first two years of the Committee's work and stressed the strong impact of the environment on health. He referred to the UK national environmental health action plan (see page 212), which was being circulated to other members.

(ii)   *Executive Board*

In May, at the World Health Assembly, the Chief Medical Officer was elected to the WHO Executive Board. The 98th meeting of the Board took place directly after the Assembly. The Chief Medical Officer was appointed by the Board to a working group to evaluate the Programme Development Committee and the Administration Budget and Finance Committee. The Board noted a report which agreed priorities for the 1998-99 programme budget, which would include the eradication and prevention of specific communicable diseases and the promotion of primary health care. The Director General was asked to produce a document on priority setting for the next meeting of the Executive Board in January 1997.

(iii) *World Health Assembly*

The 49th World Health Assembly, the annual meeting of the Member States of the WHO, took place in Geneva in May. The UK delegation was led by the Chief Medical Officer and included the Chief Nursing Officer and officials from DH, the Overseas Development Administration and the UK Mission in Geneva.

At the Assembly, the Chief Medical Officer was elected to a three-year term of office on the WHO Executive Board.

The *World Health Report 1996*[1], which focused on communicable diseases as the world's leading cause of death, was commended. Delegates strongly supported the very high priority being given to work in this area, including the eradication and elimination of certain diseases such as polio and leprosy.

The UK and Japan jointly sponsored a resolution to limit the tenure of future Director Generals of the WHO to a maximum of two five-year terms of office.

In view of concerns about the financing of WHO activities, the UK supported a resolution calling for the prompt payment of contributions from Member States, and for a financial plan to be drawn up to bring expenditure into line with expected income, with minimisation of internal borrowing.

Reference

1.   World Health Organization. *World health report 1996: fighting disease, fostering development.* Geneva: World Health Organization, 1996.

APPENDIX

Appendix Tables and their content

Appendix Table 1: *Population age and sex structure, England, mid-1996, and changes by age, 1981-91, 1991-92, 1992-93, 1993-94, 1994-95 and 1995-96.*

This Table is described in Chapter 1 (see page 59).

Appendix Table 2: *Five main causes of death for males and females at different ages, England, 1996.*

This Table contrasts the main causes of death in different age-groups for males and females alike.

It should be noted that the rankings are dependent upon how diseases are grouped. The 9th revision of the International Classification of Diseases (ICD9) is divided into 17 broad chapters, covering different types of diseases - for example respiratory diseases. Within these chapters, individual diseases or groups of diseases are given a 3-digit code, which in most cases can be further broken down into 4-digit codes. For the purposes of producing these Tables, distinct diseases have been used in most cases - vague remainder categories have been avoided, even if there were a higher number of deaths, in order to make the data more meaningful and useful. However, for the 1-14 years age-group, where the numbers of deaths are very small, the rankings are based on whole chapters of the ICD.

At the age of 35 years and over, the major burden of mortality derives from circulatory disease and malignant neoplasms. At the age of 75 years and over, respiratory diseases also contribute strongly. At ages 15-34 years, suicide and undetermined injury and motor vehicle traffic accidents are the leading causes of death for males and females alike. The leading cause of death among children is external causes of injury and poisoning (mostly accidents).

Appendix Table 3: *Relative mortality from various conditions when presented as numbers of deaths and future years of 'working life' lost, England and Wales, 1996.*

The total number of deaths at all ages attributed to selected causes are given. The percentage distribution of deaths demonstrates the major impact of circulatory disease and cancer in both sexes. In 1996, over 80% of deaths occurred at the age of 65 years and over.

259

Years of 'working life' lost between the ages of 15 and 64 years indicate the impact of various causes of death occurring at younger ages. For this table, a death occurring under the age of 15 years accounts for the loss of the full 50-year period beween the ages of 15 and 64 years, whereas a death at age 60 years contributes a loss of only 5 years of 'working life'. Thus weight is given to the age at death as well as the number of deaths, and emphasis is given to the burden of deaths occurring at younger ages.

For males, although circulatory disease and cancer still contribute substantially to loss of 'working life', other causes become more prominent. These include accidents and suicide and undetermined injury, and also those deaths occurring early in life - particularly infant death. For both sexes combined, infant deaths account for about 15% of years of 'working life' lost.

For females, the total years of future 'working life' lost from all causes combined is much less than for males, reflecting considerably lower death rates in females. Cancer - particularly of the breast, cervix, uterus and ovary - is a major contributor to loss of life in females aged under 65 years. In 1996, cancer accounted for 23% of all female deaths, but 40% of years of 'working life' lost. By contrast, although causing 43% of the total number of deaths, circulatory disease accounted for only 16% of the years of 'working life' lost. In other respects, the pattern is broadly similar to that for males, although accidents and suicide account for a smaller proportion of deaths among females.

Appendix Table 4: *Trends in 'avoidable' deaths, England, 1979-96.*

The concept of 'avoidable' deaths was discussed in detail in the Report of 1987[1]. These indicators - developed in this country by Professor Walter Holland and his colleagues[2] - have been chosen to identify selected causes of mortality amenable to health service intervention, either preventive or curative. They might best be called 'potentially avoidable' deaths as, while it might not be possible to prevent every death deemed avoidable, it is expected that a substantial proportion could be avoided. The indicators are now published as part of the Public Health Common Data Set.

The Table presents recent secular trends of nine categories of 'avoidable' deaths. The data are presented as age-standardised mortality ratios, which adjust for differences in the age structure in the years compared. During the period 1979-96, substantial declines are evident in all of the categories presented; since 1979, the age-standardised mortality ratio for all 'avoidable' deaths has fallen by just over 50%.

Appendix Table 5: *Live births, stillbirths, infant mortality and abortions, England, 1960, 1970 and 1975-96.*

Trends are discussed in Chapter 1 (see page 60).

Appendix Table 6: *Congenital anomalies, England, 1986, 1991, 1995 and 1996.*

This Table shows the numbers of babies notified with selected congenital anomalies. In the past, the Table referred to the number of mentions of selected anomalies, but this was difficult to interpret as a baby can have more than one congenital anomaly. The data for 1986, 1991 and 1995 have been re-calculated to enable comparisons over time, but it should be noted (see Chapter 1, page 64) that changes to the notifications list in January 1990 affected the following groups: ear and eye malformations, cardiovascular malformations and talipes.

Appendix Table 7: *Cancer registrations by age and site, males, England and Wales, 1991.*

The Table indicates the distribution of cancer registrations in men at different ages. At all ages combined, cancers of the lung, large intestine (including rectum) and prostate account for half of the registrations. In childhood, a high proportion of cancers are attributable to leukaemias, lymphomas, tumours of the central nervous system, and embryonic tumours such as neuroblastomas and retinoblastomas. At older ages, cancer of the lung is the major cause registered. In the oldest age-group presented (85 years and over), prostate cancer accounts for slightly more registrations than lung cancer. (See also page 71.)

Appendix Table 8: *Cancer registrations by age and site, females, England and Wales, 1991.*

In childhood, the pattern of female cancers is broadly similar to that in males. However, in the 25-44 years age-group cancers of the breast (41%) and cervix (17%) predominate. At older ages, breast cancer continues to account for many registrations, although cancers of the lung, large intestine and skin (non-melonoma skin cancers are not included in the Table) also occur in substantial numbers. (See also page 71.)

Appendix Table 9: *Immunisation uptake, England, 1980-1995/96.*

The information presented in this Table is discussed in Chapter 6 (see page 196).

Appendix Table 10: *Cumulative total of AIDS cases by exposure category, England, to 31 December 1996.*

Recent trends in AIDS cases are discussed in Chapter 6 (see page 188).

Appendix Table 11: *Expectation of life at birth, all-cause mortality rates and infant mortality, England and other European countries, circa 1995.*

This Table includes two key overall measures of general health: expectation of life and infant mortality. Recent data are presented for various European countries. Although problems often exist with regard to comparability of data, international comparisons provide an important perspective to the assessment of overall progress. In particular, such comparisons can highlight the scope for improvement and help to stimulate action to achieve progress.

In 1995, average life expectancy at birth in England was 74.3 years in males. Recent figures from our European neighbours ranged from 71.3 years in Portugal to 76.3 years in Sweden. The equivalent figure for females in England was 79.5 years, which compares with a European Union (EU) range from 78.2 years in Ireland to 82.8 years in France.

The infant mortality rate is also often used as a key descriptor of the overall health of a country. In 1995, the rate in England was 6.1 per 1,000 live births. This figure was approximately average for EU countries at that time, contrasting with a rate in Greece in 1995 of 8.2. Nevertheless, there is no scope for complacency, with lower rates achieved in some other European countries (eg, 4.0 per 1,000 live births in Finland and Sweden).

Additional information is presented on the age-standardised all-cause mortality rates for EU countries, with particular reference to deaths occurring under the age of 65 years. For males, the English death rate is well below the EU average and is only bettered by the Netherlands and Sweden. However, for women the mortality rate is above the EU average.

All international comparisons need to be made with some caution given possible differences in data collection and recording procedures. However, the indicators presented here are among the most robust for the purposes of comparison.

Appendix Figure 1: *Weekly deaths, England and Wales, 1995 and 1996, and expected deaths, 1996.*

This Figure illustrates the week-by-week registrations of deaths from all causes at ages one year and over for 1996. These are compared with the observed values in 1995 and expected values in 1996. The expected numbers of deaths for 1996 are calculated as an average of the deaths registered in the same week over the previous five-year period, 1991-95.

References

1. Department of Health and Social Security. *On the State of the Public Health: the annual report of the Chief Medical Officer of the Department of Health and Social Security for the year 1987.* London: HMSO, 1988; 4, 72-82.
2. Charlton JR, Hartley RM, Silver R, Holland WW. Geographical variation in mortality from conditions amenable to medical intervention in England and Wales. *Lancet* 1983; **i:** 691-6.

Table A.1: *Population age and sex structure, England, mid-1996, and changes by age, 1981-91, 1991-92, 1992-93, 1993-94, 1994-95 and 1995-96*

Age (in years)	Resident population at mid-1996 (thousands)			Percentage changes (persons)					
	Persons	Males	Females	1981-91	1991-92	1992-93	1993-94	1994-95	1995-96
Under 1	603	309	293	10.9	-1.0	-3.6	0.2	-3.1	-1.9
1-4	2543	1304	1239	15.2	1.2	0.2	-0.4	-0.4	-1.8
5-15	6907	3545	3362	-13.1	1.2	1.8	1.6	1.0	0.9
16-29	9287	4760	4527	4.7	-2.0	-2.5	-2.5	-1.9	-1.6
30-44	10842	5495	5347	11.5	-0.1	0.8	1.5	1.7	1.9
45-64/59*	9985	5548	4437	-0.2	3.0	2.3	1.8	1.4	1.2
65/60-74†	5380	1931	3449	-3.2	0.3	0.7	0.5	-1.8	-1.2
75-84	2629	1002	1627	17.6	-1.3	-2.7	-2.4	3.5	2.4
85+	913	235	678	49.2	4.7	5.1	3.0	3.4	2.2
All ages	49089	24129	24960	3.0	0.4	0.3	0.4	0.4	0.4

* 45-64 years for males and 45-59 years for females.
† 65-74 years for males and 60-74 years for females.

Note: Figures may not add precisely to totals due to rounding.

Source: ONS

Table A.2 Five main causes of death for males and females at different ages (and percentages of all causes of death), England, 1996

Rank	All ages - 1 & over Males	All ages - 1 & over Females	1-14 years Males	1-14 years Females	15-34 years Males	15-34 years Females	35-54 years Males	35-54 years Females	55-74 years Males	55-74 years Females	75 years & over Males	75 years & over Females
1	410-414 Ischaemic heart disease — 27%	410-414 Ischaemic heart disease — 21%	E800-E999 External causes of injury & poisoning — 32%	E800-E999 External causes of injury & poisoning — 22%	E950-E959 Suicide and undetermined injury* — 22%	E950-E959 Suicide and undetermined injury* — 11%	410-414 Ischaemic heart disease — 24%	174 MN of female breast — 19%	410-414 Ischaemic heart disease — 31%	410-414 Ischaemic heart disease — 21%	410-414 Ischaemic heart disease — 25%	410-414 Ischaemic heart disease — 22%
2	430-438 Cerebro-vascular disease — 8%	430-438 Cerebro-vascular disease — 13%	140-239 Neoplasms — 18%	140-239 Neoplasms — 18%	E810-E819 Motor vehicle traffic accidents — 16%	E810-E819 Motor vehicle traffic accidents — 10%	150-159 MN of digestive organs and peritoneum — 8%	179-189 MN of genito-urinary organs — 9%	162 MN of trachea, bronchus & lung — 11%	150-159 MN of digestive organs and peritoneum — 9%	480-486 Pneumonia — 12%	430-438 Cerebro-vascular disease — 15%
3	480-486 Pneumonia — 8%	480-486 Pneumonia — 11%	320-389 Diseases of the nervous system and sense organs — 11%	740-759 Congenital anomalies — 13%	E850- E869 Accidental poisoning by drugs, medicaments & biologicals — 6%	200-208 MN of lymphatic and haematopoietic tissue — 5%	E950-E959 Suicide and undetermined injury* — 8%	150-159 MN of digestive organs and peritoneum — 7%	150-159 MN of digestive organs and peritoneum — 10%	430-438 Cerebro-vascular disease — 8%	430-438 Cerebro-vascular disease — 10%	480-486 Pneumonia — 15%
4	150-159 MN of digestive organs and peritoneum — 8%	150-159 MN of digestive organs and peritoneum — 6%	001-139 Infectious and parasitic diseases — 9%	320-389 Diseases of the nervous system and sense organs — 11%	001-139 Infectious & parasitic diseases — 5%	174 MN of female breast — 5%	162 MN of trachea, bronchus & lung — 6%	410-414 Ischaemic heart disease — 7%	430-438 Cerebro-vascular disease — 6%	162 MN of trachea, bronchus & lung — 8%	490-496 Chronic obstructive pulmonary disease and allied conditions — 10%	415-429 Diseases of pulmonary circulation & other forms of heart disease — 15%
5	162 MN of trachea, bronchus & lung — 8%	415-429 Diseases of pulmonary circulation & other forms of heart disease — 6%	740-759 Congenital anomalies — 8%	001-139 Infectious and parasitic diseases — 9%	200-208 MN of lymphatic and haematopoietic tissue — 4%	179-189 MN of genito-urinary organs — 5%	430-438 Cerebro-vascular disease — 5%	162 MN of trachea, bronchus & lung — 6%	490-496 Chronic obstructive pulmonary disease and allied conditions — 6%	174 MN of female breast — 7%	150-159 MN of digestive organs and peritoneum — 6%	150-159 MN of digestive organs and peritoneum — 5%
Remainder	42%	43%	21%	26%	47%	63%	49%	51%	36%	46%	39%	37%
All causes	252458	2722863	918	703	6041	2549	17935	11774	98015	66551	129549	191286

*Suicide and undetermined injury=(E950-E959)+(E980-E989) excluding E988.8.
MN = Malignant neoplasm.
Note: percentages may not add up to 100 due to rounding.

Source: ONS

Table A.3: *Relative mortality from various conditions when presented as numbers of deaths and future years of 'working life' lost, England and Wales, 1996*

Cause (ICD9 code)	Males				Females			
	Number of deaths (thousands)		Years of 'working life' lost (thousands)		Number of deaths (thousands)		Years of 'working life' lost (thousands)	
	All ages	(%)	Age 15-64	(%)	All ages	(%)	Age 15-64	(%)
All causes, all ages	270		882		293		529	
All causes, 28 days and over	268	(100)	805	(100)	292	(100)	472	(100)
All malignant neoplasms* (140-208)	72	(27)	172	(21)	66	(23)	187	(40)
Trachea, bronchus and lung cancer (162)	20	(7)	35	(4)	11	(4)	20	(4)
Breast cancer† (174)	0	(0)	0	(0)	12	(4)	55	(12)
Genito-urinary cancer (179-189)	14	(5)	15	(2)	10	(3)	33	(7)
Leukaemia (204-208)	2	(1)	11	(1)	2	(1)	9	(2)
Circulatory disease* (390-459)	114	(43)	183	(23)	124	(43)	74	(16)
Ischaemic heart disease (410-414)	71	(26)	119	(15)	59	(20)	27	(6)
Cerebrovascular disease (430-438)	22	(8)	26	(3)	38	(13)	23	(5)
Respiratory disease* (460-519)	41	(15)	47	(6)	49	(17)	27	(6)
Pneumonia (480-486)	21	(8)	25	(3)	33	(11)	13	(3)
Bronchitis, emphysema and asthma (490-493)	3	(1)	8	(1)	2	(1)	5	(1)
Sudden infant death syndrome (798.0)	0	(0)	10	(1)	0	(0)	7	(2)
All accidental deaths* (E800-E949)	6	(2)	116	(14)	4	(2)	36	(8)
Motor vehicle traffic accidents (E810-E819)	2	(1)	61	(8)	1	(0)	18	(4)
Suicide and undetermined injury(E950-E959 plus E980-E989 excluding E988.8)	4	(1)	83	(10)	1	(0)	23	(5)

* These conditions are ranked as well as selected causes within the broader headings.   † Not calculated for male breast cancer.

Deaths under 28 days excluded, except from 'All causes, all ages'.   Method of calculation has been changed to that set out in DH1 (Mortality Statistics: General: England and Wales).

Source: ONS

Table A.4: Trends in 'avoidable' deaths, England, 1979-96. Age-standardised mortality ratios (1979 = 100)

Condition	SMR[1]													Actual number of deaths[2]	
	1979	1985	1986	1987	1988	1989	1990	1991	1992	1993[3]	1994[3]	1995	1996[4]	1979	1996[5]
Hypertension/cerebrovascular (ages 35-64)	100	76	73	69	63	60	57	58	55	52	49	49	49	8811	4361
Perinatal mortality[6]	100	67	65	61	60	57	56	55	52	52[7]	52[7]	51[7]	49[7]	8839	4418[7]
Cervical cancer (ages 15-64)	100	90	96	90	86	81	78	72	68	64	54	56	57	1060	625
Hodgkin's disease (ages 5-64)	100	77	75	84	74	65	60	58	57	60	39	49	41	340	153
Respiratory diseases (ages 1-14)	100	50	41	44	42	41	39	42	28	44	47	36	36	308	115
Surgical diseases[8] (ages 5-64)	100	65	71	58	75	51	58	58	61	55	45	52	50	247	123
Asthma (ages 5-44)	100	115	114	114	110	94	86	91	70	68	66	47	61	231	152
Tuberculosis (ages 5-64)	100	67	60	67	56	57	48	46	47	52	51	56	43	208	93
Chronic rheumatic heart disease (ages 5-44)	100	34	35	34	20	28	23	19	14	17	19	17	13	118	18
Total 'avoidable' deaths	100	72	70	66	63	60	57	57	54	53	50	50	49	20138[9]	10045[9]
All causes: ages 0-14 years	100	75	74	73	72	67	64	59	52	52	49	49	49	10502	5279
All causes: ages 15-64 years	100	88	86	84	82	80	79	76	74	73	70	70	69	119158	83333
All causes: all ages	100	92	89	86	85	85	82	82	79	81	77	78	77	554840	526650

1   The standardised mortality ratio (SMR) for a condition is calculated by dividing the observed number of deaths by the expected number of deaths based on 1979 death rates.

2   Excluding deaths of visitors to England.

3   SMRs recalculated since last year's publication using mortality registration data.

4   To calculate the 1996 SMRs, 1996 population projections (1994 based) were used because estimates for 1996 are not yet available.

5   From 1993 the mortality data for some causes of death are not directly comparable with those for 1992 and earlier years as a result of coding changes.

6   Stillbirths are included in the figures for perinatal mortality and total 'avoidable' deaths, but not in deaths from all causes.

7   The definition of stillbirth changed on 1 October 1992 to include 24 to 27 weeks gestation; to provide a comparable trend, these stillbirths are excluded from the figures for 1993 (848), 1994 (832), 1995 (842) and 1996 (893).

8   Appendicitis, abdominal hernia, cholelithiasis and cholecystitis.

9   Figures for total 'avoidable' deaths take account of deaths from asthma in the 5-14 years age-band which are also included in the figures for respiratory diseases.

Source: Department of Health (SD2F), from data supplied by ONS

Table A.5: *Live births, stillbirths, infant mortality and abortions, England[1], 1960, 1970 and 1975-96*

Year	Live births Number	Stillbirths Number	Stillbirths Rate[2]	Early neonatal mortality (deaths under 1 week) Number	Early neonatal mortality Rate[3]	Perinatal mortality (stillbirths plus deaths under 1 week) Rate[2]	Post-neonatal mortality (deaths 4 weeks to under 1 year) Rate[3]	Infant mortality (deaths under 1 year) Rate[3]	Abortions[1] Rate[4]
1960	740859	14753	19.5	9772	13.2	32.5	6.3	21.6	-
1970	741999	9708	12.9	7864	10.6	23.4	5.9	18.2	87.6
1975	568900*	5918	10.3*	5154	9.1	19.3*	5.0	15.7	149.9
1976	550383*	5339	9.6	4468	8.1	17.6	4.6	14.2	148.7
1977	536953	5087	9.4	4070	7.6	16.9	4.5	13.7	152.7
1978	562589	4791	8.4	3975	7.1	15.4	4.4	13.1	157.7
1979	601316	4811	7.9	4028	6.7	14.6	4.6*	12.8	158.8
1980	618371*	4523	7.3	3793	6.1	13.4	4.4	12.0	164.5
1981	598163	3939	6.5	3105	5.2	11.7	4.3	10.9	168.8
1982	589711	3731	6.3	2939	5.0	11.2	4.5	10.8	171.1
1983	593255	3412	5.7	2746	4.6	10.3	4.2	10.0	169.2
1984	600573	3425	5.7	2640	4.4	10.0	3.9	9.4	177.3
1985	619301	3426	5.5	2674	4.3	9.8	3.9	9.2	177.6
1986	623609	3337	5.3	2640	4.2	9.5	4.2	9.5	183.5
1987	643330	3224	5.0	2518	3.9	8.9	4.0	9.1	187.7
1988	654363*	3188	4.8	2543	3.9	8.7	4.1	9.1	196.6
1989	649357	3056	4.7	2368	3.6	8.3	3.7	8.4	200.0
1990	666920	3068	4.6	2382	3.6	8.1	3.3	7.9	199.0
1991	660806	3072	4.6	2260	3.4	8.0	3.0	7.3	194.4
1992	651784	2777†	4.2†	2174	3.3	7.6†	2.3	6.5	190.1
1993	636473*	3621*	5.7	2074*	3.3	8.9	2.1	6.3	190.8
1994	628956*	3583*	5.7	2011*	3.2	8.8*	2.0	6.1	191.4
1995	613257	3406	5.5	1991	3.2	8.8	1.9	6.1	193.4
1996[5]	614184	3345	5.4	1980	3.2	8.7	2.0	6.1	-

1 Relates to England residents. 2 Per 1,000 live births and stillbirths. 3 Per 1,000 live births. 4 Per 1,000 conceptions (live births, stillbirths and abortions). 5 Provisional.

* These figures have been incorrectly cited in previous Reports.

† 1992 figures exclude 198 stillbirths of between 24 and 27 completed weeks gestation registered between 1 October 1992 and 31 December 1992, following the introduction of new legislation (see Chapter 1), and are consistent with those for earlier years. The figures for later years are on the new (wider) definition of stillbirths.

Source: ONS

Table A.6: *Congenital anomalies, England, 1986, 1991*, 1995* and 1996**

ICD codes	Anomaly	Live births†				Stillbirths§			
		1986	1991	1995¶	1996¶	1986	1991	1995¶	1996¶
	Babies born with anomalies								
	Number	12133	6481	5079	4948	255	179	166	155
	Rate	194.6	98.1	82.8	80.6	4.1	2.7	2.7	2.5
320.0-359.9, 740.0-742.9 (Q00.0-Q07.9)	Central nervous system								
	Number	481	237	177	154	83	40	48	49
	Rate	7.7	3.6	2.9	2.5	1.3	0.6	0.8	0.8
360.0-379.9, 743.0-743.9, 744.3 (Q10.0-Q17.9)	Ear and eye								
	Number	689	290	190	192	18	9	9	6
	Rate	11.0	4.4	3.1	3.1	0.2	0.1	0.1	0.1
749.0-749.2 (Q35.0-Q37.9)	Cleft lip/cleft palate								
	Number	794	714	531	516	21	13	6	13
	Rate	12.7	10.8	8.7	8.4	0.3	0.2	0.1	0.2
390.0-459.9, 745.0-747.9 (Q20.0-Q28.9)	Cardiovascular								
	Number	676	432	404	394	7	14	13	20
	Rate	10.8	6.5	6.6	6.4	0.1	0.2	0.2	0.3
752.6 (Q54.0-Q54.9, Q64.0)	Hypospadias/epispadias								
	Number	959	691	470	483	1	2	-	-
	Rate	15.4	10.5	7.7	7.9	0.0	0.0	-	-
755.2-755.4 (Q71.0-Q73.8)	Reduction deformities of limbs								
	Number	242	223	174	180	16	6	5	9
	Rate	3.9	3.4	2.8	2.9	3.9	3.4	2.8	2.9
754.5-754.7 (Q66.0, Q66.1, Q66.4, Q66.8)	Talipes								
	Number	1823	856	659	545	16	5	5	10
	Rate	29.2	13.0	10.7	8.9	0.5	0.2	0.2	0.1
758.0-758.9 (Q90.0-Q99.9)	Chromosomal								
	Number	511	497	364	384	19	21	27	24
	Rate	8.2	7.5	5.9	6.3	0.3	0.3	0.4	0.4

* From January 1990 certain minor malformations are no longer notified, and have been excluded from the figures shown. For example, club foot of positional origin is now excluded from the category 'Talipes'. ICD9 codes 754.5-754.7. This change in notification practice largely accounts for the decrease in numbers of malformations reported in some categories. From 1995, ICD10 codes (in brackets) are in use.
† Rates per 10,000 live births. § Rates per 10,000 total births. ¶Data as at 30 May 1997.

Source: ONS

Table A.7: Cancer* registrations by age and site, males, England and Wales, 1991

Numbers and percentages
Age-group (years)

	All ages	%	0-14 years	%	15-24 years	%	25-44 years	%	45-64 years	%	65-74 years	%	75-84 years	%	85 years and over	%
Eye, brain, and other nervous system	2115	2	142	21	80	10	320	7	824	3	496	1	230	1	23	0
Mouth and pharynx	2146	2	5	1	15	2	129	3	923	4	603	2	406	1	65	1
Oesophagus	3134	3	0	0	0	0	68	2	872	3	1160	3	821	3	213	3
Lung	24751	24	2	0	4	1	328	7	6195	24	9500	27	7277	24	1445	20
Stomach	6138	6	0	0	2	0	103	2	1493	6	2068	6	1981	7	491	7
Pancreas	3051	3	1	0	1	0	61	1	799	3	1071	3	912	3	206	3
Large intestine and rectum	13895	13	1	0	6	1	375	8	3733	14	4772	14	4034	13	974	13
Prostate	13940	13	3	0	2	0	11	0	1590	6	4816	14	5835	20	1683	23
Bladder	8289	8	2	0	6	1	162	4	2044	8	2896	8	2517	8	662	9
Skin (melanoma only)	1468	1	3	0	41	5	316	7	562	2	295	1	195	1	56	1
Leukaemias and lymphomas	8509	8	318	47	307	39	924	21	2246	9	2216	6	1964	7	534	7
All other cancer†	16774	16	196	29	319	41	1685	38	4716	18	5118	15	3738	12	1002	14
Total cancer†	104210	100	673	100	783	100	4482	100	25997	100	35011	100	29910	100	7354	100

* Cancer = malignant neoplasm.

† Excludes figures for non-melanoma skin cancer (ICD 9 code 173), which are greatly under-registered.

Note: Percentages may not add up to 100 due to rounding.

Source: ONS

Table A.8: *Cancer* registrations by age and site, females, England and Wales, 1991*

Numbers and percentages
Age-group (years)

	All ages	%	0-14 years	%	15-24 years	%	25-44 years	%	45-64 years	%	65-74 years	%	75-84 years	%	85 years and over	%
Eye, brain, and other nervous system	1636	2	139	26	60	9	250	3	576	2	361	1	209	1	41	0
Mouth and pharynx	1185	1	7	1	5	1	87	1	341	1	303	1	299	1	143	1
Oesophagus	2226	2	0	0	0	0	23	0	378	1	583	2	839	3	403	4
Breast	30595	28	1	0	27	4	3470	41	13512	42	6328	23	5021	19	2236	19
Lung	11754	11	0	0	7	1	173	2	2961	9	4438	16	3323	12	852	7
Stomach	3924	4	0	0	7	1	82	1	540	2	965	3	1474	6	862	8
Pancreas	3216	3	1	0	2	0	45	1	590	2	918	3	1132	4	528	5
Large intestine and rectum	13844	13	1	0	10	1	325	4	2769	9	3841	14	4631	17	2267	20
Ovary	5277	5	3	1	44	7	450	5	2089	6	1373	5	1013	4	305	3
Cervix	3768	3	0	0	49	7	1403	17	1147	4	651	2	416	2	102	1
Other uterus	4282	4	1	0	8	1	167	2	1668	5	1241	4	882	3	315	3
Bladder	3180	3	0	0	6	1	61	1	597	2	945	3	1088	4	483	4
Skin (melanoma only)	2235	2	7	1	82	12	598	7	685	2	395	1	344	1	124	1
Leukaemias and lymphomas	7013	7	208	39	231	34	577	7	1520	5	1745	6	1950	7	782	7
All other cancer†	13724	13	172	32	139	21	764	9	2803	9	3656	13	4149	15	2041	18
Total cancer †	107859	100	540	100	671	100	8475	100	32176	100	27743	100	26770	100	11484	100

* Cancer = malignant neoplasm.

†Excludes figures for non-melanoma skin cancer (ICD9 code 173), which are greatly under-registered.

Note: Percentages may not add up to 100 due to rounding.

Source: ONS

271

Table A.9: *Immunisation uptake (percentage of children immunised by their 2nd birthday and of children given BCG vaccine by their 14th birthday), England, 1980-95/96*

Year	Diphtheria	Tetanus	Polio	Whooping cough	Measles	Mumps/ rubella	BCG[1]	Haemophilus influenzae b (Hib)
1980[2]	81	81	81	41	53	-	82	-
1981[2]	83	83	82	46	55	-	78	-
1982[2]	84	84	84	53	58	-	75	-
1983[2]	84	84	84	59	60	-	76	-
1984[2]	84	84	84	65	63	-	71	-
1985[2]	85	85	85	65	68	-	77	-
1986[2]	85	85	85	67	71	-	76	-
1987/88[2]	87	87	87	73	76	-	76	-
1988/89	87	87	87	75	80	7	71	-
1989/90	89	89	89	78	84	68	36[3]	-
1990/91	92	92	92	84	87	86	90[3]	-
1991/92	93	93	93	88	90	90	86[3]	-
1992/93	95	95	95	92	92	92	74	-
1993/94	95	95	95	93	91	91	79	75
1994/95	95	95	95	93	91	91	52[4]	91
1995/96	96	96	96	94	92	92	95[4]	94

[1] Estimated percentage of children given BCG vaccine by their 14th birthday.

[2] Estimated percentage immunised by the end of the second year after birth (excludes BCG).

[3] The school BCG programme was suspended in 1989 because there were insufficient supplies of BCG vaccine; figures for the subsequent two years were relatively higher as a result.

[4] The school BCG programme for 1994-95 was delayed because of the measles/rubella immunisation campaign.

Sources: 1980-87/88: Form SBL 607; 1988/89 onwards: Form KC51 (except BCG), Form KC50 (BCG).

Table A.10: *Cumulative totals of AIDS cases by exposure category, England, to 31 December 1996*

(Numbers subject to revision as further data are received or duplicates identified)

How persons probably acquired the virus	Number of cases			
	Male	Female	Total	%[§]
Sexual intercourse:				
Between men	9057	-	9057	72
Between men and women				
Exposure to				
'high risk' partner[*]	37	133	170	1
Exposure abroad[†]	847	650	1497	12
Exposure in the UK	75	74	149	1
Investigation continuing/closed	22	10	32	<1
Injecting drug use (IDU)	379	160	539	4
IDU and sexual intercourse				
between men	228	-	228	2
Blood factor treatment				
(eg for haemophilia)	533	5	538	4
Blood or tissue transfer				
(eg, transfusion)				
Abroad	21	44	65	<1
UK	21	24	45	<1
Mother to infant	98	100	198	2
Other or investigation continuing/				
closed	111	15	126	1
Total	11429	1215	12644	100

[*] Partner(s) exposed to HIV infection through sexual intercourse between men, IDU, blood factor treatment or blood/tissue transfer.

[†] Individuals from abroad and individuals from the UK who have lived or visited abroad, for whom there is no evidence of 'high risk' partners.

[§] Total does not add up to 100 because of rounding.

Source: CDSC/PHLS

273

Table A.11: *Expectation of life at birth, all-cause mortality rates and infant mortality, England and other European Union countries, circa 1995*

Country	Year	Expectation of life at birth		All cause mortality rate*		Infant mortality rate†
		Males	Females	Males	Females	
England	1995	74.3‡	79.5‡	280.8§	171.7§	6.1§
United Kingdom	1995	74.1	79.5	294.5	178.5	6.2
Austria	1996	73.8	80.4	343.8	159.1	5.4
Belgium	1992	73.1	79.9	338.9	175.3	8.2
Denmark	1994	72.9	78.3	359.9	223.5	5.5
Finland	1995	72.9	80.4	364.8	148.3	4.0
France	1994	74.4	82.8	356.8	146.1	5.9
Germany	1995	73.4	80.0	347.2	166.2	5.3
Greece	1995	75.2	80.5	289.5	131.0	8.2
Ireland	1993	72.6	78.2	330.2	184.7	6.1
Italy	1993	74.6	81.1	302.3	145.2	7.1
Luxembourg	1995	73.6	81.1	339.5	153.3	4.1
Netherlands	1995	74.7	80.6	269.4	160.8	5.5
Portugal	1995	71.3	78.7	409.9	176.2	7.5
Spain	1993	74.1	81.4	333.9	137.1	6.7
Sweden	1995	76.3	81.8	238.1	139.2	4.0
EU average	*1995*	*74.0*	*80.7*	*326.3*	*157.9*	*6.1*

* Per 100,000 population aged 0-64 years, age-standardised.

† Per 1,000 live births.

‡ Figures for England calculated by Government Actuary's Department by slightly different methodology to WHO figures.

§ England data provided by Office for National Statistics (ONS).

Source: WHO European Office 'Health for All' statistical database

Figure A.1: *Weekly deaths, England and Wales, 1995 and 1996, and expected deaths, 1996*

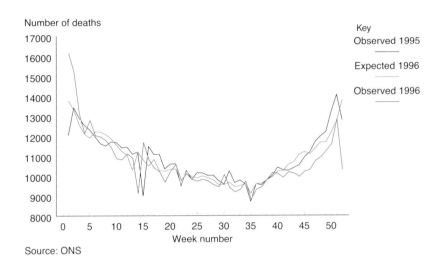

Number of deaths

Source: ONS

Printed in the UK for The Stationery Office
J24194/1 C28 9/97 13110